Settling with the Indians

Settling With The Indians

The Meeting of English and Indian Cultures in America, 1580-1640

KAREN ORDAHL KUPPERMAN

ROWMAN AND LITTLEFIELD
Totowa, New Jersey

Copyright © **Karen Kupperman**, 1980

All rights reserved. No part of this publication may be reproduced or transmitted, in any form or by any means, without permission.

Library of Congress Cataloging in Publication Data

Kupperman, Karen Ordahl, 1939-
   Settling with the Indians.

   Bibliography: p.
   Includes index.
   1. Indians of North America—First contact with Occidental civilization. 2. America—Discovery and exploration—English. 3. United States—History—Colonial period, ca. 1600-1775. I. Title.
E58.K86   970′.02   79-9543
ISBN 0-8476-6210-1

Printed in the United States of America

Contents

	Preface	vii
	Acknowledgements	ix
	Note on References	x

Part I ENGLISH WRITERS DESCRIBE THE INDIANS

1	The Scene and the Participants	1
2	Indian Appearance	33
3	Indian Society and Government	45
4	Indian Religion	64
5	Indian Technology	80

Part II ENGLISH CULTURE CONFRONTS INDIAN CULTURE

6	Were the Indians Alien?	107
7	English Social Ideals and Indian Culture	141
8	England's Special Relationship with North America	159
9	The Nature of the Relationship	169
	Appendix: Profiles of the Writers	189
	Bibliography	197
	Index	219

Preface

How do we describe people from a culture different from our own? How do we choose from among the hundreds of cues we see and hear those which tell us what is centrally important about other people? These questions were very important to me as I read and analyzed descriptions of America written for English readers in the early years of colonization. It very quickly became clear that not only was there a very great interest in the American natives, but also general agreement on what constituted a good description. There were felt to be clear and definite traits or patterns to be looked for when describing people from another culture, and societies were classified on the basis of the presence or absence of these traits and patterns. Thus in reading descriptions of the American Indians, we can learn a great deal about what English people thought were the essential elements of a society or culture worthy of the name.

Modern descriptions of the meeting between the Indians and the English colonists generally agree that the English were abruptly dismissive of Indian culture, that they were either totally uninterested or else saw it as something to be shunned or even destroyed as the work of the devil. My reading of the early descriptions of the Indians yielded a very different result, and one which seemed to me to make better sense of this early cross-cultural confrontation. Some English colonists were just not interested in an alien culture, though none of these dismissed the Indians as being cultureless. But many colonists were fascinated by the Indians, their government, social organization, and religion. Despite the language barrier, they struggled mightily to understand this culture. Moreover, they were writing for an audience in England which was hungry for such information and analysis. Many of their writings were published, frequently in multiple editions.

English people of the late 16th and early 17th centuries believed that their society was rapidly changing for the worse, that all the old social controls and supports were breaking down. Many of the reports from America reflect this fear. They worried about how their society would be affected by the very act of transplantation and by the availability of land in America. Most of all they feared the tearing down of distinctions between people. When they described the Indians they frequently held them up as an example of a society which had not lost its social moorings as English society had done. England could learn a better way, or could recapture the good old ways by looking at Indian society.

Whether or not the colonists thought Indian society worthy of destruction, the effect of their coming was the destruction, physically and culturally, of most of the Indians of the east coast of America. Much of this was accomplished during the period under consideration here. One question which is always intriguing to the historian is whether the past could have been different. Here is where I diverge most strongly from the picture usually presented by historians. The confrontation between the American Indians and the English colonists is almost always presented as a meeting between admirable but extremely primitive people and the representatives of a vastly superior culture. Thus, though the record could have varied in its details and the English record could have been more honorable, the domination of the Indians by the English is portrayed as virtually inevitable. I do not think this is the way the English saw it at the time. When they describe Indian technology it is with admiration born of experience. In the American environment Indian technology was frequently superior to English and the colonists made no secret of their continuing dependence on Indian aid. Nor did the rank and file colonists have a much more sophisticated understanding of the operation of the universe than their Indian counterparts. They interpreted natural phenomena in very much the same ways. European diseases, not European technology, conquered the Indians. Even with the diseases, which killed the Indians in appalling numbers, the relationship between colonists and natives was very delicately balanced for many years in each colony, and much of the writing about the Indians is tinged with fear. They feared not only the military attacks of the Indians or the withdrawal of technological support, but also that the Indians might use magic against them. It is very easy to overdraw the modernity of the English. They and the Indians believed in a world peopled with supernatural forces which could affect their lives. Though English people of this period were like modern people in their curiosity about alien peoples, we must take care not to see them as modern people in their view of the world and its operation. They saw the universe and man's place in it much as people had done for many centuries before them. Only when we understand the similarities of Indian and English culture, as well as the differences between them, can we see their interaction as it really was.

Acknowledgements

My greatest debt of gratitude is owed to Quentin Skinner and to my husband, Joel Kupperman. Prof. Skinner has given advice unstintingly and has repeatedly gone far beyond what I had a right to ask in reading this work in various drafts and criticizing it. More important than his willingness to help and criticize, though, is the example of his immense learnedness and his creative response to ideas. To discuss a subject with him is to have its possibilities open before your eyes. Joel Kupperman has read this book many times and has been extremely helpful at every stage, as sounding board and as editor. My colleague, Harry S. Stout, read chapter one and made many helpful suggestions, though he and I have agreed to disagree about some of the arguments of that chapter. My colleague Irene Q. Brown suggested the book's title.

My parents, Grace and Stafford Ordahl, helped make it possible for me to go to England to study. The American Association of University Women gave me a generous Dissertation Fellowship to sponsor the year of writing on the dissertation which was the parent of this book.

Parts of my article, "English Perceptions of Treachery, 1583–1640: The Case of the American 'Savages,' " *The Historical Journal,* 20, 2 (1977), appear in chapters six and nine. I thank the editors for permission to use this material.

Note on References

References to the sources on which my conclusions are based appear in the text in parentheses. Inessential references have been trimmed and those which remain have been grouped at the ends of paragraphs where that was possible, to spare the reader. In some cases it was important to the argument to demonstrate that conclusions are not based on isolated instances but on a wide number of sources. In these cases where there are many references and especially when they could not logically go at the end of a paragraph, they have been converted into footnotes. A full bibliography is included to give all details on parenthetical references.

Settling with the Indians

1

The Scene and the Participants

Americans usually picture the discovery and colonization of America as a confrontation between civilized, almost modern, Europeans and Stone Age savages. Many historians contrast the dynamic, acquisitive complex European with the simple, repetitive life of the Indians, who had occupied the same land from time immemorial, living in peace with nature and man. It is as if America were a stage tableau, with the arrival of Europeans as the raising of the curtain and the beginning of the action. Some writers stress the ecologically sound principles of Indian life and their integration of religion with all aspects of life. Others, less favorable to the Indians, picture them as perching on a rich land which they could only begin to appreciate and use as it should be used, a land that was, for all practical purposes, empty. This second line of reasoning points to the technological superiority of the English and the consequent inevitability of European domination of America, the virgin land.[1]

Much of this involves romanticism. It romanticizes the situation of the English as much as that of the Indians. This book proposes to look at the people actually involved in the first sixty years of English colonization of North America, both English and Indians. All the sources from the period were written by Englishmen, so we can assess their attitudes toward native American culture in very great detail. Along the way the careful reader can also begin to understand how the Indians viewed the English. We will also look at the technology of both cultures and examine the notion that European technology was in every circumstance superior to crude Indian methods. We will compare the two cultures as they interpret man's place in the universe and

---

1. See for example Philip L. Barbour, *The Three Worlds of Captain John Smith* (Boston, 1964), Chap. 9; Daniel Boorstin, "The birth of exploration," *The Listener*, 13 Nov., 1975, p. 636.

the natural phenomena around them. More specifically, we will look at the Indian's mental world, filled with supernatural forces which controlled his life and which much of his culture was devoted to propitiating. Does this really form a contrast to the mental world of the 16th and 17th century English person? Despite the Renaissance and Reformation and all they imply about the spirit of rational inquiry in European thought, it is also true that resort to magic and witchcraft as well as accusations of practicing witchcraft were an important part of English culture at this time. Moreover magical activity was on the increase during the period we are examining. The English also found themselves confronted by a universe apparently in the control of supernatural forces which might act malevolently or capriciously and which human magical activity could propitiate or even control. The English colonists feared Indian witches and medicine men precisely because they assumed these "conjurors" would have supernatural powers which could be used against the English.

When the English wrote about Indian culture they frequently made careful distinctions between Indians of the "better sort" and the common people. This reflected their view of human society in general. In England status and occupational distinctions were of prime importance in one person's assessment of another. Englishmen of this period, as they reveal in their discussions of Indian society, were overwhelmingly concerned with the maintenance of distinctions between people in a clear and public way. It is the argument of this book that neither savagery nor race was the important category for Englishmen looking at Indians. That is, English colonists assumed that Indians were racially similar to themselves and that savagery was a temporary condition which the Indians would quickly lose. The really important category was status.

English society of this period was characterized by one fundamental division; that separating the gentry from the rest of the population. The aristocracy was the upper end of the gentry, all of which consisted of only about 5% of the population. The other 95% ranged from substantial farmers and urban entrepreneurs to landless laborers.[2] One of the most striking features of the early colonization literature is not the writers' view of Indian society, but their view of their fellow Englishmen. The early colonies which were set up as military outposts,

---

2. For descriptions of the class structure of late 16th and early 17th century England on which this section is based, see Charles Wilson, *England's Apprenticeship, 1603-1763* (New York, 1965), part I; L.A. Clarkson, *The Pre-Industrial Economy in England, 1500-1750* (London, 1971); Peter Laslett, *The World We Have Lost* (New York, 1965); Christopher Hill, *The Century of Revolution, 1603-1714* (Edinburgh, 1961), part I; Lawrence Stone, "Social Mobility in England, 1500-1700," *Past and Present*, 33 (1966).

particularly Roanoke and Jamestown, were composed of military leaders from the gentry or aristocracy and humble people, many of whom had been pressed into service more or less against their will. The ordinary colonists in Jamestown were regularly referred to as "the very scumme of the earth." England was in a period of economic upheaval, with many small farmers being forced off the land. Writers on social issues believed part of England's problems could be traced to over-population and that America offered a solution to this problem. America could be a drain into which England's unwanted people could be poured. Such people were sent, especially to Jamestown, in large numbers. When the campaign was at its most enthusiastic, large numbers of orphans were scooped up from the streets of London and sent off. (Johnson, 1970) There is considerable evidence that when these "servants" arrived in Virginia they were ruthlessly exploited. Psychologically they were available for exploitation because they were members of the expendable category, the half of the population who, according to Gregory King late in the century, decreased the wealth of the kingdom merely by being alive.

The final Roanoke colony and Jamestown in its later period as well as the New England colonies were all family-oriented attempts to recreate English society in miniature. Whereas military colonies were populated by representatives of the extremes of English society, colonists in this new kind of venture came mostly from the middle ranks with a sprinkling of gentry. There was less raw exploitation of servants in these colonies made up of families, but belief in the necessity of distinction between people of the "better sort" and ordinary people was just as strong. In all colonies, as in England, there were sumptuary laws, laws which regulated how members of the various groups should dress so that no one would be able to slip over into a status to which he did not belong.

The care with which English writers distinguished between Indians of the "better sort" and the ordinary is not just a curiosity but is central to their response to the challenge of describing Indian society and culture. The argument which will be developed in Part II of this book is that Indians, like ordinary English men and women, were perceived as possible subjects for exploitation. At the very least, their wishes and goals were seen as less important than the plans of those colonial leaders whose ideas dominated both their own fellow colonists and the Indians. They were subject to this form of "contempt" not because they were racially different or savage, but because they were lumped in the minds of colonial leaders in the same status category as low-born English people. Frequently, though not always, Indians who were seen as being of the "better sort" were the subjects of lavish praise for their great majesty and dignity. John Smith reported that when Pocahontas appeared at the court of the English king, the courtiers thought she was both more beautiful and more beautifully mannered than many English ladies. When Pocahontas told Smith that now they were both in England, she would call him father, Smith wrote: "I durst not allow of that title, because she was a Kings daughter" (Smith, 1624, 533-534). This is an exceptionally clear illustration of the English principle that status is fundamental to all other categories.

There is another way of seeing that Indians and low-born English people were lumped together. That is by examining the kinds of crimes and character defects of which both groups are accused. It is here that historians usually see the racism of the English showing up most clearly. The English are said to have seen the Indians as forever set apart by their savagery, and this judgement is most clearly revealed in accusations that the Indians are treacherous, lazy, or disgusting in some way. More colorfully, some historians say the Indians were seen by colonists as beast-like or ranging over the land like animals, cultureless and by implication incapable of culture.[3] This problem, like the preceding one, cannot be approached head-on, but must be dealt with by analogy. The method employed here is to compare English attitudes toward Indians with expressed English attitudes toward their fellow colonists. In fact, colonists saw or feared all the same defects in their fellow Englishmen and women which they saw in the Indians. In both cases these defects were part of the justification for exploitation. The Indians are set apart in exactly the same way that these colonists were set apart.

In fact many colonists were extraordinarily interested in Indian society and culture and functioned as competent ethnographers. The volume of writing on the subject even for this early period testifies to the great interest of the English reading public in the subject of the Indians and all of America. Detailed descriptions which some colonists wrote about Indian life and culture were in response to this demand from home. English colonists had very definite ideas about what was

3. For full statements of this position, see Margaret T. Hodgen, *Early Anthropology in the Sixteenth and Seventeenth Centuries* (Philadelphia, 1964), 361-70, 405-13; Francis Jennings, *The Invasion of America* (Chapel Hill, 1975), 46-51, 57, 59, 76, 127; John H. Rowe, "Ethnography and Ethnology in the 16th Century," *Kroeber Anthropological Society Papers*, 30 (1964), p. 5; Gary B. Nash, *Red, White, and Black: The Peoples of Early America* (Englewood Cliffs, 1974), 38-9; Roy Harvey Pearce, *The Savages of America: A Study of the Indian and the Idea of Civilization*, rev. ed. (Baltimore, 1965), 5-7; Wilbur Jacobs, *Dispossessing the American Indian: Indians and Whites on the Colonial Frontier* (New York, 1972), 110; Boorstin, "Birth of exploration," *The Listener*, 13 Nov., 1975, 634.

required to produce a society that was worthy of the name and they applied these tests to the Indian societies they described. No writer who actually went to America ever denied that the Indians lived in organized civil communities, and that they therefore had the minimum attributes of human life. Many were very enthusiastic about Indian society, even hoping that readers could learn to improve their own society by reading about the Indians. No writer saw the Indians as racially set apart from themselves. During the early period of colonization no eyewitness of Indian culture saw the Indians as permanently set apart by savagery. All English people were ethnocentric, of course. All saw English culture as superior to Indian and they assumed that the Indians would recognize this superiority and would quickly adapt themselves to English culture. There was no inherent bar to such adaptation and assimilation.

The ancestors of the Indians who met early English colonists had migrated to America from Asia over a land bridge through the Bering Strait. The land bridge existed because more of the world's water was in ice at that period. The ice melted and the land bridge disappeared 10,000 years ago. It had been open and used as much as 40,000 years ago. It is assumed that a relatively small number of people actually survived the arduous centuries of migration, so all the Indians in the Americas are descended from a small base population. This accounts for the fact that they are more racially uniform than any other population in the world. The closing of the land bridge means that, except for a handful of boats blown off course, or exploring voyages from Scandinavia or Ireland during the Middle Ages, the Indians lived and developed in isolation for 10,000 years.⁴

Many diseases were endemic around the whole world in the 16th and 17th centuries, except in America. These included plague, typhus, measles, dysentery, typhoid, smallpox, and tuberculosis. None of these existed in America. The prolonged isolation of the American population meant they had no resistance to European disease. Syphilis was the one killer disease which was native to the Western hemisphere, but even this was introduced into North America by Europeans.

The subject of disease is absolutely crucial, because it was really European diseases and not superior European technology which defeated the Indians in the early years. So many Indians died from the new diseases that it is difficult even to estimate the size of the Indian

---

4. The best treatment of the subject covered in these paragraphs occurs in Alfred W. Crosby, Jr., *The Columbian Exchange: Biological and Cultural Consequences of 1492* (Westport, Conn.: 1972) 22-3, 30.

population on the eve of colonization. We know that population decline because of disease after colonization was catastrophic, but we do not know how many Indians died of diseases spread from early exploring expeditions before colonization actually began. One Plymouth colonist said that "the twentieth person is scarce left alive." (Cushman, 1622, A3) Squanto, who lived with and helped the Pilgrims at Plymouth, was the last member of his tribe. Modern estimates hold that the Indian population must have declined by somewhere between 75% and 90% during the 17th century. As a result of new studies of Indian population and rates of decline, scholars are pushing up estimates of the size of the Indian population. In the 15th century, Henry F. Dobyns argues, the population of the entire hemisphere may have been as high as 100 million, with a population in North America of 10 to 12 million. (Cook, 1973, 499, 501, 505; Jennings, 1975, 28; McCary, 1957, 78; Dobyns, 1966, 414)

The epidemics of European diseases were catastrophic culturally as well as physically. Indians and Englishmen alike were accustomed to explaining extraordinary events in terms of the operation of supernatural forces. When the Indians died in massive numbers of diseases which appeared to select them and leave the English alone, it was natural for both sides to assume that God or some other controlling force favored the English and their enterprises over the Indians. This belief was by no means confined to Puritans or even to English people. Many Indians are reported to have seen the diseases in this way. The perception of the diseases as magical was reinforced by the fact that Indians who had been exposed and were coming down with diseases might go among groups who had never seen the English and bring the disease with them. This made it look as though the English had the power to make the diseases strike by remote control without any physical contact at all. (Hariot, 1588, 380; Winslow, 1624, 10-11) Finally the diseases were destructive of Indian culture in that the medicine men were unable to cure them by their traditional methods. The medicine men were central to Indian culture and government. Much of their power came from their contact with supernatural powers which gave them control of physical phenomena on earth. When they could not cure disease, it was assumed they had lost their supernatural powers and there was no way for the Indians to replace this central pole in their social and political structure. All this gave weight to the idea, shared by colonists and many Indians, that God had forsaken the Indians and favored the English.

Anthropologists group the Indians in North America by languages. All the Indians who lived in the parts of North America originally settled by the English were of the Algonquian language group. The Algonquians had moved into the east coast area as much as a century, possibly longer, before the arrival of the English colonists. They had migrated from the northwest. Later, Iroquois tribes had moved from the southwest into the New York and Pennsylvania areas and forced out the Algonquians living there. The Algonquians were thus split into northern and southern groups. West and south of the southern Algonquians, there were various Iroquoian and Siouan tribes. The southern Algonquians extended to the present-day Carolinas. Roanoke colony in North Carolina confronted Indians of this group as did the Virginia and Maryland colonies. The first settlers in New England met Indians of the northern Algonquian group. The Wampanoags, sometimes called the Massasoits in early writings after their chief, helped the Pilgrims of Plymouth colony.

Political relationships between Indians of the east coast were not static. In fact, there had been considerable movement in both Virginia and New England just before English settlement. The Mahicans of the upper Hudson River, an Algonquian tribe, had split and one segment of the tribe was moving into areas held by other Algonquian tribes. During the late 16th century, this group of Mahicans moved down the Connecticut River to the coast. This feared tribe was named Pequot, "destroyer," by the other Algonquians of New England. In 1636 Massachusetts Bay Colony, with at least the nominal assistance of other New England colonies and several rival tribes, went to war against the Pequots in what was presented as a pre-emptive strike. The Pequot War resulted in the elimination of the powerful Pequots and the increased domination by English colonists over the remaining Indian tribes, just as the Pequots had predicted. (Bradford, 1953, 294-295)

Thomas Jefferson coined the term "Powhatan Confederacy" for the political relationships among Virginia Indians. The early 17th century Jamestown colonists were more accurate when they wrote of the "Great Emperor Powhatan." Powhatan's real name was Wahunsonacock. The English extended the name Powhatan, which meant "falls in a current of water," to him and to all the tribes under his dominion. The actual Powhatans were a small tribe living at the falls in the James River at the present-day site of Richmond, Virginia. Powhatan had inherited the overlordship of six tribes. In the period just before the settlement of Jamestown, he had enlarged his empire to include, finally, more than thirty tribes. This had apparently been accomplished by conquest and intimidation. In 1607 he controlled most of tidewater Virginia, except for the Chesapeake Indians. It is believed that Powhatan caused that tribe to be exterminated shortly before the arrival of the Jamestown colonists in 1607 because he feared the possibility of their producing a political rival to him. (Quinn, 1974a, 453-454) Powhatan had a variety of relationships to the tribes under his sway, some having a great degree of autonomy. (McCary, 1957, 10-11; Swanton, 1952, 66; Morgan, 1975, 49) Powhatan's concept of himself and his authority emerged clearly when the English offered to crown him, thereby hoping to make him a vassal of King James. They wanted him to come to Jamestown for the ceremony. In refusing, Powhatan said, "If your king have sent me presents, I also am a king, and this my land, 8 daies I will stay to receave them, your father is to come to me, not I to him, nor yet to your fort . . ." (Smith, 1612b, 413) Powhatan had enemies among tribes living in the piedmont region to the west. Nancy Oestreich Lurie offers, as an explanation for the initial welcome offered by the Virginia Indians to the colonists and the subsequent alternation of friendliness and hostility, the concern of Powhatan over the threat of his western enemies. His treatment of the English, she argues, was calculated to win their aid against his enemies without at the same time allowing the English to become dominant in the tidewater area. (Lurie in Smith, 1959, 33-50) The English, of course, interpreted Indian behavior according to their own preconceptions. They saw Powhatan as a formidable foe and so were keenly interested in his plans and the thinking behind them. They misinterpreted Powhatan frequently, but they underestimated him only at great cost. Part I of this book will analyze the way in which English colonists reported on and interpreted Indian culture, social organization, religion, and technology.

At the end of the 16th and the beginning of the 17th centuries when Englishmen first began to think of colonies in America, Europe was in the midst of a century and a half of very rapid population growth and economic inflation.[5] Use of farmland showed the effects of this as landholders consolidated their holdings into sizeable fields which could be farmed more efficiently than the small plots formerly worked by tenants and copyholders. Consolidation, along with the use of new scientific agricultural techniques, helped to feed the enlarged population, but at the price of sending many people off the land. These people, "masterless men," looked for work in the towns and cities or became reliant on poor relief. The Poor Law required each parish to be responsible for its own poor, so wandering poor people were shipped, often with punishments, from parish to parish until they found one that would claim them. Humble people in general found themselves

---

5. This treatment draws on the sources in note 2 above.

squeezed as food prices rose disastrously. Many people of all walks of life looked back nostalgically, and with a good deal of romanticism, to a settled past where everyone had had a place in society and money meant less than place. This nostalgia had an impact on colonization. Gentry or aristocratic colonial leaders sometimes came to America looking for a chance to recreate such a society, organized semi-feudally around the lord of the manor, the proprietor of the colony. At the other end of the social scale, the rank and file colonists were often made up of these poor people who lacked any other place to go or who felt they lacked economic opportunity in England. In some cases they were sent against their will. Others were skilled farmers or artisans who came looking for a chance to use their skills.

Not all Englishmen were unhappy about the emerging capitalism in England. Many influential people felt that it was high time England became part of the modern world. These men saw their country as backward and inconsequential. Many of them had lived on the continent of Europe and so had a base of comparison. Colonization in America had been the way to wealth and power for Spain. The fishing industry had been the way to wealth and power for Holland. Writers such as both Richard Hakluyts hammered on this theme constantly. They pointed out that both the best fishing and unlimited colonization possibilities were offered by North America which was just waiting for the English to come. To some extent the Hakluyts acted as agents for Sir Francis Walsingham, so they had encouragement from the highest government circles. (1589c, I, xx) None of these men said it would be easy. They believed England would have to pull itself together before it could make a success of colonies. They suggested the two universities, Oxford and Cambridge, should move away from the traditional medieval curriculum and teach the geography and mathematics which would enable the English to produce their own ship pilots and free English colonial ventures from dependence on Portuguese pilots. England's traditionalism was holding her back. (Hakluyt, 1582a, 14-17)

In the beginning there was much confusion over the purpose and character of colonies. The earliest colonies were set up as military outposts to explore and maintain claims to territory. People who went to them saw their life in America as temporary, assuming that their places would be taken by others when they were sent home. These colonists usually traded with Indians for food and often for furs. Some colonial promoters, those who hoped for rich commodities from Indians in the interior, expected England to establish a series of trading posts along the North American coast. Colonies toward the south had another purpose—to act as a base for privateering ventures against

Spanish treasure ships coming out of the Caribbean.[6] Privateering was given tacit endorsement by the English government and many exploring ventures also indulged in attacks on treasure ships when they could. Until this confusion of goals was resolved, the colonies faced too many problems. Colonies such as Raleigh's Roanoke were placed farther south than they should have been in order to be a better base for privateering. Being close enough for privateering also made them more vulnerable to Spanish attack. The crews of English ships expected to be able to supplement their incomes with the fruits of privateering. They would therefore divert voyages meant to bring crucial supplies to colonies if they saw a rich prize. John White, the leader of Raleigh's last colony at Roanoke, believed that such diversions helped kill the colony. Only when colonization itself became the focus of expectations could colonies get the steady kind of support they needed. This did not happen until colonies also changed in character. No colony was successful until after they were transformed from military outposts into miniature recreations of English society. The Virginia Company came to believe that only when women were in the colony would men come to identify with the land and build a colony they could stay in rather than just hoping to make a quick fortune and then spend it in England. All promoters of colonization eventually came to see that it was this permanent commitment which was crucial for success. (Va. Co. Recs. I, 256-257, 268-269, 391, 566; III, 160, 493, 505, 526, 640)

There was a similar change in the character of promotion and backing for colonies.[7] The earliest colonies were the enterprises of just one man or a small group. Raleigh is symbolic of this style of colonization. He held the patent for Virginia, which at that time meant the entire coast of America, and the Roanoke colonies were his ventures. His primary goal, as in the case of all colonial promoters, was to make money, but he also was in search of glory for himself and for England. Individual promoters such as Raleigh and Sir Humphrey Gilbert—who died trying to found a colony in Newfoundland—evoke the image of the swashbuckling Elizabethan who contributed to England's prestige by individual exploits of great daring and skill. This was not destined to be the pattern of the successful English colony. Colonization required such a massive initial investment that the

---

6. The best treatment of the link between privateering and colonization is that of K.R. Andrews, *Elizabethan Privateering* (Cambridge, 1964).

7. See Theodore K. Rabb, *Enterprise and Empire: Merchant and Gentry Investment in the Expansion of England, 1575-1630* (Cambridge, Mass., 1967) and Wesley Frank Craven, *Dissolution of the Virginia Company* (1932, rpt. Gloucester, Mass., 1964).

resources of a small group around an individual were not equal to it, particularly as people learned that colonies required sustaining infusions of funds and supplies over several years. Joint-stock companies, capitalist organizations in which people bought shares, were formed to provide this steady aid. The Virginia Company of London was the first and most famous of these in colonization. National prestige was a strong motive for investors, but they expected to reap a steady income from their shares. Few investors in colonial companies actually got any return on their investments during the period under consideration. The Pilgrims who left Leyden to found Plymouth colony were funded by a joint-stock company, which insisted that they take a large load of non-Puritans chosen for their skills. Joint-stock organization did not mean a complete break with the aristocratic image of colonization. The Virginia Company had a good many members of the gentry and nobility in it and these men were often given shares and high office simply because of their station in life. They were set over the merchants, who provided most of the money, in order to give prestige to the venture and because they alone had the entrée at court which would give them access to the people around the king who actually issued patents and controlled policy.

Joint-stock companies, being capitalist organizations, sound modern; but care must be taken not to over-emphasize the modernity of economic venture in England at this time. The king's court controlled the economy because ventures required patents, and the king customarily rewarded people he favored with monopoly control of the manufacture or importation of products vital to the economy. This was seen as a constriction on economic opportunity for those well-to-do people who saw investment as their way to wealth. People of all sorts were becoming estranged from the royal government in the decades before the English Civil War broke out in the early 1640's. Many of these invested in or came to America. We are most familiar with the estrangement of the Puritans, who were increasingly excluded from public life before 1640, but they are not the only group. Though James I and Charles I were considered by some to be too pro-Catholic, Roman Catholics also thought in terms of creating refuges in America for their co-religionists. Many English people of the poor or "middling sort" felt excluded from traditional occupations and sought a better opportunity in America. The period from 1630 to 1640 is the time of Great Migration of Puritans to Massachusetts Bay in which between 1000 and 3000 colonists came each year. They were fleeing the increasing restrictions which Charles I and his archbishop, William Laud, were putting on the lives of Puritans. It is important to notice, though, that

1000 people a year went to Virginia during the same decade. The 1620's and 1630's were a period of depression in which real wages were lower than they had been for the preceding century. Constriction of opportunity and high prices must have been a powerful combination pushing people toward emigration. University-trained men also found opportunities constricted for them, largely because of corruption within the church. (Curtis, 1962, 25-43) During its first decade Massachusetts Bay had the highest proportion of university-trained men of any society in the history of the world. Dissastisfaction in England eventually led to civil war and the execution of the king. While it was building up it contributed greatly to the development of English colonies in America. It is highly significant that in the decades before the Civil War, England was seen as burdened by overpopulation and America as the receptacle for her unwanted people. In the latter part of the 17th century, despite an absolute rise in population, England was seen as underpopulated, unable to supply her commercial enterprises with sufficient labor.

This study covers the first sixty years of colonizing activity. It ends in 1640 on the eve of the Civil War. This is an important date for America as well. From 1640 the flow of immigration slowed to a trickle. Many colonists returned to England. (Stout, 1976) When colonization resumed after the restoration of the Stuarts in 1660, it was different in character just as England was different. The years 1580 to 1640 are a period of relative unity of outlook on the part of colonists and their English backers. England's relationship to America was very different after the Civil War.

Looking back to the 17th century there is an air of inevitability about English colonization of North America, but this was by no means the way it looked to contemporaries. Professor David Quinn argues that the English may actually have discovered America as early as 1481, well before the famous voyage of Columbus. Columbus may even have known about the discoveries by a ship from Bristol which Quinn believes landed in Newfoundland. Failure to publicize the discovery was a result of the Bristol fishermen's desire to exploit the rich area without competition.[8] The English-sponsored voyage of John Cabot

---

8. The best source on early English colonization of North America is D.B. Quinn, *England and the Discovery of America, 1481-1620* (London, 1974). On the subject of early colonization see also Alexander Brown, *The Genesis of the United States* (1980, rpt. New York, 1964), C.R. Boxer, *The Portuguese Seaborne Empire, 1415-1815* (Harmondsworth, 1973) and *The Dutch Seaborne Empire, 1600-1800* (Harmondsworth, 1973); K.G. Davies, *The North Atlantic World in the Seventeenth Century* (Minneapolis, 1974); J.H. Parry, *Europe and a Wider World, 1415-1715*, 3rd ed. rev. (London, 1969) and *The Spanish Seaborne Empire* (1966, rpt. Harmondsworth, 1973). Information in the pages which follow is drawn from reading in these books.

THE SCENE AND THE PARTICIPANTS 13

made the first documented contact with northern North America in 1497. His son, Sebastian, made the first long voyage along the coast of North America, probably going at least as far south as Chesapeake Bay, in about 1508. Giovanni da Verrazano repeated this coastwise venture for France in 1524. It was not clear to 16th century Europeans that God had reserved North America for the English as proponents of English colonization claimed. All the European countries which were active in colonization had North American interests. The earliest and the most international venture was the development of the Newfoundland fisheries. Throughout the 16th century, Portuguese, French, and English fishing boats frequented the area every summer. By the end of the 16th century 500 ships came each year. Basque and Breton sailors dominated the walrus fisheries in the St. Lawrence area. A late 16th century English colonization effort there ended in failure. France founded settlements in Acadia, now Nova Scotia, and French Canada early in the 17th century. A French attempt to found a Jesuit mission farther south in Maine was ended by an expedition sent from Jamestown in 1613 under the command of Samuel Argall. Argall also attacked the Nova Scotia settlements. A French post in modern South Carolina and Huguenot attempts to found a colony in Florida in the 1560's also ended in failure, in both cases because of Spanish attacks. Spain occupied Florida from 1565 on. The Spanish had been active in the Chesapeake Bay area, the area later settled by the Jamestown colony, first in the 1520's and later in the 1570's and 1580's. A Jesuit missionary colony there in 1570-1572 was "extinguished" by the Indians. Spanish interest continued. English colonization of Virginia would have been foreclosed as French efforts had been but for the sea war between England and Spain.

Argall, in his punitive expedition to French Jesuit colonies in the north, visited a small Dutch colony on the Hudson River. New Netherlands flourished there between 1624 and 1664. Finally, the Swedes founded New Sweden on the Delaware River in 1628, a colony which also contained a large number of Finns. There was no reason to assume, after the failure of Roanoke and the prolonged weakness of Jamestown, that England would naturally dominate the coast of North America. Whether or not they were first in discovery, the English were keenly aware that they were late on the scene in the colonization of America. As will be shown later, they believed this to be the more important because the greatest strides in colonization and thus in conversion of heathen peoples had been made by Roman Catholic nations. Nationalism and religion united to create a powerful stimulus to found and sustain colonies in North America.

England's first full-fledged effort to found a colony was in Newfoundland, the area the English knew best because of their fishing interests. Anthony Parkhurst had been trying to spark interest in a permanent base there from the 1570's. Sir Humphrey Gilbert, thinking partly in terms of a colonial refuge for Roman Catholics, led the first colony in 1582. Though he had intended to locate the colony in New England, he landed first in Newfoundland and decided it was superior. Edward Hayes, who accompanied the Gilbert expedition, reported Gilbert as saying, "this voyage had wonne his heart from the South, and that he was now become a Northern man altogether." Gilbert died on the return voyage, and efforts to continue the venture failed. (Hayes, 1583, 418)

Gilbert's half-brother, Sir Walter Raleigh, sponsored the next wave of colonization efforts. Raleigh's monopoly patent covered the coast from modern North Carolina to New England, all of which was then called Virginia. He chose a southern location, at Roanoke in modern North Carolina. Though this colony ultimately failed, Raleigh continued his interest in it for twenty years. Included under the general name of Roanoke are several separate attempts at a permanent settlement. The area was reconnoitered first by a voyage under the command of Philip Amadas and Arthur Barlowe in 1584. Barlowe's enthusiastic description pictured a land where "The earth bringeth foorth all things in aboundance, as in the first creation, without toile or labour." (Barlowe, 1584, 108) In the following year, Raleigh sent a colony of 108 men under Ralph Lane, which was meant to be a permanent colony. This expedition included Thomas Hariot, the scientist, and the painter John White. Their charge was to make accurate maps, and learn about the natives and commodities of Virginia. Supplies ran low, because the expected ships from England did not arrive and because friction with the Indians cut down on the amounts of food available from that source. When Sir Francis Drake stopped at Roanoke on his return to England from the West Indies, the colony decided to leave with him. Three men who had gone into the interior were abandoned. Drake may have left a group of several hundred Africans and Indians he had accumulated in the West Indies. Supplies did arrive with Grenville shortly thereafter. He left 15 men in the deserted colony as a holding party, which is sometimes referred to as the first lost colony. None of the people left behind was ever seen again.

The next colony, sent to Roanoke in 1587, marked a change of policy. This group, under John White, included women and children and was expected to be a true community, not just a military outpost. The economic base of the effort thus changed from emphasis on privateering and toward exploitation of America's natural resources. But the past confusion of privateering with colonization continued to haunt the colony. The skilled pilot on whom many of these voyages depended was a Portuguese, Simao Fernandes, known in England as Simon Ferdinando or Simon Fernandez. White complained bitterly about Fernandes's manipulation of the voyage to Roanoke, manipulation which he charged amounted to treachery. Raleigh, after hearing the Lane colony's reports of the year at Roanoke, had decided that the new colony should locate farther north at Chesapeake Bay, where the Jamestown colony was eventually founded. The colony landed first at Roanoke to look for Grenville's holding party. Fernandes then refused to take them further, and White thought the reason was that he wanted to get on with his privateering. Nor was this the last problem for the colony caused by the sailors' belief that colonization voyages meant an opportunity for privateering. White, at the insistence of his colonists, returned to England to hurry the sending of supplies. The colony he left behind included his daughter and newborn granddaughter, Virginia Dare. White's efforts to bring supplies, or at least make contact with the colony, were complicated by the need for ships to meet the Spanish Armada of 1588 and were completely frustrated by the diversion of the voyages to privateering. When White finally reached Roanoke in 1590, the colony was deserted. Prearranged signals were carved in the trees indicating that the colonists had gone to the friendly Croatoan Indians to the south. The agreed signal for their having left in distress was missing. Foul weather and the loss of all but one anchor made the mariners prevail against White's desire to search further. (White, 1587, 520-523, 525, 531-535; 1588, 564-569; 1590, 599-609, 613-617)

Professor Quinn, in his exhaustive examination of all the evidence, concludes that the colony split into two groups. The larger went north to the Chesapeake Bay area as originally planned. A smaller group then stayed behind at the nearby location to meet the supply ships and inform them of the colony's new location. White's colony is the famous Lost Colony of Roanoke. None of the lost colonists was seen again by English people. Further efforts to contact the colonists were made before Raleigh's imprisonment in 1603. Raleigh may have postponed efforts to search for the colonists because his patent would expire if he did not have a settlement in existence in America. As long as the colonists were not proved dead, he could claim that he was fulfilling the patent's conditions, and therefore control all colonization efforts along the entire eastern coast of the present United States. If the colonists did reach the Chesapeake area, Professor Quinn suggests they may have been killed by Powhatan along with the Chesapeake Indians just before the settlement of Jamestown. In fact, the Chesapeakes' friendliness to the Europeans may have motivated the massacre. Colonial leaders in Jamestown and in London eventually came to believe that Powhatan was responsible for the deaths of the Roanoke colonists. Throughout the early history of Jamestown, there are persistent reports of scattered Europeans or of people who dress like Europeans. They may refer to survivors of Powhatan's attempt to kill off the earlier colony, or survivors of one of the other groups left behind earlier. (Quinn, 1974a, 300, 434-456, 479-480, 492)

The first years of the 17th century also saw some tentative interest in New England, particularly in Maine, the northernmost part. Bartholomew Gosnold was sent in 1602 to the area originally aimed at by Gilbert. His intention to leave a small post there was foiled by the refusal of his men to stay. He returned praising Massachusetts as a prospect for settlement, a conclusion publicized by John Brereton. Raleigh was indignant over this venture, because the proposed settlement fell within his patent. In 1605 after Raleigh's patent had been resumed by the king, George Waymouth was also sent to look for Gilbert's original target, this time with the same intention as Gilbert, that of finding a place of refuge for Roman Catholics. James Rosier wrote this voyage's report.

A completely new phase of venturing began in 1606, in the atmosphere of peace with Spain. The dual Virginia Company was founded to combine the resources of individual adventurers and sustain colonies over the first hard years. The London company was to sponsor the new attempt to colonize Virginia and the western merchants were to assume responsibility for New England colonies. The first attempt to colonize New England under the new patent was inspired by Lord Chief Justice Popham. This Sagadahoc colony in Maine was governed by George Popham, with Ralegh Gilbert as his lieutenant. The colony lasted only one year, 1607-1608. (Preston, 1953, 140-148)

Jamestown was the first attempt by the London Virginia Company. Its foundation begins a new era, as Jamestown was the first English colony to survive in North America. Jamestown's early years were so beset with difficulties that no impartial contemporary would have selected it to be the one that would succeed. Whether or not the Roanoke colonists actually made their way to Chesapeake Bay, Europeans were not unfamiliar to the Indians there. They had been in contact with various Europeans for at least 60 years when the first party of settlers arrived at Jamestown. These first settlers were largely soldiers, their object to set up a post from which to explore the territory. Capt. John Smith was a member of this first party. The London Council had named a council to govern in Virginia, which would elect its own president. Despite the experience gathered from earlier failures, these colonists were poorly prepared for erecting and sustaining a colony. The basic fact that was not recognized, and which Jamestown clearly demonstrated, was that a colony must be carefully nurtured for several years before it could be hoped to begin paying its way.[9] The Virginia Company's failure to grasp this unwelcome fact can be inferred from the inclusion of goldsmiths, jewelers, and other specialized craftsmen in the original group of colonists. Despite the lessons of experience, it was still hoped that a quick return would be possible. Confusion about what life on the colonial frontier would really be like and the dominance of military aims is seen in the number of gentlemen sent to Jamestown. Gentlemen, who did not do any manual labor, were six times as numerous proportionally in Virginia as in England. Not only was the colony poorly prepared, but the choice of site was bad. The *Instructions given by way of advice* which the Virginia Company sent with the settlers emphasized that they should settle on a navigable river, as far upstream as a bark of 50 tons could go. It went on to caution them, "neither must You plant in a low and moist place because it will prove unhealthful." (Va. Co., 1606, 50, 52) In the event they satisfied the goal of the first part of the *Instructions* by settling on the James River in a site which offered ease of contact with English ships and protection against attacks by other Europeans. Their peninsula also offered the best chance of defence against Indian attack. To get these advantages, however, they settled in low, swampy ground. Much of the endemic disease that decimated each new group of settlers has been traced to this mistake. At the end of the first year, only 38 of the original 108 settlers were alive. During this and the next several years, the colony grew almost none of its own food.

   At the end of this year of experience with the realities of colonization, Christopher Newport arrived with supplies, new settlers, and instructions. The gap between the experience of the decimated colony and its London backers was re-emphasized. The new settlers were as ill-suited to the work as the first had been. The backers had said that Newport was not to return without finding gold, finding the passage to the South Sea, or learning about the fate of the Roanoke colonists. John Smith, who took command of the colony in 1608, sent a letter to the Council of

---

   9. A good summary of Jamestown's early years can be found in Alden T. Vaughan, *American Genesis: Captain John Smith and the Founding of Virginia* (Boston, 1975) and in Edmund S. Morgan, *American Slavery-American Freedom: The Ordeal of Colonial Virginia* (New York, 1975).

the London Company in which he expressed his anger over their expectations and the supplies and men they sent to Jamestown. He said the colonists have begun to set up works to make "Pitch and Tarre, Glasse, Sope-ashes, and Clapboord," but the Company cannot expect more than samples of these: "you must not expect from us any such matter, which are but a many of ignorant miserable soules, that are scarce able to get wherewith to live, and defend our selves against the inconstant Salvages." Finally he suggested: "When you send againe I intreat you rather send but thirty Carpenters, husbandmen, gardiners, fisher men, blacksmiths, masons, and diggers up of trees, roots, well provided; then a thousand of such as we have." The London Company's requiring gold was harmful, according to Smith, because the colony had to maintain Newport's mariners who waited while the fruitless search was carried on and he had to "see all necessarie businesse neglected, to fraught such a drunken ship with so much gilded durt." (Smith, 1624, 443-444)

During Smith's administration his tight military discipline improved the situation in the colony, but in 1609, under a new charter, the merchants sent out a new government with Sir Thomas Gates as governor. It was this great fleet which was shipwrecked in Bermuda by the hurricane which inspired Shakespeare's *The Tempest.* One ship managed to reach Jamestown and, after a period of maneuvering, Smith was removed from authority and made to leave the colony. Those who had cast up on Bermuda arrived in the colony 9 months later to a scene of desolation. The winter of 1609 was the notorious starving time in Virginia, when the population dropped from 500 to 60 in 6 months. The colonists, with the refugees from Bermuda, were actually on shipboard and sailing down the James with the intention of abandoning the colony when a new fleet under yet another governor, Thomas West, Lord de la Warr, arrived with supplies. The entire saga became, in the hands of Virginia Company propagandists, a story of divine testing and deliverance.

Very rigorous military discipline under the next governor, Sir Thomas Dale, held the colony together. Improvement in the basic situation which created hope for the future came through the agency of John Rolfe. In 1614 he married Pocahontas, the daughter of Powhatan, who had been kidnapped and held in Jamestown to induce Powhatan's cooperation. This marriage initiated a truce period which gave the colonists much greater freedom in moving around the neighborhood than they had had for many years. It was also Rolfe who experimented with West Indian tobacco and succeeded in growing tobacco in Virginia that could rival Spanish exports. Tobacco finally solved the colony's problem of paying for supplies. During the initial boom period some planters became truly wealthy. In the long run, however, when the market subsided, Virginia's dependence on a single crop made for an unhealthy economy. Tobacco's success kept the Virginians from organizing their economy on a sounder basis. More serious was their unwillingness to divert land to growing food to make the colony self-sufficient.

An effort to give colonists a greater stake in the future of Virginia was made in 1618 and the years following. Land was to be given to settlers who paid for another's passage. Large stockholders were given the right to set up "particular plantations" peopled with their own tenants. As the colonists became more confident, they responded to the need for large amounts of land for tobacco growing by spreading along the James in particular plantations. In 1619 representatives from these plantations "met at a generall Assembly," as reported by John Rolfe. Many historians have pointed to the irony of the fact that the paragraph in which the first representative assembly in America is reported is followed by Rolfe's mention of a "dutch man of warre that sold us twenty Negars," the first black slaves in Virginia. (Smith, 1624, 541)

Powhatan died in 1618. His brother Opechancanough, alarmed by the growth of the colony, shattered the general truce. The Massacre of 1622 hit the plantations strung out for 70 miles along both sides of the river simultaneously and killed 347 settlers. A long struggle for control of the London Council of the Virginia Company culminated shortly thereafter in the resumption of the charter by the crown. In 1624, Virginia became a royal colony. In fact, the mortality caused by the massacre was minor compared to that throughout the colony's history from other causes. At least 6000 went to Virginia between 1607 and 1624. In 1625, there were 1200 people there. (Craven, 1971, 3) In the three years immediately preceding the Massacre, 3,570 persons were sent, according to an angry member of the Virginia Company. With the 700 people already there, they made 4,270. At the time of the Massacre, 1,240 were alive. 3000 people had been lost during those three years. (Va. Co. Recs., III, 536-537; IV, 158-159) Moreover, the high mortality rate continued throughout the century. Typically the new resident went through a seasoning of about two years. If he survived this period, his chances for survival were good. Morgan estimates that the death rate for immigrants continued to be over 50% between 1625 and 1640. Further, as Anita and Darrett Rutman demonstrate, the mortality rate was much higher in the Chesapeake area than in New England during the entire 17th century. (Rutman and Rutman, 1976, 49; Morgan, 1975, 158-159) Jamestown colony's early history was certainly as difficult and troubled as any colony's, but it did survive to be the oldest of the English North American colonies.[10]

New England was settled by Puritan groups. In 1607 at the same time as the foundation of Jamestown, a group of separatist Puritans was preparing to leave for Holland.[11] In 1620 part of this congregation founded the colony of Plymouth Plantation on Cape Cod in present-day Massachusetts. They considered an invitation to settle in New Netherland, but the patent they sailed under actually gave them the right to found a particular plantation in Virginia. Financial backing came from a company of merchant-adventurers for whom the colony was of purely economic interest. Landing in New England, outside the jurisdiction of the London company, meant that they had no patent. The colony never had any legal standing and was finally absorbed by Massachusetts Bay in 1692. The patent which the colony did receive from the Council for New England, which replaced the western merchants' Virginia Company in 1620, was not signed by the king. Their landing on Cape Cod also meant economic difficulty for the colony. The land was barren and rocky and their attempts to pay off their debts by fishing ended in failure. The fur trade became the only good source of cash for the colony, and the problem of simply feeding itself loomed large for the first several years. As in the case of Jamestown, Plymouth had a great mortality during the first winter. Squanto, a Pawtuxet Indian who had been twice kidnapped and taken to England and who returned to find his entire tribe dead of European disease, stayed with the colony and was important in helping them to adapt to American conditions. He was the first Puritan convert.

There was no possibility that Cape Cod would become a purely Puritan preserve under the Pilgrims. Their original band was small, so the merchant-adventurers chose a group of colonists to fill out the first shipment. These "strangers" outnumbered the separatists from the beginning. It was the presence of these "strangers" and the lack of a patent for New England that led the Pilgrims and their fellow colonists to agree before leaving their ship, the Mayflower, to "combine ourselves together into a civil body politic" to make laws by which to conduct their lives. The Mayflower Compact was signed by all the adult free men. Throughout its history Plymouth was characterized by a

10. For a discussion of the causes of death in early Jamestown and the interplay between them, see Karen Ordahl Kupperman, "Apathy and Death in Early Jamestown," *Journal of American History*, 66, 1 (1979), 24-40.

11. The full story of Plymouth colony can be read best in George F. Willison, *Saints and Strangers: The Story of the Mayflower and the Plymouth Colony* (London, 1966), and George Langdon, Jr., *Pilgrim Colony: A History of New Plymouth, 1620-1691* (New Haven, 1966).

relatively wide participation in the political life of the colony. Other groups also tried to settle on Cape Cod. One of these colonies, at Wessagusset, was forced to disband by Pilgrim manipulation of Indian relations. Another, that of Thomas Morton, who was accused of licentiousness and of selling guns and liquor to the Indians, was twice destroyed by forces from Plymouth. (Willison, 1966, 118-136, 163-168)

At the end of its first decade, Plymouth was dwarfed by the arrival of the other Puritan colony, that of Massachusetts Bay, which centered on Boston. Advance parties had been sent to Salem as early as 1628. The Great Migration brought 1000 people in its first year, 1630, which was 3 times the entire migration to Plymouth in the preceding decade, and the rate continued high until 1640. Settlement for the colony of Massachusetts Bay was made easier, as it had been for Plymouth, by the fact that they were initially able to occupy lands cleared by Indians who had died of European diseases. (Willison, 1966, 160; Vaughan, 1965, 93-97; Rutman, 1967, 14)

The Charter of the Massachusetts Bay Company was issued by the Council for New England, the successor of the western merchants' Virginia Company, and this charter was confirmed by a royal grant. (Morgan, 1958, 34-36) Since the charter did not specify where the meeting of its governing council be held, Mathew Cradock, M.P. for London and first governor of the Massachusetts Bay Company, suggested the charter be taken to New England and future meetings of the company take place there. This meant that Massachusetts Bay Colony developed in relative freedom from royal control. (Mass. Bay Recs, I, 49-51) John Winthrop was the first governor of the company after it moved to New England. There were several settlements in Connecticut, each under a separate government. As the numbers of colonists grew in Massachusetts Bay colony, they spread over the Bay area and down the Connecticut River, initially founding Hartford and spreading from there. New Haven was also settled by emigration from Massachusetts Bay. John Winthrop's son, John Winthrop, Jr., was governor of a semi-feudal domain set up at Saybrook at the mouth of the Connecticut River under the sponsorship of Lord Saye and Sele and Lord Brooke.

Some expansion from the colony resulted from the expulsion of dissidents. The Puritans of Massachusetts Bay were determined to arrest the development of Puritan thought at the degree of radicalism which it had attained with the colony's founders. More extreme Puritans, those who paralleled the sectarians of the post-Civil War period in England, were censured or eliminated from Massachusetts Bay. Two upheavals of this sort took place before 1640. Roger

Williams, at first welcomed by the colony, tried to push its religious leaders in the direction of formal separation from the Church of England by refusing to worship in the presence of the unregenerate. After his expulsion, he founded the colony of Providence in modern Rhode Island, where he allowed liberty of conscience. (Morgan, 1958, 115-133) Anne Hutchinson, who had traveled to New England in order to hear the minister who had inspired her and many others, John Cotton, was the chief mover behind the Antinomian Crisis of 1636. This proved difficult for the colony because she claimed it was Cotton himself who was the source of her opinions. He was a leading minister in Massachusetts Bay. The younger Henry Vane, who was for a brief period governor of the colony, supported Mrs. Hutchinson. Her movement brought up the issue of lay involvement in preaching, which in turn reinforced the fundamental fear that the established order might disintegrate under frontier conditions. After a lengthy trial, Mrs. Hutchinson and several of her followers were expelled. (Morgan, 1958, 134-154; Battis, 1962) At the same time that the internal peace of the colony was shattered by these two eruptions, Massachusetts Bay was also involved in the Pequot War. This war, begun by an English "pre-emptive strike," resulted in the elimination of the powerful Pequots, the climax being the burning of their principal fort with all its inhabitants, estimated to be as many as 700 men, women, and children. The removal of the Pequots opened the Connecticut Valley to expansion and clearly established the dominance of Massachusetts Bay over other English colonies in New England.[12]

Permanent colonization of Newfoundland began in 1611, but the effort remained small. In the 1620's George Calvert, Lord Baltimore, revived Gilbert's idea of founding a refuge for Roman Catholics in Newfoundland. His colony was at Ferryland. Though the small colony continued, Baltimore decided to settle elsewhere at the end of his first Newfoundland winter. Negotiations for a particular plantation in Virginia were unsuccessful, so the second Lord Baltimore in 1632 founded a totally separate colony just north of Virginia and named it Maryland. As it would have been dangerous to attempt to discriminate against Church of England men, Maryland became the second North American English colony to offer religious toleration. (Quinn, 1974a, 394-396)

Many people wrote home about their experiences in America and

---

12. For diametrically opposed interpretations of the motives and actions of the Puritans in the causation and conduct of the Pequot War, see Alden Vaughan, *New England Frontier: Puritans and Indians, 1620-1675* (Boston, 1965), Chap. 5 and Jennings, *Invasion of America*, Chap. 13.

their impressions of the country and its people. That the English public was very greatly interested in America can be inferred from the vast number of writings on it which were published in the period before 1640, beginning with the eyewitness report of Edward Hayes on the 1583 Gilbert voyage to Newfoundland. Many commentators on America wrote their impressions and published them as individual books. Many more were printed as part of vast collections of works on America published by a few men. Publication was often a matter of chance. Sometimes very ambitious projects, such as William Strachey's *Historie of Travell into Virginia Britania,* never found the backing necessary for publication. On the other hand some people who had written letters home to friends and families were surprised to find that they had been printed in a compilation or used as the core of a treatise.

America, and the entire subject of exploration and colonization, was brought massively to the public attention with the work of Richard Hakluyt the younger. His interest in geography was first stimulated by his older cousin, the lawyer of the same name. While he was thoroughly committed to pushing the tardy English into new endeavors, Hakluyt's outlook was international. Much of his effort went into putting reports of the ventures of other countries before the public; "For he who proclaims the praises of foreigners, rouses his own countrymen, if they be not dolts." (Hakluyt, 1587a, 365) The travel descriptions he published were meant to stimulate imagination as well as to provide information for future explorers. He did this in his first compilation, *Divers Voyages touching the discoverie of America,* 1582, and in his *The Principall Navigations, Voiages, and Discoveries of the English Nation,* first published in 1589 and published in a much larger second edition of 1598-1600. Samuel Purchas, like Hakluyt a minister, saw himself as Hakluyt's successor and he carried on the practice of collecting documents to tell the story of American colonial efforts, as well as those in other parts of the world. He also published many reports which Hakluyt had collected but had not published. His theological outlook is pronounced and colors the picture of the struggle to establish an English presence in America found in his compilations. His major works on colonization were *Purchas his Pilgrimage,* first published in 1613, and the multi-volume *Hakluytus Posthumus or Purchas his Pilgrimes,* whose first edition was in 1625.

Neither Hakluyt nor Purchas ever went to America. One eyewitness, Capt. John Smith, published a similar compilation of documents. Smith was the only major figure in pre-1640 America who was clearly of a yeoman family. After grammar school and a brief time as a merchant's apprentice, Smith went to fight in the European wars at about the age of 16. His European career involved fighting against the Turks, in the course of which he won a grant of arms from Sigismundus Bathori. He was later captured and made a slave at Constantinople. He was in Russia and North Africa before returning to England, and later he spent some time in Ireland. At the age of 24, when he went to Virginia, he was already a man experienced in surviving in cultures very different from his own.[13] Smith published several accounts of Jamestown colony during the early struggling period. His *A True Relation of such occurences of noate as hath hapned in Virginia* of 1608 and *A Map of Virginia,* Parts I and II, of 1612 were all written to set the record straight about the true state of affairs in the colony and especially about his role in the early years. He was consciously attempting to refute some of the Virginia Company's own pamphlets, as well as the stories of other leaders in America. Smith was obviously a born controversialist. He was almost executed for mutiny before the first party even reached Jamestown. He saw plots against him everywhere throughout his life. He sometimes felt himself discriminated against for his lack of social status and he, for his part, expressed his contempt for men whose experience came from books alone and who crumpled before the hardships of colonial life. His next several books were about New England, attempting to gain backing for a large expedition there under his command. Late in life he returned to the subject of the controversies of early Virginia in his great work of compilation, *The Generall Historie of Virginia, New-England, and the Summer Isles,* published in 1624. In this, as in his earlier *Map of Virginia,* Part II, he used the writings of many people woven together to make a coherent narrative and to support his version of motives and events. He was less scrupulous than Purchas and Hakluyt about making clear which passages are his alone and which are the words of others.

The great majority of other men who wrote about their own experiences in America were from the upper ranks of English society. If they were not actually of gentry or aristocratic status, they were people who were in positions of command or authority.[14] Most were from families of substantial means or influence. Many had been to Oxford, Cambridge, or the Inns of Court, or to some university on the continent. Several had attended more than one university. A substantial minority had had that other important education, travel or service

---

13. On the life of Capt. John Smith, see Vaughan, *American Genesis,* and the works of Philip L. Barbour.

14. Gentry status is assigned on the basis of the requirements set forth in Ruth Kelso, *The Doctrine of the English Gentleman in the Sixteenth Century* (1929; rpt. Gloucester, Mass, 1964), 27.

on the continent or in Ireland. For these, strange cultures would not be a new experience. One large group among the writers was ministers. Another was made up of military men and mariners. Others were merchants, lawyers and men of affairs. Many were interesting men. Thomas Hariot, a great scientific figure, was engaged by Sir Walter Raleigh from the time Hariot was a young man to work on mathematical and geographical projects for him. He, with the watercolorist John White, went to Roanoke colony and produced a remarkable record of Indian life and flora and fauna, which is, even today, the best ethnographical source for the vanished Carolina Algonquians. The name John White occurs twice. The second John White, a minister, was an important force in the organization of the Massachusetts Bay Company, though he himself did not go to America. Jamestown had two colonists with literary ambitions. George Sandys and William Strachey both came to Virginia with the idea that living there would give breadth to their experience. Both had already traveled in Europe and the middle east. Sandys worked on his translation of Ovid's *Metamorphoses* in Jamestown. Strachey wrote a long description of Virginia and the life of English and Indians there which was presented to potential patrons with elaborate dedications and hand-colored frontispieces. Though other works were published by him, his masterpiece, the *Historie of Travell into Virginia Britania,* was not published until the twentieth century. One of the peculiarities of literary conventions of the 16th and 17th centuries is illustrated by Strachey's book, and that is that much of it is borrowed from John Smith's *Map of Virginia*. This is not uncommon. Sometimes authors changed borrowed material, sometimes they incorporated it verbatim into their own prose. This borrowing apparently had nothing to do with the failure of Strachey to get his book published.

Two very remarkable descriptions of Indian life and culture came from New England during this period, those of William Wood and Thomas Morton. Wood is a man about whom almost nothing is known, except that he probably came to Massachusetts Bay with the initial group in 1628 and he indicates by his writing that he was a man of education. Several William Woods studied at Cambridge and it can be assumed that he was one of them. He says he stayed in New England for four years. Thomas Morton, a lawyer, set himself up as the opposite of everything that his Puritan neighbors, both at Plymouth and Massachusetts Bay, stood for. He took over a plantation at Quincy, which he renamed Ma-re Mount and which the Pilgrims called Merry-mount. There he presided over a society which included Englishmen and Indians of both sexes. He competed with the Pilgrims of Plymouth in the fur trade, command of which the Pilgrims needed to pay off their backers at home. When he erected a maypole, a symbol of traditional sports and of social levelling, and of pre-Christian fertility rites as well, the Pilgrims attacked. Three times he was imprisoned by authorities in Massachusetts. Many times historians have seen the vicious punishments enforced on Morton as symptomatic of the Puritans' fear of losing their civilization on the frontier, of "going native." (Zuckerman, 1977b; Slotkin, 1973, 58-65) This was doubtless part of their motivation. Morton, though, also represented all that was wrong with the old England which they had left. He was the archetypal Elizabethan adventurer. The maypole was a political symbol in 17th century England. Royalists celebrated their victories in the English Civil War with maypoles. (Hill, 1964, 184-187) Furthermore, he represented a political threat to the Puritans of Massachusetts Bay. Morton associated himself with Sir Ferdinando Gorges in England, director of the company which was successor to the western merchants' Virginia Company, the one which claimed the right to control all of New England. Morton's book, the *New English Canaan,* satirized the Puritans and characterized them as rebellious subjects of the king and all this was useful in Gorges' campaign to invalidate the Massachusetts Bay charter. Edward Winslow, an important Plymouth colony leader and author, was thrown into prison when he returned to England on colonial business as a result of information given by Morton. More importantly, the Massachusetts Bay charter was revoked in 1637, again partly because of Morton's work. The colonists stalled when ordered to return the charter to England for cancellation and the civil war soon diverted the English government's attention. (Connors, 1969, Chaps. 1 & 2)

What is important for our purposes is to see that Wood and Morton, despite their obvious differences in background, wrote similar kinds of descriptions of the New England Indians. The two books are very different in style and tone, but they are similar in that both men are fundamentally interested in the Indians. They find them sometimes amusing, sometimes awe-inspiring, and sometimes alien, but never contemptible. As both men are open to new experiences, so they both celebrate the new land thay have come to. Wood and Morton are both essentially optimistic men.

Evidence that judgements about the Indians reflect individual psychology also comes from the work of Robert Cushman and Alexander Whitaker. Cushman was a founder of the Pilgrim colony at Plymouth, though he arrived after the first winter and actually stayed in the colony only three weeks. He was an important agent for the colony before and after its founding. Whitaker, the son of a Cambridge University professor, was a moderate Puritan who went to Virginia as a minister. He died there of drowning at a young age. Both these men took a harsh and censorious stand in describing the Indians. Each wrote about them in curt generalizations and seemed little interested in the details of Indian culture. What is striking about their writings, however, is that these men also take a no less harsh and censorious view of the evil tendencies of their fellow Englishmen. Cushman is perpetually complaining to Governor Bradford of Plymouth of his mistreatment and of those who are working against him. Whitaker's book is filled with vivid passages about the sins into which England has fallen. (Cushman, 1622, A2v, 11, 18; Bradford and Winslow, 1622, 72; Bradford, 1953, 45, 55, 56, 109, 128, 365-366; Whitaker, 1613, 6, 11, 22, 27-8, 39)

Religion is unrecorded for most of these writers. A few were strong supporters of the orthodox Church of England and a handful, those associated with the founding of Maryland and a few others, can be clearly identified as Roman Catholics. A more sizeable minority, including the founders of Massachusetts Bay and Plymouth, were known to be Puritans. The others were probably men who at least conformed to the Church of England. The important question is whether there are significant differences between members of different religious groups on the important ethnographical questions. It is frequently asserted that the Puritan view of unregenerate human nature as depraved led Puritan writers to be especially antipathetic to Indian culture, to denounce it without attempting to understand it.[15] Some historians draw a contrast between the secular outlook of the Virginians and the theological cast of New England thought.[16] Finally, some scholars, by writing of New England alone, imply that themes and attitudes which are typical of Englishmen of the period are instead unique to Puritanism.[17] In practice differences in assessments of Indian culture were individual, and membership in one religious or

---

15. See for example Pearce, *Savages of America*, 25-26, 28; Richard L. Slotkin, *Regeneration through Violence: The Mythology of the American Frontier, 1600-1860* (Middletown, Conn., 1973), 42; Howard H. Peckham, *The Colonial Wars, 1689-1762* (Chicago, 1964), 19.

16. Alden T. Vaughan, "The Evolution of Virginia History: Early Historians of the First Colony," in *Perspectives on Early American History*, ed. A.T. Vaughan and George A. Billias (New York, 1973), 36-37; Richard S. Dunn, "Seventeenth-Century English Historians of America," in *Seventeenth-Century America: Essays in Colonial History*, ed. James Morton Smith (Chapel Hill, 1959), 196-197.

17. See Pearce, *Savages of America*; Jennings, *Invasion of America*; Peter N. Carroll, *Puritanism and the Wilderness: The Intellectual Significance of the New England Frontier, 1629-1700* (New York, 1969).

social or educational group is not a good predictor of how a person will view the Indians. In drawing the contrast between Puritans and their contemporaries too sharply we make Puritanism more monolithic than it really was, obscuring the diversity that existed within the broad movement. We also obscure the similarities that Puritans shared with their fellow English men and women. Many of the attitudes we label as Puritan really reflect the accepted practice of the period.

Much of the difficulty in interpretation comes from the fact that Puritanism has a number of meanings in the late 16th and early 17th centuries. One could be called a Puritan on some issues and not on others. (Hill, 1964, Chap. 1) In religion, of course, the name refers to the desire to simplify religious ritual, to purify the church of its remaining Roman Catholic overtones, using the simplicity of the early church as the model. Within this general movement, there was a wide variety of positions on the degree of change looked for and the means which would be appropriate to effect that change. This range led William Haller to identify a right wing, center, and left wing of the movement, particularly as it developed over time, but Haller argues that the similarities of outlook are more important to the interpretation of Puritanism than the differences. The "vital principles" are the same across the Puritan movement, even including the sects of the civil war period. (Haller, 1957, 15, 17, 174-181; Simpson, 1955, 1) These sects made explicit the radicalism which was implicit in Puritanism. They correspond to the radical sects which grew up around such figures as Anne Hutchinson, Roger Williams, and the Quaker leaders in America. All these represent developments within Puritanism.

Puritan theology centers on the belief that mankind is totally depraved, that no man can find redemption by his own efforts. God bestows grace in accordance with his own scheme. Man, lacking understanding, can only see the choice as arbitrary. Thus, the division between the elect and the rest of mankind, whether Indians or Englishmen, was absolute. One could not achieve election by living a good life, though the elect would naturally exhibit virtue in their lives in response to the gift of grace. This theology, usually associated with the work of John Calvin, was not unique to Puritans. Predestinarianism preceded the Reformation, in the writings of St. Augustine, for example. William Lamont argues that Archbishop Laud, the man credited with driving the Puritans to New England, actually shared their theology of election. Moreover, Laud wanted power as a vehicle for enforcing ethical reforms. He, like the Puritans, wanted "Godly Rule." Nor was Laud unique among Church of England leaders in his adherence to this position. Haller points out that James I agreed with the Puritans on most points of theology. (Lamont, 1969, 64-5, 68-70, 73, 158, 165; Haller, 1957, 50)

Puritans definitely differed from these figures in the established church on the issue of church government. They opposed the episcopal system retained from the Roman Catholic church. All Puritans wanted a greater degree of lay involvement in decision-making than episcopacy allowed. Some wanted total congregational self-government. This issue also produced a fissure within the Puritan movement. Moderate Puritans hoped to reform the church from within. These moderates abhorred the idea of disunity. The left wing, the Separatists, believed that the church should contain only those who were clearly elect, and therefore set up separate self-governing congregations. Plymouth colony in Massachusetts was settled by separatist Puritans. Massachusetts Bay, centered on Boston, was founded by non-separating Puritans. Virginia was a mixed, nominally Church of England, colony. (Levy,1960, 114; Langdon, 1966, 100-101; Vaughan, 1975, 136) The distinction between separatists and non-separatists became virtually meaningless in America, where all congregations were too cut off from the center of the established church to receive any real direction. It was in a letter from Virginia that Alexander Whitaker, son of the Master of St. John's College, Cambridge, pointed out that neither the surplice nor subscription, both targets of Puritan reform, were "spoken of" in Virginia. (Whitaker in Hamor, 1615, 60)

In fact, in America the picture is far more mixed than historians usually allow for. The practice of writing only about one colony or region contributes to a feeling of sharp division in the early character of the colonies which is unrealistic. Perry Miller long ago pointed out that much of what we consider distinctively Puritan is really just part of English culture of that period. (Miller and Johnson, 1963, 7) Much of the confusion stems from the fact that Americans label the group of Puritans who settled Massachusetts Bay as *the* Puritans. When writing of the Puritans in America, then, one can mean a religious movement, but one can also refer to one colony, or even to the government of that colony. The sense in which the word is being used is not always made clear. When historians write about the antinomian movement in Massachusetts Bay, these extreme Puritans are sometimes described as non-Puritan because they were opposing the government, *the* Puritans. The same problem can be seen in reference to the separatist Puritans, known to Americans as the Pilgrims, who settled Plymouth colony. They were moderate Puritans in their theology. (Haller, 1957, 188) They are sometimes distinguished from Puritans, however, because they were not part of *the* Puritans.[18] Finally, the designation of the Massachusetts Bay colonists as *the* Puritans serves to obscure the fact that Virginia and Maryland contained a great many Puritans as well. In fact the religious complexion and motivations of the Virginia Company are very similar to those of the organizers of the Puritan New England colonies. Most of the ministers who were sent to Virginia in its early years were moderate Puritans. Not only was the general religious tenor of Virginia colony low church, but also there were small avowedly nonconformist particular plantations authorized within Virginia territory. The separatist Puritans who settled Plymouth, the Pilgrims, had a patent for a Virginia settlement. The most well-known of the Puritan plantations actually founded in Virginia was Jacobopolis, whose leader was the non-separating congregationalist Henry Jacob, the former pastor of a congregation at Southwark. (Quinn, 1974a, 348-9, 362-3; Levy, 1960, 96-113; Morgan, 1975, 149-151; Langdon, 1966, 102, 109; Willison, 1966, 196; Miller, 1964, 106)

One sense in which Puritanism is often used is to designate a "puritanical" approach to personal and public standards. Many writers have pointed out that this is inappropriate in early America, that much which we see as Puritan is simply the normal standard of the times. It was a puritanical age. Certainly Virginia was as rigorous in punishing moral offenses as was New England, and Virginia required much more in the way of church attendance and enforced it more harshly than Massachusetts colonies did.

The Jamestown venture provides two extremely good examples of puritanical attitudes among non-Puritans. One of these is Nicholas Ferrar, a high-church Anglican who, with other members of his family, was a director of the Virginia Company. He founded a religious community for his extended family at Little Gidding in Huntingdonshire in which they lived an austere but purposeful life of devotion, dressing in a special way to distinguish themselves from the uncommitted, just as Puritans did. (Maycock, 1963)

The other example is Capt. John Smith. When Smith took parties away from Jamestown, he held daily religious services. His "he that will not worke shall not eate" policy was a deliberate echo of 2 Thessalonians, 3, 10. It was Smith as president who poured a can of cold water down a man's sleeve for every oath uttered each day, and Smith was revolted by the "Saint-seeming worthies of Virginia," who stole from the common stock. Finally Smith tells of his entertainment by thirty painted but naked young Indian women dancing. He calls them

---

18. Jennings, *Invasion of America,* 187; Willison, *Saints and Strangers,* xi; Peckham, *Colonial Wars,* 19.

"These feindes." Later "all these Nimphes more tormented him then ever, with crowding, and pressing, and hanging upon him mostly tediously crying, love you not mee." Smith, like most Englishmen of his day, was extremely puritanical. (Smith, 1612b, 408, 413, 417, 441)

The most full and meticulous eyewitness accounts of the Indians and their culture were those of Thomas Hariot of 1588, John Smith of 1608 to 1631, Edward Winslow of 1622 and 1624, William Wood of 1634, the *Relation of Maryland* of 1635, and Thomas Morton of 1637. These vary greatly in style and according to the interests of the individual author, but they are similar in that they are all interested in the Indians, and anxious to transmit an accurate picture of their life. Some writers value Indian culture more than others, but none of these men dismisses it out of hand. Hariot was accused of atheism by, among others, Lord Chief Justice Popham after his return from America. (Shirley, ed., 1974, 23-5, 27) Smith was an Anglican. Winslow was one of the separatist Puritans of Plymouth colony, while Wood came in the advance party of the Puritans of Massachusetts Bay. The writer of the *Relation of Maryland* is presumed to have been a Roman Catholic. Thomas Morton was an Anglican. Attempts to portray him as the apostle of pagan libertinism are made at the cost of labeling all his religious allusions as ironic or as "a disguise" or by seeing his classical references as unique to him, which does not accord with the facts.[19] Of all these the account which is most skeptical of the value of Indian culture is that of the conventional Church of England man, John Smith. The most sympathetic of these very lengthy accounts are those of William Wood and the *Relation of Maryland*. It is as misleading to dismiss Wood as "sketchy" (Pearce, 1965, 25) as it is to see him as unique. (Zolla, 1973, 49) Many shorter accounts, such as that of William Morrell, an Anglican minister, and Christopher Levett, a sea captain, are very sympathetic to Indian life. Together these accounts make a good ethnographic resource on the vanished cultures of the eastern woodland Algonquians.

A favorite example of Puritan bigotry in America for many historians is their understanding of the plague which decimated the New England Indians and presented the Puritans who settled there with cleared fields to plant and weakened natives to oppose them. That Puritan writers thought God had cleared away the "savages" for them is undeniable. But what is equally undeniable is that the distinguished

---

19. Slotkin, *Regeneration Through Violence*, 59-60; Larzer Ziff, *Puritanism in America: New Culture in a New World* (New York, 1973), 41; Elémire Zolla, *The Writer and the Shaman: A Morphology of the American Indian*, trans. Raymond Rosenthal (New York, 1973), 24-25.

scientist, Thomas Hariot, and Thomas Morton, the Plymouth Puritan's enemy, thought similarly about the strange disease that attacked the Indians. It was Morton who labeled the plague, "the hand of God." Many of the views which are seen as derived from Puritanism are by no means exclusive to Puritans. The result of the great mortality among the Indians according to Morton is that "the place is made so much the more fitt, for the English Nation to inhabit in, and erect in it Temples to the Glory of God." (Morton, 1637, 18-19; Hariot, 1588, 378-381)

2

Indian Appearance

There is a puzzle in early English discussions of American Indian appearance, best seen in the strange career of the watercolors of John White. White, who was sent by Raleigh to Roanoke colony to paint the natives and natural commodities of America, produced a remarkable set of pictures of Indians and their daily life. He was meticulous in his effort to render an exact likeness. His Indians are tanned, they assume postures which are ungainly to Western eyes, and their faces are somewhat Oriental with low foreheads. Their hair is straight and black. These watercolors were not published until the twentieth century. What the contemporary English public did see was engravings of them done by the continental publisher Theodore deBry and his assistants. Thomas Hariot, who had worked with White at Roanoke, had published his account of the natives and commodities of Virginia as *The Briefe and True Report of the New Found Land* in 1588. DeBry's edition, which was published in 1590 at the urging of Richard Hakluyt and with the cooperation of Hariot, reprinted the *Briefe and True Report* and presented the deBry engravings of White's watercolors with notes on the pictures written by Hariot.[1] These engravings retained White's meticulous attention to detail in dress, hair style, and body decoration, but changed the faces, postures, and bodies of the Indians in dramatic ways. The faces were sweetened, softened, and Europeanized. With their new high foreheads, puckered mouths and ringleted hair they resemble the classical figures in the German engraving tradition.

---

1. The White watercolors and deBry engravings can be compared in Paul Hulton and D.B. Quinn, eds., *The American Drawings of John White, 1577-1590* (London, 1964), which also includes the best scholarly discussion of the works. See also D.B. Quinn and R.A. Skelton, "Introduction," to Richard Hakluyt, *The Principall Navigations, Voiages, and Discoveries of the English Nation* (1589 facsimile rpt. Cambridge, 1965), I, xxxiii.

Crouching and ungainly postures were largely eliminated. The long thin feet and large hands of White's Indians became short and fat.

How can this difference be accounted for? Both White and deBry were anxious to encourage interest in America. White's meticulous and accurate rendering of American natives was not intended to make them repugnant to European eyes. He was himself the governor of Raleigh's next expedition to Roanoke and was concerned to provide a favorable picture of Virginia life. Why, then, did deBry change his pictures in the way he did? It is important to notice that deBry was quite faithful in rendering the extremely detailed dress and tattooing patterns of the watercolors. The minor variations in body decoration which do occur may be White's own. He did a second set of the watercolors, now lost, from which deBry worked. One possible explanation is that deBry thought the exotic qualities of White's Indians would be unacceptable to the European public, that they would make them repugnant. This would be consistent with his making them "prettier" as well as more familiar to Western eyes. The other possible explanation is that, while dress and other external kinds of decoration were seen as extremely important, faces and posture were not important enough to preserve. The engravers, then, simply rendered these as they were accustomed to do. There is a kind of negative evidence for this second explanation as typical. This is the almost total lack of interest in native faces and unusual postures through the rest of the period, despite the often extensive descriptions of other aspects of their appearance. Apparently these were not important ingredients in the picture which the English public demanded.

Englishmen did want to know what the Indians looked like. When colonists and travelers introduced the American natives to their audiences they usually began with descriptions of Indian appearance and many devoted most of their attention to it. Naturally appearance was the initial focus of writers because it was most accessible, but that was not the only reason for its prominence. Appearance was important to the travelers and their audience because it was the key communicator of the truth about one's character and status. This can be seen in the fact that there is general agreement among writers on what aspects of appearance are important and what not. Some writers unashamedly borrowed from others, usually without acknowledgement, but even when there was no borrowing, the descriptions conform to a standard format. Though all aspects of appearance were equally accessible, only some were important indicators. These are the ones we see described again and again.

If a modern traveler were to describe an alien culture to people who had never seen representatives of that culture, he would begin by describing the faces of the people, that part of appearance which we believe most closely reflects the true character of a person. Clothes and decoration, especially if exotic, would be interesting to the traveler describing an alien culture because they would complete the picture and would add color, but they would not tell the truth about the culture in the same way. To put this another way, we would concentrate on those aspects of a people which we would see as intrinsic, as basic to the character of those people. Above all we would concentrate on aspects of appearance which are not subject to manipulation. We would want to know what the truth is, not what the people are trying to make us believe by their way of presenting themselves.

Exactly the reverse is true of those Englishmen who came to America in the early period and who wrote home of their experiences. Indian faces are virtually never described.[2] Faces clearly are not interesting. What is described at very great length is Indian clothes and hair styles, tattooing and jewelry, posture, and skin color. In short the descriptions concentrate almost exclusively on aspects of appearance which were within the control of the person described. Early modern Englishmen believed that people can create their own identity, and that therefore one communicates to the world through signals such as dress and other forms of decoration who one is, what group or category one belongs to. Therefore, such intrinsic elements as facial or bone structure are not interesting because they tell nothing about the identity one has created.

When they look at individual Indians, English people are anxious to know their status and quality. This is communicated through dress, hair styles, and decoration. What the writers are interested in is distinctions which occur according to social class, age, marital status, sex, tribe, occupation, or season. English society of this period had distinctive dress for each of these classifications, if tribe is replaced by locale. When early writers look at Indian society they want to know whether that culture also makes distinctions between kinds of people. Englishmen, concerned about the breakdown of order and distinctions in their own society, wanted to know how boundary lines between groups were handled in Indian society. It was determiners and maintainers of status, not intrinsic character judgements, which interested early colonists and travelers.

Skin color was an interesting example of fabrication of identity for these writers. Most Englishmen described the Indians as being tawny or tanned. What was important for them was their belief that this color

---

2. William Strachey, *The Historie of Travell into Virginia Britania*, ed. Louis B. Wright and Virginia Freund (1612, rpt. London, 1953), 71, is an exception to this generalization.

was artifically produced. In fact, skin color attracted much more attention as an "accidental" attribute than it would have done if it had been considered natural. Color symbolism was extremely important to Englishmen of this period. Blackness was seen as the antithesis of purity, virtue, and goodness. It was the color of evil. (Jordan, 1969, 7; Heather, 1948, 175-176, 178) The "blackness" of the African was seen as the result of "natural infection," one popular theory being that it proceeded from the sin of Cham. It is important, therefore, that the writers do not picture the Indians as black. In fact the proof that blackness resulted from sin rather than from the experience of living in hot regions was that natives of America in the same latitudes as Africa were light-skinned. (Best in Hakluyt, 1598-1600 rpt. 1904, VII, 261-265)

One reason for concern over the darkness of the Indians' skin was the fear that Englishmen might be affected by living in hotter regions than they were accustomed to. William Crashaw specifically says that Englishmen who have lived many years in Virginia have not been altered by the climate. William Wood assured his readers that the English are keeping their natural color, though they do somewhat tan during the summer. In a burst of regional chauvinism, he asserts that the sun is actually making Virginia colonists more pale, as it is drying up their blood.[3]

There were no red men in the early colonies. Red was not used to describe Indian color before the end of the 17th century. (Craven, 1971, 41) Though the standard description involved the words tawny or tanned, many writers add the information that the Indians are born white and that the darker color is artificially produced. (Pringe, 1603, 325; Smith, 1612a, 354; Morrell, 1625, 20; Wood, 1634, 63) Thomas Morton of New England said that infant Indians are "of complexion white as our nation." (Morton, 1637, 24) The Rev. William Crashaw saw a "Virginean" living in England whose skin "was so farre from a Moores or East or West Indians, that it was little more blacke or tawnie, then one of ours would be if he should go naked in the South of England." (Crashaw, 1610, 35) So little were the Indians set apart by color that when the Pilgrims discovered a blond-haired corpse carefully buried by Indians, they were genuinely puzzled. "There was a varietie of opinions amongst us about the embalmed person; some thought it was an Indian Lord and King; others sayd, the Indians have all blacke hayre, and never any was seene with browne or yellow hayre;

---

3. This pallor may have been due to pellagra. See Kupperman, "Apathy and Death," *Journal of American History*, 66, 1 (1979), 32.

some thought, it was a Christian of some speciall note, . . ." (Bradford and Winslow, 1622, 12)

Color, then, was a manipulable attribute. Writers mostly referred to the tan color of the Indians as the "Sun's livery." (Wood, 1634, 63) Thomas Morton believed it was even more deliberately produced by dipping infants in a bath of walnut leaves and husks which "will staine their skinne for ever." (Morton, 1637, 24) However color was produced, the important fact was that the Indians were naturally white like Englishmen and were therefore of similar racial stock. Their darker color was part of a deliberately produced identity which the Indians chose for themselves, because they considered it beautiful or to protect themselves from the elements.

Indian physique was a subject of praise. Their "perfect constitution" as John Brereton put it, is seen in their strength, agility, and straight posture as well as in the fact that there are no physical defects to be found among the Indians. (Brereton, 1602, 11) Wood says, "I have been in many places, yet did I never see one that was borne either in redundance or defect a monster, or any that sicknesse had deformed, or casualtie made decrepit, saving one that had a bleared eye, and an other that had a wenne on his cheeke." (Wood, 1634, 63) Many writers referred to the Indians as well-proportioned, but there is some controversy over whether they are medium height like the English, or tall, and whether they are slender or fat. Most commonly, the writers remark that they are taller than the English. There is no controversy about the admirable straight posture of the Indians, as "straight as arrows" according to John Underhill. (Underhill, 1638, 5) Thomas Morton thought their straight backs were a result of their mothers' carrying them on their backs "by the help of a cradle made of a board forket at both ends, whereon the childe is fast bound, and wrapped in furres." As he says, ". . . to give their character in a worde, they are as proper men and women for feature and limbes as can be found, for flesh and bloud as active." (Morton, 1637, 24) John Smith similarly described a Susquehannock as "the goodliest man that ever we beheld." Some of the writers made social distinctions, reserving their highest praise for Indians of the "better sort." Typical is John Smith in his descriptions of Powhatan and Pocahontas. Smith reported the courtiers who saw Pocahontas thought "many English Ladies worse favoured, proportioned, and behavioured." (Smith, 1612a, 343: 1624, 534)

Clothes were the single most important indicator of status and identity as well as the best boundary maintainer. Colonists assumed that Indians would have distinctive dress depending on whether or not one was married, on where one came from, on what occupation one practiced, and on age, sex and status. They made this assumption because this was true for English society of this period. Not only were there the standardized changes at great moments such as marriage, but there were all sorts of subtle changes in identity which could be communicated by changes in one's clothes. John Underhill, who had misused the Puritans' trust by going over to sectarianism and debauchery after they had given him a position of responsibility in Massachusetts Bay, returned finally to beg their forgiveness. When he came into the meeting house, "he came in his worst clothes (being accustomed to take great pride in his bravery and neatness) without a band, in a foul linen cap pulled close to his eyes." (Winthrop, 1908, II, 12) His dress, far from being an affront to the dignity of the religious gathering, was the sincerest possible indication of his reformation. The Puritans as a group signified their internal change of heart by adopting their plain black and white dress and short hair in an age when men and women dressed opulently. The Indians whom the first English colonists met understood and participated in the language of clothes. After the massacre of 1622 the Virginia Indians signified their desire for peace by sending back a prisoner, Mrs. Boyse, "appareled like one of theire Queens, which they desired wee should take notice of." (Va. Co. Recs., IV, 98)

When early modern Englishmen described Indian culture in terms of the clothes the people wore, they were, in their own eyes, telling the fundamental truth about the Indians. Not only do clothes tell the truth about one's situation, but also the writers strongly imply that the message one communicates by one's clothes must be true. A Jesuit report from Maryland cautioned against imagining that Indian kings were properly compared to kings in Europe. Though Indian kings are described as having absolute power over their subjects, yet they are not true kings because they do not look like kings, in fact they are indistinguishable from their subjects except for an ornamented badge they wear. For this writer the degree of power is less important than whether one looks like a king. (Jesuit letters, 1639, 125) Similarly, Robert Cushman reported from Plymouth colony that the young Indians are so tractable that their conversion would be accomplished "if we had meanes to apparel them, and wholly to retain them with us . . ." (Cushman, 1622, sig A4) One could not become a Christian if one could not dress like a Christian. In some sense, clothes really did make the man.

This preoccupation with clothes as symbols and the need to get the symbols right is most graphically demonstrated in the case of Thomas

Hall of Virginia, who told the authorities that he was both man and woman. He testified that he had been christened Thomasine and had dressed as a girl up to the age of 22. He then cut his hair and went with his brother as a soldier to the Isle of Rhe. When he returned to England, he once again put on women's clothes and lived by doing needlework. When he decided to go to Virginia, he put on men's clothes and shipped as Thomas Hall. After several physical examinations of this unfortunate person, the General Court of Virginia decreed that he was in fact both man and woman and they decided that his clothes must represent this fact. He was ordered to dress in man's clothes but to wear a woman's cap and apron and the order expressly states as its purpose that all the inhabitants should be able to know the truth about his sexual status. (Minutes Va. Council and Gen. Ct., 194-5)

It is not surprising then that, for writers who wrote relatively little about Indians, descriptions of Indian clothes and hair styles predominate. They concentrate on details of clothing which change with the seasons, with age or marriage, or with higher or lower status. Their chief concern is to know that Indian clothes do perform a social function and they are satisfied on this point. This is an important index to the civility of the Indians.

There is a further complication in discussions of Indian dress. Many of the writers described Indian clothes in some detail. Many more used the single word "naked" in describing the Indians. Moreover often a single writer gives both sorts of description. Hariot, for instance, calls the Indians naked despite his later full description of their clothes. (Hariot, 1588, 368-369; White, 1587, 530) The problem lies in the fact that naked meant a variety of things to Englishmen of this period. In the case of Hariot and the others who use the word naked as well as describing Indian clothes, it means that the Indians wear fewer and less elaborate clothes than Europeans do. Most of the writers who seem to contradict themselves actually say, as does *Mourt's Relation*, that the Indians are naked but for a "skin around their middles." (Bradford and Winslow, 1622, 32, 34, 62) It is clear that they do not mean, when they say the Indians are naked, that they are literally without clothes. Several of the writers say, on the contrary, that the Indians are extremely modest. William Wood is one of these, although several times elsewhere he says they are naked and in "Adams livery." Thomas Morton, after describing separately the modesty of Indian men and women, and reinforcing the point in marginal notes, says, "they seeme to have as much modesty as civilized people, and deserve to be applauded for it." (Wood, 1634, 96; Morton, 1637, 22-23)

There is a parallel to the issue of nakedness in discussions of the hairiness of the Indians. Many historians assert that early English colonists compared the Indians to the Medieval Wild Man; but the Wild Man was not only naked, he was covered with a coat of hair which was the source of his superhuman strength. (Bernheimer, 1952, 10, 86; Hodgen, 1964, 362) The best evidence that the Englishmen who went to America during this period did not associate the Indian with the legendary Wild Man is that the Indian was depicted as being less hairy than Europeans. Again and again they comment on the thin beards of native men, even claiming that the natives pluck out what does grow on their chins because they know they do not have enough to make a proper beard. Mosco, the bearded Indian who helped John Smith, was assumed by both Indians and English to have had a French father. His beard led him to adopt the word for stranger as his name, the same word the Indians used for Europeans. (Smith, 1624, 424, 430) The full Indian has neither the nakedness nor the hairiness of the Wild Man.

There is a minority of writers who do seem to use the word naked literally. When this happens, the writer is always attempting to demonstrate that the American climate is suitable for Englishmen. The idea that the American natives can live without clothes is the best proof that America is not inhospitable. (Whitbourne, 1620 rpt. 1622, 55; Best in Hakluyt, 1598-1600 rpt. 1904, VII, 260-261) The other line of reasoning which runs with a literal use of the word naked is the mercantilist one. The Indians, being naked, will be pleased to trade the commodities of America for English woolen cloth. Both sides would benefit from such trade. Several writers looked to American sales for a revival of the English cloth industry, so that benefiting the American Indian would also benefit the English poor. Even these apparently literal uses of the word naked, however, do not necessarily imply more than skimpiness and simplicity of clothes. Certainly they represent a minority opinion on the general question.

The nakedness of the Indians involved varied meanings which had little to do with clothes. The frequent use of the word shows its importance in the English mind. More important, the nakedness of the Indians is the only aspect of Indian appearance that noneyewitnesses feel they may safely comment on. So sure was the armchair traveler Samuel Purchas of his picture of the naked Indian that he shortened James Rosier's description of Indian women wearing beaver skins to the single word "naked." (Rosier, 1605, C2; Purchas, 1625 repr. 1906, XVIII, 343) Naked meant, in addition to unclothed, poor and wretched, or defenceless and unprotected. This picture of the impoverished and defenceless Indian was obviously what those writers who stayed in England had in their minds when they asserted his nakedness. Indian poverty implied a warm welcome for the English and their trading goods and Indian lack of weapons and armor implied inability seriously to threaten the colonies. The nakedness of the Indians was the guarantee of English superiority. Early writers, particularly those who never came to America, thought it would be an easy matter to overcome the "naked and unarmed people in Virginea." (Anon, 1584-5, 130; Peckham, 1583, 471; Hakluyt, 1587b, 377)

There is a further dimension to the issue of nakedness which appears only indirectly in these writers, and that is their belief that opulence and luxury represent sin. The Puritans adopted plain severe clothing to show that they were separating themselves from the sinfulness of the world. Moreover, according to the Bible, clothes became necessary for man when he had sinned. Therefore the writers faced the implicit possibility that the simple clothes of the Indians represented a culture which was morally superior, not degenerate or primitive. Only Thomas Morton of New England, the enemy of the Puritans at Plymouth, endorsed the biblically orthodox view when discussing Indian clothes. First he maintains that the Indians are ashamed of their nakedness, but later he ridicules any meaning attached to clothes beyond the utilitarian one:

Now since it is but foode and rayment that men that live needeth (though not all alike,) why should not the Natives of New England be sayd to live richly having no want of either: Cloathes are the badge of sinne, and the more variety of fashions is but the greater abuse of the Creature . . .

Moreover both he and William Wood introduce the idea that the clothes the Indians wear are better suited to their bodies and way of life than English clothes would be, that they are superior clothes in the American environment. Both men argue that Indians should not be encouraged to abandon their traditional ways of dressing. Morton finished his description of Indian dress by saying:

and in this kinde of ornament, (they doe seeme to me) to be hansomer, then when they are in English apparell, their gesture being answerable to their one habit and not unto ours. (Morton, 1637, 23, 39)

Wood says the Americans do not want any English clothes except "a good course blanket, thorough which they cannot see . . ." or a piece of "broade cloth . . . they love not to be imprisoned in our English fashion." The reasons he gives are interesting. They do not want to spend a lot of time in dressing. More important, they do not want English clothes "because their women cannot wash them when they bee soyled, and their meanes will not reach to buy new when they have done with their old . . . therefore they had rather goe naked than be lousie, and bring their bodies out of their old tune, making them more tender by a new acquired habit, which poverty would constraine them to leave." (Wood, 1634, 65) Since the English probably did not wash these clothes either, the clear implication is that the Indians were cleaner in their habits. Certainly there is plenty of testimony that 17th century Englishmen did not concern themselves unduly about being lousy.

Since clothes were the most important badge of identity for these writers, Wood and Morton are advocating a momentous policy change. Not only are they defending Indian ways of dressing as being well suited to the American environment and the Indian life, but they are also indicating that the Indians were members of a separate culture which should not be obliterated unthinkingly. Both Wood and Morton advocated converting the Indians to Christianity, but they apparently, alone among their fellow colonists, believed the Indians could continue to live their traditional life as Christians. Their advocacy of Indian dress for Indians meant that they looked for a parallel but separate Indian culture to continue even after conversion.

The monstrous does not appear when eyewitnesses discuss the Indians they knew "experimentally." Their interest in accuracy made them distinguish between information they had gathered personally and that which came from another source, and usually the other source is identified. None of the writers portrays the American natives as being anything but fully human, and often admirable. The monstrous savage survives in eyewitness writings in just one type of case. Occasionally the Indians who live beyond the circle of English settlement are described as monstrous. These Indians are said to be not only more savage in their behavior, but they are also physically different from the natives the English writers know. David Ingram was one of 100 sailors set ashore by John Hawkins in the Gulf of Mexico. He claimed to have walked with two other men from there to Acadia in one year, 1568-1569. His *Relation,* a mixture apparently of genuine observations and remembered stories and experiences of other areas, was mentioned by George Peckham in his *True Reporte,* and was printed in the first edition of Hakluyt's *Principall Navigations.* Ingram reported that the Indians he knew were enemies of the "Canibals or men eaters," who "have teeth like dogs teeth, and thereby you may know them." (Ingram, 1582, 287) George Peckham presented the desire to "ayde the Savages against the Canniballs" as a good reason for colonization. He quoted Ingram in this connection, and emphasized that the cannibals had teeth like dogs. (Peckham, 1583, 452) Samuel Purchas's *Pilgrimage* passed on rumors from the short-lived Sagadahoc colony in New England in the early 17th century of cannibals with teeth three inches long, though the colonists admitted they did not see these men. (Purchas, 1614, 756) John Smith did see some of the Susquehannocks, whom he described as giants, sounding like "a great voice in a vault, or cave, as an Eccho." The largest of these men was "the goodliest man that ever we beheld." (Smith, 1612a, 342-343)

Smith was unique in having actually seen the larger than life people he described. The others are transmitting reports made to them by their Indian friends or, sometimes, by European travelers. The physical peculiarities of these unknown Indians were always in the direction of making them stronger and more fearsome than the known Indians. They were often described as being fearless fighters too. Clearly this is partly a function of the fact that the nearby Indians were the source of information. The Indians thus described were always of a different language group from those telling the stories and were often the latter's enemies. The Susquehannocks, for instance, were Iroquoians, while the Powhatans, whom the English in Virginia knew best, were all Algonquians. The situation in New England was similar. The Indians neighboring on English settlements were all of the Algonquian group. The Indians described as monstrous were the Iroquoian Mohawks of upper New York and the Tarrentines, who were the Abnaki of western Maine. Philip Vincent says the "Mowhacks" are "cruell bloody Canniballs," and that all the other Indians are afraid of them. During the war between the Pequots and the English, the "cruell, but wily" Mohawks mutilated some Pequot refugees and sent parts of them back to the English. (Vincent, 1637, 16-17) The Mohawks may have practiced ritual cannibalism. Mohawk is the anglicization of the Algonquian epithet "man-eaters." (Jennings, 1975, 161) William Wood began his discussion of the New England Indians with a description of the "cruell bloody" Mohawks, who "come downe upon their poore neighbours with more than bruitish savagenesse." These cruel cannibals sometimes ate parts of a man in front of him while he was still living. Wood saw the scarred arm of an Indian who had been their captive. He had been painted and "hem'd in with a ring of bare skinned morris dancers" every morning. Later, "when they had sported enough about this walking Maypole, a rough hewne satyre cutteth a gobbit of flesh from his brawnie arme, eating it in his view . . ." The Mohawks are so strong that Wood has heard from an "honest gentleman" that he saw one of them "with a fillippe with his finger kill a dogge . . ." The Mohawks are desperate fighters, with their war cry of "*Hadree Hadree succomee succommee*, we come we come to sucke your blood." They fight with "Tamahaukes" and javelins, disdaining bows and arrows as cowardly. The Tarrentines are almost as bad: "saving that they eate not mans flesh, are lettle lesse savage, and cruell than these Canniballs." (Wood, 1634, 57-60)

Thus there were a few reports of culturally and physically monstrous natives in America. Except for John Smith, however, the writers did not claim first-hand knowledge of the monstrous natives. Smith's giants were not portrayed as culturally vicious. Moreover, even at the time, doubts were cast on the veracity of some of these stories. Samuel Purchas explained that Ingram's *Relation* was dropped from the second edition of the *Principal Navigations* because of "some incredibilities of his reports . . ." (Quinn, ed., 1940, II, 283) Purchas himself cast doubt on the reports of cannibals with three-inch teeth from Sagadahoc when he printed the story. His marginal note said: "These seem to be the deformed Armouchiquois made in the telling more dreadfull." (Purchas, 1614, 756) Finally Wood ends his description of the Mohawks, Tarrantines, and Pequots by saying: "But to leave strangers, and come to declare what is experimentally knowne of the Indians, amongst whom we live." (Wood, 1634, 62) He affirms that he has seen no vicious monsters.

So, the critical outlook of the writers reasserted itself almost immediately. The fact that there are few of these reports and that they do not figure prominently when they do appear, along with the writers' making clear that the information is not first-hand, reinforces the general impression that the documents give. That is, that the writers were overwhelmingly concerned to show the Indians as they themselves had seen them, and that they were impressed by their common humanity with these Indians. The picture of the typical Indian that was transmitted to the English public in the first period of colonization was of a graceful figure, dressed and ornamented in a way which was very different from the English way, but which was usually thought to recognize all the distinctions which English dress recognized and preserved. Indians, like the English, divided people into categories and maintained boundaries between these categories. Therefore they exhibited one of the prime marks of civility.

3

Indian Society and Government

Henry Spelman was a boy who traveled to America shortly after Jamestown was founded, possibly as a ship's cabin boy. In Virginia he was part of a group sent to explore the James River under Capt. John Smith, a trip partly designed to set up contacts with Indians in the vicinity of the colony. To his surprise and without his consent, Spelman was left behind with the son of Powhatan. Though several boys were left temporarily with Indians, usually to learn Indian languages and in return for Indians taken to England, Spelman ever after thought he had been sold to Tanx-Powhatan in return for an Indian village which Smith wanted for an outpost. He was rescued by Capt. Samuel Argall after he had spent about a year with various Indians. He, like the other boys who lived with Virginia Indians for a time, grew up to be an interpreter for the colony. Shortly after his rescue he was in England and there he wrote an account of the Virginia Indians and their society. In it he says he did not attempt to understand Indian government and laws because he was too young and because "I thought that Infidels wear lawless." He goes on to say that the only operation of the laws he saw was the execution of several people for murder and theft. (Spelman, 1613, cx-cxi; Smith, 1608, 171, 193-4; and 1612b, 391-392, 423, 462; and 1624, 606; Purchas, 1625 rpt. 1906, XIX, 158; Barbour, 1964, 275)

Henry Spelman's childish assumption is important because it gives us a chance to look at the preconceptions with which Englishmen first looked at American Indians. What sort of life did they think was normal for "savages?" One image which all Europeans had inherited from the Middle Ages was that of the Wild Man. The Wild Man was the subject of popular legend reinforced by reports of actual wild men found living deep in the European woods. The Wild Man was a renegade from human society. He lived alone or with his mate only. Since he lived out of society, he needed no government. Since he had no need to communicate with his fellow man he had no language. Since he was ignorant of man's place in the universe, he had no religion. He was indeed a man who was more like a brute than a man. We have already seen that the American Indian was not reported as resembling the Wild Man physically. Since the English were met by sizeable groups of Indians, it also was clear that they were not wild men in the sense of the European solitary Wild Man.[1]

The question still remained for English writers, though, of whether the Indians were wild or savage in the original meaning of the word. Robert Johnson, a Virginia Company propagandist who never went to America, offered a description of the American Indians as wild:

> It is inhabited with wild and savage people, that live and lie up and downe in troupes like heards of Deare in a Forrest: they have no law but nature, their apparell skinnes of beasts, but most goe naked: the better sort have houses, but poore ones, they have no Arts nor Science, yet they live under superior command such as it is. (Johnson, 1609, 11)

If the American Indians were to meet English expectations of them as wild or savage, then, they would live as nomads ranging over the land in search of game; in fact they would resemble the beasts they hunted. They would be without law or proper government. Their language and understanding of the world would be simple and possibly defective.

It has become a commonplace among historians that English colonists found their preconceptions confirmed when they looked at the American Indians, that they rejected Indian culture out of hand without attempting to describe or understand it adequately. To confirm this contention, historians point to writings of men such as Robert Johnson. But Johnson, and others who endorsed his view, never visited America. Among Englishmen who actually came to America, no one ever denied that the American "savages" were recognizable as men in their level of social and political organization. They had a set of tests in mind which they could apply to determine whether the Indians were civil men. These tests included having a complex language, government by an hereditary hierarchy, organization of society in towns, and the tilling of the soil with its accompanying care for the morrow. Englishmen of this period believed that town life was superior to any kind of scattered life. They believed man was

---

1. An extremely interesting treatment of the Wild Man can be found in Richard Bernheimer, *Wild Men in the Middle Ages: A Study in Art, Sentiment, and Demonology* (Cambridge, Mass., 1952).

meant to live in association with other men. All other requirements were in support of this main one. In order to live in company together, people must have ways of communicating with their fellows, and there must be ways of regulating relations between people, not only to settle disputes but also so that the functions and responsibilities of each member of society can be known. An orderly life was the sign of a healthy society and the best way to achieve order was to have government based on an hereditary hierarchy of royalty, aristocracy, and common people so that no member of society could question the place he occupied. Not only did English colonists make every effort to describe accurately the Indian culture they saw, but the number of books published and re-published in several editions testifies to the fact that the English public demanded information about these aspects of social organization among the natives of America.

Far from characterizing the Indians as sub-human brutes who lacked government, eyewitness writers did not have the least doubt that the Indians were organized in a civil society. The first requirement for such organization was language. There was widespread interest in Indian languages, partly because they constituted evidence of the level of development of the American natives, but also because knowledge of Indian languages would be the bridge between the two cultures. Thomas Hariot, one of the earliest eyewitness writers, felt Indian language was so important that he had developed a working knowledge of Carolina Algonquian before he went to Roanoke colony. Hariot responded to English interest in Indian languages by including the Indian name for each product he described and by demonstrating the formation of plural words. He stressed that full understanding of Indian culture, especially their religion, could not come without a greater competence in the Algonquian tongue. Even after his general interest in America waned, Hariot's interest in the language continued. (Hariot, 1588; Shirley, ed. 1974, 39, 48) Though few colonists made the effort to become fluent in the various dialects of Algonquian, the basic language group all along the English coast of America, interest in the native language remained high throughout the period. Clearly the English public wanted to know about how the Indians communicated with each other. For those actually in America, there were additional practical reasons why they needed command of Indian languages. Not only would it make their mutual occupation of the land easier, but the Indians were also the most important source of information about the geography and natural resources of America. The colonists were being pressed from England for accurate information on both, particularly about the hoped-for passage to the Pacific Ocean.

Were the Algonquian tongues recognizable by these Englishmen as being equivalent to European languages, though not possessing a written form? John Smith found the Indians used the word *werowance* for commanders of all ranks and therefore said their language was poor in words. (Smith, 1612a, 371) Some writers, disturbed by the fact that Indians from different parts of the coast could not communicate with each other, referred to their "confused tongues." (Johnson, 1612, 8; Hariot, 1588, 370; Smith, 1612a, 344) Christopher Levett said the New England Indians spoke to each other in broken English, but he pointed out that the same difficulty in communication would occur in a meeting between a Welsh and an English speaker in Britain. (Levett, 1624, 22) William Wood also reminded his readers of the confusion of languages between the north, west, and south of England. (Wood, 1634, 92) Edward Winslow and John Smith believed Indians from different parts of New England could communicate, a belief supported by modern research. (Winslow, 1624, 60-61; Smith, 1631, 938; Vaughan, 1965, 30)

Many writers hoped to go beyond basic communication to an understanding of Indian culture. The British Library copy of Smith's *True Relation* has this hand-written marginal note: "This author I find in many errors, which they do impute to his not well understanding the language." (Smith, 1608, ed. Barbour, 189) Thomas Morton of New England pointed to other errors growing out of insufficient knowledge of each other's languages. The English had formerly believed that great hairy beasts described by the Indians were men. The error grew because "wee were but slender proficients in the language of the Natives." Morton says that each side is now more skilled in the language of the other. (Morton, 1637, 66) Those who spent considerable time in America agreed with Edward Winslow of Plymouth that the Indian language was "copious, large, and difficult." (Winslow, 1624, 60-61) William Wood said their language "is hard to learne; few of the English being able to speake any of it, or capable of the right pronunciation, which is the chiefe grace of their tongue." (Wood, 1634, 91) Very few would have joined the three-week New England resident Robert Cushman in dismissing "their barbarous language." (Cushman, 1622, 18)

Englishmen in the Tudor-Stuart period were not democrats. For most of them the best government was one which, while respecting the ancient rights of the people, governed with the greatest degree of authority and command. Weak authority was a sign of decay and led to disorder. When Englishmen of this period describe Indian society, the characteristic on which they lavish the most praise is the great authority of the kings and the reverence of the governed for them. There was no doubt on the part of anyone who actually saw Indian society that they had fully recognizable civil government. Again and again the writers refer to the Indian kings, usually using the native word—*sachem, sagamore, bashabes, werowance*—along with an English equivalent—king, lord, commander, prince. Many writers endeavored to render the complexity they saw in Indian government and law. The Virginia Company sternly objected to the use of the word king for Powhatan, saying Virginia knew no king but King James, and chided them for seeming to recognize the sovereignty of Opechancanough, Powhatan's successor. The colonists themselves could afford to indulge in no such wordplay. The word king is constantly used from Virginia, even when the colonists are discussing plans for revenge against the Indians. (Va. Co. Recs., II, 41, 94-95, 115-116, 482; III, 438; IV, 89, 98, 102) William Strachey believed that Powhatan was so much a king that he, and all Christian kings, were God's "ymediate Instruments on earth" and therefore Powhatan had an "infused kynd of divinenes." His sovereignty indicated that he was God's annointed, despite the fact that he was a heathen. Strachey believed that this was the cause of his majesty and presence, "which oftentimes strykes awe and sufficient wonder into our people, presenting themselves before him." A Jesuit report from Maryland claimed with pride that Father Andrew White was living in the "metropolis of Pascatoa" in the "palace with the emperor himself." (Strachey, 1953, 60-1; Jesuit letter, 1639, 124)

The writers agree that the native system of government is complex, involving far more than a simple tribal chief and his immediate followers. In their attempt to describe this complexity, they use a variety of European terms as similes. They usually conveyed their perception that some kings had the overlordship of several lesser kings by the word imperial. Powhatan's control of the entire Chesapeake area earned him and his successors the title of the Great Emperor. John Martin, a Virginia colonist, wrote a plan for making Virginia a royal colony. In it he portrayed Virginia under the Indians as a series of towns with their surrounding fields resembling shires in England. The great king, he said, commanded 32 of these small kingdoms. (Va. Co. Recs., III, 708) Reports from Roanoke, Maryland, and New England also refer to Great Kings or Emperors. In New England, the colonists sometimes recognized the Sachems' sovereignty by having them carry out punishments decreed against Indians for injuries committed against Englishmen. This was convenient but it was also recognition that sachems were responsible for their own people. (Winthrop, 1908, I, 89, 193)

Despite general agreement on the great authority of the Indian rulers, many writers indicated that they were bound to follow the advice of councils made up of the chief and wisest men of the community. Again, such reports came from all along the coast. In one case, that of the Chickahominies of Virginia, there was no king and the entire government was said to have been conducted by a council of priests. These Indians, loosely tied to Powhatan, but anxious to keep from becoming fully part of his empire, agreed to ally themselves with the English, thus becoming "King James his men." King James is said to be the first king they ever acknowledged.

Many writers believed that hereditary rank or social class was recognized in Indian society just as in English culture. The king's council was chosen from the chief men, the aristocrats. Many writers indicated that the nobility or "better sort" were set apart by their dress, by their physical proximity to the king, or by special trading privileges. Again, it is said that Indians marry only people of their own rank. Rank was such an important organizing principle to the English that some believed Indians and Englishmen of the "better sort" could recognize each other as such without any prior introduction.

All these eyewitness writers agree that native Americans have a monarchical form of government growing out of a social hierarchy. Some do dispute whether the European similes are being correctly applied, whether the writers have their terminology right. Some writers object that the terms, such as *sagamore* and *werowance,* which are being translated as king actually refer to anyone in authority and cannot be assumed to refer to the one in supreme command. (Lane, 1586, 281; Levett, 1624, 20) Other writers express doubt as to whether "king" and "nobility" correctly describe the system they have seen. (Smith, 1608, 171, 191-192; and 1612a, 371; and 1612b, 380; Morton, 1637, 23, 27-28, 34, 53) None of this doubt, however, is about whether there is a hierarchical social system and government in Indian society. The doubts concern whether the European similes are conveying the exact truth.

Most writers were satisfied with translating native words for chief as king, just as they believed in the imperial simile. The reason for this is not only that the kings governed with great authority, but also that the people held them in great reverence and that they themselves possessed such great dignity and majesty. Gravity is the quality most important in word portraits of Indian chief men. "Grave and majesticall" or "grave and wise" are frequent combinations in English descriptions. In short, Indian kings acted like kings. This sense is conveyed in many ways. A Virginia colonist, in telling a story about Powhatan, began it, "The greate Werowance Powhawtan in his annuall progress through his pettye provinces . . ." (Va. Co. Recs., III, 438) Another time the colonists there referred to events which took place in Opechancanough's "courte." Henry Spelman wrote of the annual planting day in which his subjects planted corn for Powhatan, which was followed in the fall by a harvest day. After the work, Powhatan went among the people and distributed beads. Spelman says the people "shew much reverence to him." (Spelman, 1613, cxii-cxiii)

In 1603 the majestic Queen Elizabeth I died and with her the Tudor line of monarchs. She was succeeded by James VI of Scotland, who became James I of England and the first of the English Stuart kings. James, who ruled until 1625 and was succeeded by his son, Charles I, was not considered grave or majestical. His trunk was too big for his spindly legs, so he walked with an uneasy gait. His manners were "crude and uncivil." He slobbered when he ate and he was dirty. John Smith's report of Powhatan washing his hands before and after each meal can be contrasted with the practice of King James as reported by a contemporary: "His skin was as soft as taffeta sarsnet, which felt so, because he never washed his hands." He lavished affection on his succession of male favorites in public to the disgust of many of his subjects. The most powerful favorite, Buckingham, closed a letter to James with: "And so I kiss your dirty hands." He liked strong drink and he presided over an unruly and often drunken court. James was one of the most learned of English kings, but he was not wise. As his subjects became increasingly alienated from him, he withdrew himself from all but his court. When the public pressed around him and he was told they just desired a look at his face, he is said to have replied: "God's wounds! I will pull down my breeches and they shall also see my arse!" (Willson, 1956, 27, 53, 379, 386; Kenyon, 1967, Chap. II, esp. p. 50-51; Smith, 1612a, 370-371)

When English writers say that Indian kings are so dignified that even the English are awestruck before them, they are saying a great deal. Whether they realized it or not, they were claiming qualities for the Indian kings which were lacked by the man who was the English king during the time many of them were writing. John Smith's earliest work described his first meeting with the Emperor Powhatan:

This proude salvage, having his finest women, and the principall of his chiefe men assembled, sate in rankes as before is expressed, himselfe as upon a

Throne at the upper ende of the house, with such a Majestie as I cannot expresse, nor yet have often seene, either in Pagan or Christian. (Smith, 1608, 191)

When another chief, striving too hard for dignity, looks foolish, this is recorded as an exception. (Archer, 1607c, 92) In New England the Plymouth leaders described the Sachem Iyanough similarly: "a man not exceeding twentie-six yeeres of age, but very personable, gentle, courteous, and fayre conditioned . . ." (Bradford and Winslow, 1622, 50) Massachusetts Bay colonists also wrote about the wisdom and dignity of the Indian chiefs they dealt with. (Winthrop, 1908, I, 59, 186) These descriptive words—civility, dignity, gravity—would have carried a tremendous load of meaning to readers of the period. Indians governed by such men were easily recognizable as fellow participants in civil society with the Europeans who wrote about them.

Many who wrote from America, not content with demonstrating that the Indians did indeed live in civil society, went on to describe various aspects of their political and social life in some detail. Many did so because they found the society interesting in its correspondences to and divergences from familiar European societies. Mixed with this interest was the search for information about the Indians that would make their approach and manipulation more effective. This further information about Indian customs and society falls into several categories which appear again and again regardless of the area being described.

The writers were most interested in the institutions which regulated relations between individuals and between groups of individuals. As they wanted to understand how the society functioned and preserved order, they also reported on how the society dealt with tensions and violations. Regulation of society, resolution of tensions, and the preservation of relationships and proper distance between individuals were major concerns in Elizabethan and Stuart England. The travelers reflected their belief that these three were the major functions of society when they selected topics for their American reports. Indian society, as presented by these writers, succeeded at least as well as English society in the all-important maintenance of order and propriety. Many of the writers specifically assert that the Americans are more orderly and respectful of their society's institutions than are the English as will be demonstrated later. Functionally, Indian society was worthy of respect.

Management of inheritance, especially when royal power was at stake, was a subject of great interest to English writers. Orderly passing on of power is one mark of civility. Some writers assert that royal inheritance among the American Indians parallels European practices—the eldest son inheriting, followed by other sons in order and then daughters. Others insist that inheritance goes through the female line. John Smith says the sons of the Virginia Algonquian kings do not inherit. In his earliest work, he says the inheritance goes to the sisters of the king and their heirs. In the *Map of Virginia,* published four years later, he says the brothers of the king inherit first, then his sisters. (Smith, 1608, 189; and 1612a, 371) Powhatan's brothers did inherit his empire after his death in 1618. The *Relation of Maryland* says the royal line passes to the sons of the werowance's daughters, "for they hold that the issue of the daughters hath more of his blood in them than the issue of his sonnes." (Anon, 1635, 33, 35) What is important about all this is that the writers are doing a decent job of describing a matrilineal system, a form with which they were unfamiliar. (Hudson, 1976) When they come up against a strange way of proceeding, they neither scoff nor dismiss. They obviously place value on getting the description right, which indicates that they wanted to understand this alien culture.

References to child kings and the regents who governed for them reinforce the picture of orderly succession of power. (Fr. White, 1634, 41) On the other hand, there are instances of conquest and disputes over the royal power in the literature. Powhatan, according to John Smith, inherited six of the territories he governed. The rest "have beene his severall conquests." (Smith, 1612a, 369) Leonard Calvert reported Portobacco became "Emperor of Paskattaway" by killing his eldest brother who had been emperor. (Calvert, 1638, 159) John Pory reported a more amicable resolution of such a problem in Virginia. The "laughing King at Accomack" gave his younger brother most of the authority in his dominion because his brother was "more affected by the people than himselfe." (Smith, 1624, 569-570) The writers do not indicate a mad or savage scramble for power when there is a question about its distribution.

Indian law was a subject which pointed up in an acute way the basic ambivalence of English writers about the alien culture they were describing. The existence of law along with the tacit agreement of the community to abide by it makes civilized life possible. Therefore it is significant that several writers rendered the fact that the Indians had no written law as an absence of law altogether. Many argue that the will of the king is the only law and that this law is absolute.[2] On the other hand, mankind needs law for civil life only because mankind is depraved. Was it possible that the Indians needed no or few laws because they lived in peace and harmony without them? The Roman Catholic writer of the *Relation of Maryland* certainly thought so:

> hee that sees them, may know how men lived whilest the world was under the Law of Nature; and, as by nature, so amongst them, all men are free, but yet subject to command for publike defence. (Anon., 1635, 32)

The Anglican minister William Morrell also claimed the Indians needed no bonds to keep their promises because they "love equitie." (Morrell, 1622, 18, 22) William Wood, who came to Massachusetts Bay in the vanguard of the Puritan migration, also called up images of a time closer to the infancy of the world when men had lived virtuously without the restraints of political society: "For their Lawes, as their evill courses come short of many other Nations, so they have not so many Lawes, though they be not without some . . ." (Wood, 1634, 80)

That law which is discussed by English writers is criminal law. Most writers agree that Indian kings do not punish any except important crimes such as murder, theft, and, possibly, adultery, and that the punishment is death, often carried out by the chief himself. Thomas Hariot shows a greater degree of sophistication in his description of criminal law among the Indians near Roanoke colony. He says there is a range of punishments to match the significance of the crimes committed. (Hariot, 1588, 374-375)

Just as Indian law is seen as regulating relationships within the community, so some writers indicate that American Indians recognize international law which regulates relationships between nations. One such example occurred when the governor and his council in Virginia decided to accept the invitation of Opechancanough, Powhatan's successor, to join in punishing a tribe of Indians who lived beyond the falls. Their crime had been that they killed some women of Opechancanough's tribe "Contrary to ye law of Nations." (Va.Co. Recs., III, 228) Another shows an Indian leader trying to school the English in international law. At issue was the deaths of some English colonists at the hands of a group of Indians. The leaders of the Indians offered to make restitution according to the Indian method by payment of "100.

---

2. Anon., *A Relation of Maryland,* 1635, ed. Francis L. Hawks (New York, 1865), 32; Christopher Levett, *A Voyage into New England* (London, 1624), 20; Smith, *A Map of Virginia,* 1612, in Philip L. Barbour, ed., *The Jamestown Voyages Under the First Charter, 1606-1609* (Cambridge, 1969), 371; William Morrell, *New England* (London, 1625), 18, 22; William Wood, *New Englands Prospect* (London, 1634), 79.

armes length of Roanoke" for each man slain rather than delivering up the murderers as the English demanded. As the Indian ambassador argued, "since that you are heere strangers, and come into our Countrey, you should rather conforme your selves to the Customes of our Countrey, then impose yours upon us." (Anon., 1635, 43) It seems clear that, though many of the colonists came to America with the same notion as Henry Spelman, that "Infidels wear lawless," what they described for English consumption was not wild and savage lawlessness, but a life of simplicity in which complex laws were unnecessary. Such simplicity was a subject of admiration for these writers.

When relations between nations break down, war occurs. Many colonists were interested in the state of warfare among the American Indians. There were several reasons for this. It was a commonplace, especially in the early writers, that the Indians were constantly at war. This fact was comforting to prospective colonists because it offered them a handle for controlling the Indians near their settlements. If the Indians nearby were amenable, then they could offer them protection against their enemies to the west in return for amity and help. If the nearby Indians were recalcitrant, then similar offers could be made to their enemies. Either way, Indians who were fighting among themselves would be more easily controlled by Europeans. The empires, confederations, and alliance systems in which the colonists were so interested were thought to be necessitated by this constant warfare. John Smith believed at one point that Powhatan had offered his "continuall subjection" in return for military aid against his enemies to the west.

The idea that the Indians were constantly at war also fitted in with European preconceptions about savages. "Cruel" and "bloody" were words regularly used in conjunction with savage especially by writers who remained in England.[3] When Gabriel Archer described a demonstration skirmish which he witnessed in Virginia as "violent Cruell and full of Celerity," he was feeding English preconceptions. (Archer, 1607c, 91) But there is another and stronger theme which runs through discussions of Indian warfare. This is the contention that Indian wars are not very serious, that they may be more symbolic than threatening. John Underhill commented on a battle between two sets of Indians during the Pequot War. He said "they might fight seven yeares and not kill seven men." Their warfare was "more for pastime, then to conquer and subdue enemies." (Underhill, 1638, 40-41; Spelman, 1613, cxiv) In fact, as some writers pointed out, the purpose

---

3. For a discussion of the actual state of warfare among these Indians, see Jennings, *Invasion of America*, expecially Chap. 9, "Savage War."

of war among the eastern woodland Indians was either for revenge or to get women and children for captives. Because of the importance of the work women did, one writer reported the Indians as believing that the tribe which had the most women was the wealthiest. (Winslow, 1624, 58-9) All this leads to the conclusion that in the wars which English colonists knew about only enough force was used to achieve the goals of the fighting tribes. This conclusion is reinforced by the example of the Narragansett Indians of New England who had grown rich through trade and manufacturing. They do not expose themselves to "the uncertain events of warre." Other Indians say they are "Women-like men; but being uncapable of a jeare, they rest secure under the conceit of their popularitie, and seeke rather to grow rich by industrie, than famous by deeds of Chevalry." (Wood, 1634, 62, 84-86)

Colonists also described great gatherings of Indians in which they sang, danced, and feasted and during which they played games which were conducted with the seriousness of war. William Wood described their games of chance and their version of football in the greatest detail. In these games, which could go on for several days, the participants painted themselves as if for war and wagered so much that sometimes they lost all they owned. (Wood, 1634, 85-86) Morton also commented on the great seriousness with which these games were taken. (Morton, 1637, 20) The writers may have been so very interested precisely because they recognized that games of skill and chance performed some of the symbolic function of war for Indian society. (Washburn, 1975, 62) William Strachey thought the games might be similar to those described by Virgil. (Strachey, 1953, 84) Sometimes they compare the games played to English equivalents and remark that the main difference is that the Indians never fight with each other in the course of games as the English do, though Wood also claims that the English are more skilful players. (Spelman, 1613, cxiv; Strachey, 1953, 84; Wood, 1634, 86-7) Not only did the games give individual Indians an opportunity to show off their skill and bravery as war did, but they also offered a chance to win spoils. Wood refused to describe the wealth with which one football goal was hung, on the grounds that he would not be believed.

Trade is the other important way in which nations relate to each other. Discussion of Indian trade networks presented a complicated problem to colonists similar to the problem of law. Active and complicated trade patterns would obviously indicate a complex civilization, so the question was important. Even more important was the fact that Indian trade would mean access to a wide variety of goods. Since all the earliest colonies were founded to make money for their backers in

England and since it very quickly became clear that colonists did not have the skill and knowledge to find and mine precious minerals even if they existed along the American coast, the explorers looked to evidence of Indian trade networks as a source of commodities for sale at a profit in England.

Early reports were mixed. Colonists in the 1585 expedition thought the copper used in the Roanoke area came from about three weeks' journey away. Actually it came from as far away as the Lake Superior region. (Lane, 1586, 268-270; Swanton, 1946, 492) Edward Waterhouse, writing of Virginia in 1622, transmitted the report of Marmaduke Parkinson and others who saw a "China Box" at a king's house up the Potomac River. The king said he had it by trading with people who lived ten days' journey over the "great Hils," and near a great sea. That people had gotten it from men who dressed like the English and came in ships. This story convinced Waterhouse that, not only were there rich commodities to be had in the interior, but also the search for a passage to the South Sea would be successful soon. (Waterhouse, 1622, 8-9)

Other early Virginia reports offer a contradictory view. Gabriel Archer, one of the earliest colonists at Jamestown, said that not only did the Indians have no trade with other nations, but there is "no respect of profit, neither is there scarce that we call meum et tuum among them save only the kinges know their owne territoryes, & the people their severall gardens." (Archer, 1607b, 101) Here again there is the ambiguity of the English attitude toward simplicity. While Archer's note of scorn is unmistakable, it is also true that English people in this period believed that excessive concern for profit and covetousness was ruining English society and the example of people who were able to live in peace and harmony without the desire for more than they needed was a powerful one. Once more the writers had to confront the possibility that the "savageness" of Indian society was closer to a pre-lapsarian simplicity and innocence than the civilization of which they were so proud.

Later reports from Maryland and New England tell of more sophisticated trade. Not only are Indians said to trade for necessities, but they also carry on trade for novelties to wear. More importantly, they have a form of currency. English writers compare "Wampompeage," which is made from "periwinkle-shels," to the gold and silver of European commerce. The white wampompeage, which they compare to silver, is worth about one-third of the dark or violet, the equivalent of gold. William Wood and Thomas Morton say this shell money is used as currency all up and down the coast of New England. In fact, the use of wampum may have become generalized only under the influence of English contact. According to Wood, the Narragansett Indians, those who disdained war, made all the coin for the entire coast and were the "Mint-masters." Morton says the English efforts to counterfeit wampum have failed because they are not skilful enough. The Indians recognize their wampum for forgeries and they "slight them." (Smith, 1616, 192, 206; Morton, 1637, 21-22, 29-30, 37; Wood, 1634, 61; Anon., 1635, 44; Winthrop, 1908, I, 109; Swanton, 1946, 483)

There was very great curiosity among English writers about those institutions which governed relationships between individuals in Indian society. Whether and how distinctions were recognized and maintained was the great question. Marriage, and the rules surrounding it, was one subject which excited great interest. The first important point which the writers made is that marriage is well-regulated, that the choice of a mate and the actual joining of the couple is done according to recognized forms. These forms include the prospective husband getting the consent of the maid and of her parents or guardian and the paying of a dowry, though details vary, such as on whether the maid or the man pays the dowry. The writers are in general agreement that divorce is possible, though rarely done, and that it is usually for adultery. (Wood, 1634, 81; Anon., 1635, 35-36; Morton, 1637, 23; Spelman, 1613, cvii)

Several writers also make a second important point about marriage procedures, and this concerns the subject of who may marry whom. Again, the recognition of distinctions between people is the important point. Those writers who say that the Indians recognize rank in their society usually remark that those of the "better sort" marry only within their own class. John Smith quotes John Pory on the Eastern shore Indians in Virginia who approves of their taboos in marriage: "In their mariages they observe a large distance, as well in affinitie as consanguinitie." In other words, they observe regulations which keep them from marrying close relatives. This is part of the reason Pory calls them the "most civill" Indians the English have met. (Smith, 1624, 570)

The *Relation of Maryland* offers a further restriction on marriage in that the writer asserts that the age at marriage was higher among the Indians than in England. He then supports his contention that Indians live to a greater age than Europeans do by asserting that many of them are great-grandfathers. In England, few people survived to become grandparents, largely because of the late age at marriage. The writer of the *Relation of Maryland* must be reflecting the common but erroneous belief that age at marriage in England was low and dropping. William

Morrell asserted that a late age at marriage was enforced among the poor in America. (Anon., 1635, 36; Morrell, 1625, 19; Laslett, 1965, 90-94)

Not all writers present such a picture of regulation and restraint in sexual relations. John Smith was disgusted when the 30 girls who had presented a dance of welcome before him invited him into their lodging and seemed to offer themselves to him. Smith and Edward Winslow both say there are prostitutes in Indian society. (Smith, 1612b, 413; and 1624, 378; Winslow, 1624, 59) William Strachey says husbands among the Virginia Indians allow their wives sexual license, "and uncredible yt is, with what heat both Sexes of them are given over to those Intemperances, and the men to preposterous Venus, for which they are full of their owne country-disease (the Pox) very young." (Strachey, 1953, 112-3, 116) Strachey believes sexual license leads to a low birth rate, "many women deviding the body, and the Strength thereof, make yt generally unfitt to the office of Increase, rather then otherwise." Edward Maria Wingfield is reported to have asserted sexual license extended to homosexual relationships as well. (Purchas, 1614, 768)

One of the most persistent and absorbing questions was whether the Americans practiced polygamy, something which Englishmen associated with the exotic. No very clear answer emerges, probably because each writer is drawing on his own limited experience, and some are letting their preconceptions rule. Many early writers simply say that polygamy is allowed in Indian society. Often these same writers will stress that this is not uncontrolled license, that Indian husbands are constant to their wives. (Ingram, 1582, 293; Archer, 1607a, 104; Fr. White, 1634, 44) Other early writers assert that only the kings are allowed multiple wives. (Hamor, 1615, 39; Jesuit letters, 1639, 127) Having multiple wives was a status symbol for Indians as the English reported it. This accounts for the reports which say that polygamy is allowed but rarely occurs except in the case of kings. It was a status symbol precisely because only a wealthy man could afford to pay for several wives or a great warrior to win them in war, so "he that hath the most wives is the bravest fellow." (Levett, 1624, 20; Anon., 1635, 34; Spelman, 1613, cvii)

Later writers attempted to minimize reports of polygamy. William Wood consciously wrote to set the record straight: "the kings or great Powwowes, alias Conjurers, may have two or three Wives, but seldome use it. Men of ordinary Ranke, having but one; which disproves the report, that they had eight or tenne Wives apeece." (Wood, 1634, 81)

William Morell, the Anglican minister, even went so far as to argue that polygamy made sense in Indian society. Having several wives made up for the high infant mortality rate. Also, since agriculture was carried on by Indian women, multiple wives increased the corn supply. Morrell reminded his readers that corn was the most valuable thing to the Indians. (Morrell, 1625, 19-20)

Only one aspect of American social structure was unanimously censured by English writers and this was the position and treatment of women. Indian women were seen as doing all the really important work in their society. This was universally represented as inexcusable exploitation and was universally condemned. John Smith in an early work set the standard description of the sexual division of labor among Indians: "the women be verie painefull and the men often idle." (Smith, 1612a, 357) The writers describe a routine in which the women planted and took care of the corn and gardens, erected and maintained the materials for housing, and did all the household work. Indian men were seen as lazy because their chief occupations were hunting and fishing. Condemnation of Indian treatment of women reached a crescendo with William Wood's *New England's Prospect*. His chapter on Indian women included a three-page description of all their responsibilities. He pictures the squaw as working so hard she is dancing a jig "to dive for Cocles, and to digge for Clamms, Whereby her lazie husbands guts shee cramms." After raising and preparing all the food, the women wait while the men eat, dancing "a Spaniell-like attendance at their backes for their bony fragments." (Wood, 1634, 33, 68, 94-97) Ethnocentrism had much to do with this scorn. Because hunting and fishing had been reduced to the status of sports in their England, the colonists did not recognize that Indian men were involved in genuine occupations. Nancy Lurie, in fact, asserts that tasks were roughly evenly divided between men and women among the Chesapeake area Indians. (Lurie in Smith, 1959, 57; Craven, 1971, 53)

When English writers described Indian culture, they were looking at a traditional society. In economic terms this meant that tasks of production were shared among all segments of the society. Politically, economic responsibility meant power for women. England was moving away from traditional economic relationships to capitalism. Women were affected profoundly by the move away from traditional patterns. As production for exchange began to predominate, the family ceased to be the center of economic life and women, the partners who remained at home, ceased to play an equal role in the economic life of the family. With the loss of a central role, women lost status and power in other ways. This process has been pointed out in different contexts by many historians of women.[4] Colonists' descriptions of the roles of Indian women show a profound ambivalence about women's importance in that society. They recognize the contribution of women to the Indian economy, but their overpowering concern for order and distinctions meant that they feared changes in the power relationships between the sexes.

In denouncing the exploitation of native American women, Englishmen appear not to recognize at all that Indian women are made more important in Indian society because of their share in production. But such recognition does come through in other discussions. We have already seen that the wealthiest tribes were those which had the most women. Because of this, Edward Winslow reported that a wife who runs away to another tribe is always welcomed. (Winslow, 1624, 59) Not only do the writers report matrilineal descent of inheritance for some tribes, but there were woman monarchs reported and these apparently ruled as well as reigned. Pocahontas was sent by her father, Powhatan, on several diplomatic missions to Jamestown. (Smith, 1608, 206; and 1612b, 396) Women apparently had much more flexibility and independence in choice of marriage partner than English women did. John Smith reported that Indian men must learn to shoot well if they are to win a mate. Marriage meant a decisive change of status for men as well as women, with both sexes adopting a different hair and clothing style to indicate their new status. (Smith, 1612a, 359; Strachey, 1953, 83-4; Rosier, 1605, B3v)

English writers' ambivalence about the roles of Indian women is also demonstrated by their praise for the obedient behavior of these women. Despite their belief that Indian women are systematically mistreated and undervalued, they feel it is right and just that they should be subservient to their husbands. The modesty of Indian women is as praiseworthy as their work. Some writers feared that English society was losing this important source of good order. William Wood reported that Indian men were horrified at the greater freedom of English women in the colonies:

An Indian sagomore once hearing an English woman scold with her husband, her quicke utterance exceeding his apprehension, her active lungs thundering in his eares, expelled him the house; from whence he went to the next neighbour, where he related the unseemeliness of her behaviour; her language being strange to him, hee expressed it as strangely, telling them how she cryed

---

4. See for example John Kelly-Gadol, "The Social Relation of the Sexes: Methodological Implications of Women's History," *Signs*, 1 (1976), 818-819; and articles by Kelly-Gadol and Renate Bridenthal in *Conceptual Frameworks in Women's History* (Bronxville, N.Y., 1976).

Nannana Nannana Nannana Nan, saying he was a greate foole to give her the audience, and no correction for usurping his charter, and abusing him by her tongue.

Not only were English women free in criticizing their husbands, but the Indian men, as Wood put it, "doe condemne the English for their folly in spoyling good working creatures." Worst of all, English women in the colonies were corrupting Indian women, who came to their kitchens for comfort. If the husband comes "to seeke for his Squaw and beginne to bluster, the English woman betakes her to her armes which are the warlike ladle, and the scalding liquors." (Wood, 1634, 73, 97; Levett, 1624, 16)

English writers found much in Indian society which brought up subjects about which they felt ambivalent, such as the power and role of women or the apparent simplicity and innocence inherent in Indian laws and customs. On most occasions, they glossed over these subjects. What they were intent on doing was to see whether Indian society qualified for civil society according to the tests of language, government, settled habitation, and agriculture. In order to accomplish this, they interpreted what they saw to make it conform to European patterns. They believed they had seen an hereditary monarchy and nobility and wrote that. What is important for our purposes is not whether their reports were accurate but rather that they saw in Indian society the order and distinctions and regularity which they valued most of all. They saw Indian society as praiseworthy precisely because they could see it as conforming, however sketchily, to English standards. In some aspects, such as the great reverence of the people for their governors, and wives for husbands, it even exceeded English society.

Equally important is that many English writers were not content with recording surface impressions or the mere fact of organized government, but were actively probing beyond the surface to attempt to understand the inner working of Indian government and social customs. They were ethnocentric, in that they saw their own system as the standard by which all others should be judged, but this did not prevent them from attempting to understand an alien system. There is a very strong tradition in this literature, which begins early and gains strength, of correcting earlier erroneous reports, alleging that the later writer has been able to gain greater understanding of Indian culture. What all this means is that English colonists did not dismiss Indian culture as non-existent or unworthy of notice. Many wrote extensively about it. Some merely noted its existence because their interest lay elsewhere, but no writer who actually went to America denied that the American Indians lived in an organized society which was recognizable as such by all Englishmen who cared to study it.

4

Indian Religion

Important questions of many different kinds could be answered by describing the religion of the American Indians. The subject was extremely complicated for late 16th and early 17th century Englishmen. By studying their religion, one could learn something about whom the Indians were descended from. Since wild people simply accept the fruits of nature without thanks or thought, the existence of a religious system of any complexity among the Indians would also be strong evidence for their civility. Finally, the religious beliefs of the Indians would be a crucial factor in their prospects for conversion to Christianity and to European civilization on which the whole future of the colonization effort depended.

No English writer said Indian religion was anything but idolatry. There was no possible true religion except for Protestant Christianity. In this sense, all the writers dismissed any non-European religion. Those writers who remained in England were often content with a simple dismissal of Indian worship as idolatry. Many compared it to Old Testament examples. This allowed them to play on one of their favorite themes—the comparison of the English, the international leaders of Protestantism against the twin dark foes of Roman Catholicism and heathenism, with the Jews, God's Chosen People of the Old Testament who had to face trials with so many representatives of false religion.

Reports of the misery of Jamestown colony's early years were countered by a massive propaganda campaign conducted by the Virginia Company in a series of sermons, declarations, and pamphlets, which began in 1609-1610. All of these more or less official writings make the Old Testament comparison. Robert Johnson's *New Life of Virginea* begins with a recounting of the wanderings of the Jews. He then transfers the scene to "the sundrie nations of America," which "sacrifice their children to serve the divel, as those heathens did their sonnes and daughters to Molech." (Johnson, 1612, 8; Symonds, 1609, 15, 25) The English public was also urged to disregard reports of Jamestown's failures and stir itself to overturn the kingdom of Satan, to end the bondage of these people to heathenism and idolatry. Most of the writers in this campaign were not eyewitnesses.

Curt dismissals of Indian religion occur among non-eyewitness writers throughout the entire period. Often these dismissals consist of one or a few words. Richard Hakluyt was the earliest who assumed their "Paganisme and Idolatrie." (Hakluyt, 1609, 503) This formulation is typical. Samuel Purchas, in his essay, *Virginia's Verger*, is more colorful: "captivated also to Satans tyranny in foolish pieties, mad impieties." (Purchas, 1625, rpr. 1906, XIX, 231)

The division in outlook between eyewitnesses and non-eyewitnesses was not as clear-cut on Indian religion as it was on appearance and social organization. Several eyewitnesses did find Indian "Idolatrie" to be simply uninteresting. All writers, of course, saw Indian religion as false religion, but some were nevertheless interested in describing its belief system and practices. Those writers who were content to dismiss American beliefs were also those who wrote little about native life in general, and indeed who had little contact with the Indians. Frequently the allegation of heathenism and idolatry was made as part of a rhetorical flourish, as when Anthony Parkhurst calls on Englishmen to liberate the Newfoundland Indians "from out of the captivitie of that spirituall Pharao, the divell." (Parkhurst, 1578, 128) In the same paragraph he blames the lack of support in England for colonization on "the malice of wicked men, the divels instruments in this our age." Thus Englishmen were not immune from being the targets of this type of rhetoric. Sometimes writers begin with a rhetorical denunciation of Indian religion but go on to a sober discussion of its beliefs and practices. (Strachey, 1953, 55, 88ff) Some do dismiss Indian religion as devil worship, including Sir Thomas Dale and John Rolfe, the man who captured Pocahontas and the man who married her. These men are nevertheless exceptions in finding the content of the Indians' religious beliefs and practices totally lacking in interest.

Rhetorical discussions of Indian religion were complicated by the issue of human sacrifice. That the Indian civilizations of Central and South America practiced human sacrifice was well known through the writings of the Spanish. A few writers simply assumed the same was true of North American Indians. Several allegations of human sacrifice appear to be purely rhetorical. Others speak of the Indians sacrificing themselves to Satan, in which case it is probably the immortal soul and not the body of the victim which is in question. Alexander Whitaker, preacher in Jamestown colony, says Indian children are sacrificed to the devil, but adds, "(as I have heere heard)". (Whitaker, 1613, 24) No writer showed any recognition that the martyrdoms produced by the religious strife of Reformation Europe, not even those burned by the Inquisition, could also have been described as human sacrifice. Roman Catholics were accused of many of the false religious practices of infidels, but this extreme was excluded.

Actual reports from Virginia stimulated belief that North American Indians practiced child sacrifice. William White, a laborer in Jamestown, lived with the Indians for a time. He described an initiation ceremony of young boys, which became known in England as the "Blacke Boy" sacrifice. White's story was printed by John Smith, with Smith's own refinements, in the *Map of Virginia* in 1612. Samuel Purchas published White's description and separated Smith's elements in his *Pilgrimage* of 1614. White believed that some of the 14 or 15 boys involved in the initiation actually died. What he saw was a ritual which involved beating of the boys (though they were in part shielded by guards), the making of a great fire, the boys lying in a heap, and extravagant mourning by the Indian women. He was not allowed to see the boys following the ceremony. He was told that some were selected to die, though it is clear that boys who had supposedly died were seen alive years later. (Smith, 1612a, 367-368, Purchas, 1614, 766-767; Strachey, 1953, 89-90, 98-100) Henry Spelman, in a report which was not published until modern times, alleged a sacrifice of children in which the god appears and makes a sign to show which child he has selected. (Spelman, 1613, cv-cvi)

Since these reports fitted with European expectations of heathen behavior, some English writers accepted them at face value. One reason why the Indians at Pawtuxent are said to be the "most civill" Indians is that they do not "use that devilish custome in making black Boyes." John Smith and Samuel Purchas both related versions of John Pory's description of these "thriftie Savages." (Smith, 1624, 570; Purchas, 1625 repr. 1906, XIX, 168) Patrick Copland, not yet knowing that Powhatan's successor, Opechancanough, had led the disastrous 1622 attack in Virginia which killed 347 colonists, published a sermon in which he told of Opechancanough's desire to make an accommodation to English ways. He says Opechancanough knows God is angry with the Indians for their "custome of making their children blackeboys, or consecrating them to Sathan." (Copland, 1622, 29)

Modern anthropologists accept that this ceremony, later known as the *huskanaw,* was a type of initiation or rite of passage and was not designed as a human sacrifice. Among the Powhatans of Virginia both boys and girls were subjected to the initiation. (Swanton, 1946, 815) Philip L. Barbour suggests that the mock execution of John Smith, from which he thought Pocahontas had rescued him, might have been a similar type of initiation into the tribe. (Barbour, 1969, 24-25) It was the extreme mourning and grief of the women which made the interpretation of the rite as human sacrifice credible. The boys were moving from one phase of life to a new state. In this sense, they died and were reborn. The ritual of test, symbolic death, and separation from the rest of society for a time is typical of initiation rites. The mourning was part of the symbolic death. (Douglas, 1966, 96-97)

The combination of an "endurance test and of a metamorphosis through death," particularly in initiation to a special society or group, was pointed out by Richard Bernheimer in his discussion of the Wild Man Hunt of the Middle Ages:

But the ritual itself is suggestive: the masking and subsequent submergence of personality, the effort demanded in terms of running and dancing, the rough treatment against which no complaint could be made, finally the slaying and death, and the injunction to play dead while lying on a bier: all this is familiar from initiation rituals, as they have been practiced over a large part of the world. (Bernheimer, 1952, 56-57)

What is most important is that people writing at the time went beyond the simple allegation of human sacrifice and attempted to understand the meaning of this ritual. William White reported that the boys who survived the ritual lived in the wilderness for nine months. They grew up to be the society's "Priests, and conjurers." (Purchas, 1614, 766) Edward Winslow, writing of New England Indians, described the selection of young boys who were then specially hardened from an early age by a rigorous life which included beating, forced vomiting, and living in the cold. They were destined to be priests. Winslow also said the threshold from boy to manhood was crossed for the rest of the population after the doing of some notable deed. He does say children are "in some cases" killed in sacrifices. (Winslow, 1624, 55-58) By 1617 Purchas himself had some doubts about the interpretation which William White had placed on the ceremony he saw. He republished White's account in the new edition of his *Pilgrimage,* but added a marginal note expressing his skepticism about the sacrifice. Paspiha had been named by White as one boy who died in the sacrifice. In 1617 Purchas said:

this Paspiha is now alive, as Mr Rolph hath tince related to me: and the mourning of the women is not for their childrens death, but because they are for divers moneths detained from them, as we shall after see. Yea, the Virginians themselves, by false reports might delude our Men, and say they were sacrificed when they were not . . . (Barbour, ed., 1969, I, 149)

William Strachey added a different dimension to the discussion of human sacrifice among the Indians. He claimed that such sacrifice was general in the ancient world and that the English had sacrificed their children and the Scots had ritually eaten theirs before the Romans civilized them. (Strachey, 1953, 24, 90) The last, and most moderate, reference to the Black-boys during the period occurred in the *Relation of Maryland.* This account stressed the voluntary and universal nature of the experience. (Anon., 1635, 34) On the question of human sacrifice, as on other aspects of Indian culture, Englishmen were interested in probing beyond their initial reactions and their preconceptions. The drive to describe accurately and to understand was very strong in these observers.

Though it was difficult for colonists to understand Indian religion fully, the English public wanted detailed information and several writers attempted to fill this demand. The marginal note written by hand in John Smith's *True Relation* chided him for underestimating the complexity of Indian religious beliefs:

This Author I fynde in many errors which they doe impute to his not well understandinge ye language for they doe Acknowledge both God & ye Devill and yt after yei are out of this world they shall rise agayne in another world where they shall live at ease and have greate store of bread and venison & other _____. (Barbour, ed., 1969, I, 189)

Edward Winslow was sorry that an early letter of his in which he had denied the existence of Indian religion had been printed, "against my will and knowledge." He says, "therein I erred, though we could then gather no better." (Winslow, 1624, 52; Winslow and Bradford, 1622, 61) Winslow amply made up for his early error by presenting, as did many others, a full and detailed account of Indian ceremonies and beliefs.

When eyewitness writers attempt to describe Indian religion, they find the task difficult, but interesting. Several of the colonists argue, not rhetorically, but out of their own observation, that the Indians worship the devil. This had two meanings during this period. The first would be shared with writers in England, simply the idea that Indian religion was a false religion and therefore an invention of the devil. This allegation, during that emotionally charged time, was also made against Roman

Catholics. John Donne speaks of a Jesuit as having the devil for his "Intelligencer." (Donne, 1626, 35-36) The English Jesuit John Floyd's *The Overthrow of the Protestant Pulpit-Babels*, largely an attack on William Crashaw, was written to refute Protestant charges that Roman Catholics worship the Pope and think him greater than God, that they pray to rocks and stones, and that they think images better books than scriptures. For his part, Floyd exhibits the temper of the age in asserting that the English church cannot be a true church. (Floyd, 1612, 9, 11)

On the other hand several writers believed that the Indians literally worship an evil power, the devil. It is explained that they worship anything capable of doing them harm by adding that the Englishman's "ordinance, peeces, horses &c" are also the objects of worship now.[1] William Strachey compared this worship of that which is feared to ancient Roman practice. (Strachey, 1953, 88)

More often the writers render Indian religion as a dual system, with an evil and a good god. No comparisons are drawn to Christianity on this opposition of good and evil powers. The good god is usually portrayed as remote. The evil one plays a greater part in daily life and fear of him is strong. Alexander Whitaker says, "They acknowledge that there is a great good God, but know him not, having the eyes of their understanding as yet blinded; wherefore they serve the divell for feare . . . (Whitaker, 1613, 24; Strachey, 1953, 89; Fr. White, 1634, 44-45) There are several discussions of the two gods from New England. Francis Higginson and Christopher Levett say they are Squanto and Tanto (or **Squantum** and **Tantum**). William Wood and Edward Winslow say the good god is Kiehtan and the evil one is Hobbomock or Abbomocho. Both Wood and Winslow testify to the power of the evil god. Wood says the Indians call on Kiehtan first in sickness, but if cure does not result, they then turn to charms and the power of the devil. Winslow says they never turn to Kiehtan in sickness, only to Hobbomock. If the disease is curable, he says he sent it for anger. If not, he says Kiehtan sent it. Therefore, they wonder if

---

1. Smith, *Map of Virginia*, in Barbour, ed., *Jamestown Voyages*, II, 364; Gabriel Archer (?), *A breif discription of the People, ibid.*, I, 104; Francis Magnel, *Relation of what Francis Magnel, an Irishman, learned in the land of Virginia, ibid.*, 154; Arthur Barlowe, *The first voyage made to the coastes of America*, in David B. Quinn, ed.,*The Roanoke Voyages, 1584-1590* (London, 1955), I, 114; David Ingram, *The Relation of David Ingram*, in David B. Quinn, ed., *The Voyages and* Colonizing Enterprises of Sir Humphrey Gilbert (London, 1940), II, 293; Henry Spelman, *Relation of Virginia*, in Edward Arber and A.G. Bradley, eds., *Travels and Works of Captain John Smith* (Edinburgh, 1910), I, cv; Susan Myra Kingsbury, ed., *The Records of the Virginia Company of London* (Washington, D.C., 1906-1935), III, 14-15.

Kiehtan is wholly good. (Higginson, 1630, 13; Levett, 1624, 19; Winslow, 1624, 52-53; Wood, 1634, 77, 82) Carved and painted images of the Indian god reinforced the colonists' belief that the Indians worshipped the devil. English writers from southern settlements found these images evil and deformed illusions of the devil. They were, nonetheless, interesting to them. Two of John White's watercolors from Roanoke show a carved god and this image is discussed by Hariot in his notes. Hariot says the idols are only representations of the gods, though the "common sort thinke them also to be gods." (Hulton and Quinn, eds., 1964; Hariot, 1588, 373) Alexander Whitaker, a minister in Jamestown, sent an image, a "deformed monster," home to the council of the Virginia Company. (Whitaker, 1613, 24; Barlowe, 1584, 114; Smith, 1612a, 364; Spelman, 1613, cv)

Several of the writers add that the Indians have many lesser deities. A few say their principal god is the sun. Whatever the identity of the Indian deities, and many writers indicated they could not be sure, the colonists felt the existence of Indian religion was an important first step to acceptance of true religion. Orthodox Christian opinion held that the belief in a supreme being was instinctive and universal. Calvin said it quite clearly:

We lay it down as a position not to be controverted that the human mind, even by natural instinct, possesses some sense of a diety. (Calvin, McNeill, ed., 1957, 9)

Calvin refers the reader to Cicero for evidence that no men are so barbarous as to be ignorant of a god. Many who wrote from American experience cited this doctrine in their discussion of native American religion. William Morrell put it in verse: "all feare some God, some God they worship all." (Morrell, 1625, 22; Wood, 1634, 82; Smith, 1612a, 364; and 1631, 939; Strachey, 1953, 88)

For the majority of colonists who wrote about Indian religion, the important fact was this acknowledgment of a supreme being. What John White, the Puritan Patriarch of Dorchester in England, called the few "foot-steps" of the knowledge of God would be the path by which the Indians would learn of Christianity. The modern historian R.H. Pearce says the Puritans felt that "Satan had possessed the Indian until he had become virtually a beast; Indian worship was devil worship." (Pearce, 1965, 22) But several Puritan writers specifically made the more hopeful connection between Indian worship and Christianity. Several observers reported that the Indians had themselves drawn parallels between their own beliefs and Christian orthodoxy. Colonists were encouraged to be able to report the "motions of Religion" among the Indians. As Hariot said of Indian religion, "although it be farre from the truth, yet beyng as it is, there is hope it may bee the easier and sooner reformed." (Hariot, 1588, 372; Winslow, 1624, 34-35; Wood, 1634, 79; Morton, 1637, 35; Smith, 1624, 565; Anon., 1635, 40; Va.Co.Recs., III, 584)

There is one exception to the general picture of Indian religion and that is a notable one. It is Thomas Morton, the antagonist of the Puritans at Plymouth, who alone among eyewitnesses specifically denied that the Americans had a religion. This is especially noteworthy, as Morton is often a leader in finding the Indians praiseworthy in other respects. Morton supports his contention by referring to Sir William Alexander's *Encouragement to Colonies*. Alexander, the Earl of Stirling, was a man of status, but unlike Morton, he had no experience of America. Nevertheless Morton says that his observations and conversations over a long period have convinced him that Alexander, and not Cicero, is correct. He adds emphasis by asserting that he would sooner "beleeve that the Elephants (which are reported to be the most intelligible of all beasts) doe worship the moone." Despite his other references to Indian government, he also endorses Alexander's use of the "*sine fide, sine lege, & sine rege*" tag in this section of his book. Morton found some linguistic evidence that the Americans may have once worshipped Pan, "the great god of the Heathens." But now they worship nothing. (Morton, 1637, 16, 21) Alden Vaughan has endorsed Morton's position as the one that most closely accords with modern interpretations of Indian religion of that period. (Vaughan, 1965, 36-37)

Morton's statement is straightforward, but interpreting it is not. Part of the problem arises from Morton's desire to ridicule William Wood's *New Englands Prospect*. Wood, along with several other writers had asserted that, though they knew the Indians had religious beliefs, the English could not be sure what they were. (Wood, 1634, 82) Morton ridicules people who accept Indian religion without full understanding. "And me thinks, it is absurd to say they have a kinde of worship, and not able to demonstrate whome or what it is they are accustomed to worship." Wood's *New Englands Prospect* is clearly Morton's target. He finished by reasserting with a pun that Indians have no religion "and I am sure it has been so observed by those that neede not the helpe of a wodden prospect for the matter."

More importantly, Morton's dispute with other eyewitness writers seems to be more a matter of words than substance. What is most striking is that Morton gives what is in fact one of the most full accounts of Indian religion. He describes their knowledge of God "(historically)," their beliefs about the creation of man and of his fall from grace and a universal flood in which most of mankind died, and their views of the afterlife. Their chief god, Kytan, which Morton thinks may be the sun, makes their crops and the wild plants grow. Lying and stealing are forbidden by their beliefs. He also thought the priests, though they are "weak witches," do in fact produce miracles. (Morton, 1637, 21, 25-26, 34-35) To say as Vaughan does that Morton correctly interprets the picture he gives as "no real systematized religion" is to draw the definition of religion rather too narrowly, in too ethnocentric a manner.[2]

The fact that Indian religion was false religion did not mean that its priests lacked supernatural powers. The most frequent analogy made was to English witches. Just as witches in England during this period were thought capable of performing supernatural feats through the help of Satan, so the Indian priests and medicine men could do miracles "by God's permission, thorough the Devils helpe." (Wood, 1634, 83) The power of Indian priests to foretell the future and perform other feats of magic will be dealt with in a later chapter. Several writers were interested in the fact that religious leaders were also the society's doctors, and that they healed partly by charms and invocations. Wood gives a vivid description of the "Pow-wow" giving his "hideous bellowing and groaning . . . sometimes roaring like a Beare, other times groaning like a dying horse, foaming at the mouth like a chased bore, smiting on his naked brest and thighs with such violence, as if he were madde." He says the invocations may go on for half a day. (Wood, 1634, 83) Edward Winslow, like Wood, describes the medicine man leading the entire tribe in invocations for the cure of the sick. Winslow says the "Powah" then secretly treats the wound by sucking or by having an eagle or snake lick it. No one sees this but the medicine man. (Winslow, 1624, 54) John Smith earlier reported similar "Anticke actions" in cure of the sick among the Powhatans. (Smith, 1608, 188)

When English writers looked at Indian religious practices, the most important question concerned whether they gave thanks to a supreme being for their food. It was important because such thinksgiving would indicate that the Indians saw themselves as living in an orderly universe in which man's relationship to his environment was rational and not accidental. God looks after the beasts of the field, but they are insensitive to this and accept the fruits of nature without returning thanks. Indian thanksgiving is another proof of a type of civility. Discussions of this appear from the earliest reports on. Thomas Hariot,

2. See William P. Alston, "Religion," in *The Encyclopedia of Philosophy*, ed. Paul Edwards (New York, 1967), VII, 141-142.

in his note to John White's picture of Indians fishing, says they enjoy the things God has given them, "yet without givinge hym any thankes according to his desarte. So savage is this people, and deprived of the true knowledge of god. For they have none other then is mentionned before in this worke." Hariot's other references to which he refers the reader create a different impression. In the *Briefe and True Report*, which was published in 1588 and republished with the White pictures and *Notes* in 1590, he wrote of the Indians sacrifice of *Uppowoc* or tobacco to their gods over "hallowed fires." White's picture of a ceremony labeled "their manner of prainge with Rattels abowt te fyer," is described by Hariot as a ceremony performed after the escape of "any great danger by sea or lande." Hariot says he himself observed this ceremony: "For it is a strange custome, and worth the observation." (Hariot, 1588, 345; 1590, 429, 435)

Southern reports show a variety of personal thanksgivings which the Indians are seen as practicing daily. Entire tribes went down to the water's edge at sunrise and, after sprinkling tobacco, plunged into the water, probably in a purification rite. Some writers reported a table grace, usually said to consist of casting a few bits of food into the fire. Some of the personal rituals are seen as propitiatory, and are used in situations where individuals fear harm from their god. Not all the writers saw the Indian thanksgiving ceremonies as properly reverential. George Percy described the sacrifice of tobacco at sunrise and sunset, followed by prayers, as "making many Devillish gestures with a Hellish noise foming at the mouth, staring with their eyes, wagging their heads and hands in such a fashion and deformitie as it was monstrous to behold." (Smith, 1608, 188-189; and 1612a, 367; Percy, 1607, 417; Spelman, 1613, cxiii; Strachey, 1953, 95-98; Archer, 1607a, 104; Wingfield, 1608, 216)

Several writers also describe annual ceremonies of thanksgiving at harvest time. Sometimes it was a "great and solemne feaste" of supplication which brought together Indians from a wide area. (Hariot, 1590, 421-423, 428) The *Relation of Maryland* gave a sympathetic account of the Indian harvest festival:

These People acknowledge a God, who is the giver of al the good things, wherewith their life is maintained; and to him they sacrifice of the first fruits of their Corne, and of that which they get by hunting and fishing: The sacrifice is performed by an Ancient man, who makes a speech unto their God (not without something of Barbarisme) which being ended, hee burnes part of the sacrifice, and then eates of the rest, then the People that are present, eate also, and untill the Ceremony be performed, they will not touch one bit thereof. (Anon., 1635, 40)

William Wood likens their sacrifice "after their garners bee full with a good croppe" to the sacrifices "the ancient Heathen did to *Ceres.*" (Wood, 1634, 82) Several times we have seen English writers comparing the religious practices of the Indians to those of ancient cultures, as William Strachey compares their table grace to that of the ancient Egyptians. (Strachey, 1953, 88, 95, 98) This is intended as an aid to understanding, to picturing the Indians at their ceremonies. It is important because when the writers are looking for a simile, they choose cultures from ancient times which, though heathen, were high cultures and ones which their audience would think of as high cultures. If they were merely dismissive of Indian religion, they would have compared their ceremonies to those of beings less worthy of note.

Winslow also described a great sacrifice among the Narragansetts. He says they, at "certain known times," bring "almost all the riches they have to their gods, as kettles, skins, hatchets, beads, knives, &c., all which are cast by the priests into a great fire . . ." Each man gives freely, "and the more he is known to bring, hath the better esteem of all men." Other Indians attributed the Narragansetts' escape from the plague to this periodic sacrifice. (Winslow, 1624, 55)

There are a few scattered descriptions of other ceremonies. George Percy described what was apparently a ceremony of welcome to the English in which the Indians prostrated themselves. Percy remarked with an air of shrewdness: "We did thinke that they had beene at their Idolatry." (Percy, 1607, 409) James Rosier quotes Owen Griffin in his description of a religious ceremony whose purpose is not given: "One among them (the eldest of the Company as he judged) riseth right up, the other sitting still, and looking about suddenly cried with a loud voice, baugh waugh." This report from New England, then called the North Part of Virginia, was probably picked up by Shakespeare and used in Ariel's first song in *The Tempest.* (Act I, Scene 2; Rosier, 1605, C2v)

Some of the colonists attempted to penetrate beyond religious ceremonies, to find out what the Americans believed about the beginning and end of life on earth. Several discuss their beliefs about life after death. This subject was usually approached through a description of burial practices. John White painted the Indian idol and priest keeping watch over a row of corpses. Hariot's *Notes* explained that these were the bodies of their "Weroans or cheefe lordes." These bodies were prepared for burial by having the flesh removed from the bones. The dried flesh is placed in mats at the feet of the bodies. The bones are covered with leather, "and their carcase fashioned as yf their flesh wear not taken away." Their own skin is replaced over all. (Hariot,

1590, 425-427) These bodies were placed side by side on a hurdle or scaffold. John Smith described a similar type of burial for Virginia chiefs. He differs in saying the dried bodies of the kings are stuffed with their copper and beads and weapons and what is left of their wealth is put into baskets and is stored at their feet. These kings' bodies are wrapped in white sheets and then mats. They are then watched over by the priests. All other reports of burial customs concern the more familiar underground burial. John Smith follows his description of the exotic treatment of royal corpses by saying that the ordinary people are buried in deep holes in the ground and specifically says these are "graves like ours." (Smith, 1608, 189; and 1612a, 364-365; Spelman, 1613, cx)

William Morrell, in his *New England,* says the mat-wrapped bodies of all Indians are buried in a kneeling position, with their eyes to the east. (Morrell, 1625, 20) William Wood and Thomas Morton both describe underground burials, though Morton believes there is a great difference in treatment between "persons of noble, and of ignoble, or obscure or inferior discent." The nobles are buried with a plank on each of their four sides. The planks are covered with earth and "they erect some thing over the grave in forme of a hearse cloath." Morton reports the Indian belief that no great Englishmen have yet come to New England, because all their graves are alike. He is indignant that the "Plimouth planters" have defaced the grave of "Cheekatawbacks mother." He says they did so because they thought the monument superstitious, but the Indians believed the action was "impious and inhumane." (Morton, 1637, 35-36; Wood, 1634, 93)

The writers are struck by the extremity of Indian grief at death and the extravagance of their mourning. They blacken their faces in sign of their grief and lament lavishly. Several writers say the Indians blacken their faces and mourn annually. It is clear from the descriptions that there is a prescribed ritual which the bereaved follow. Thomas Morton says they abandon the place of burial because they cannot bear to be reminded of death. William Wood marveled at the longevity and good health of the Indians. Despite their long life, though, death is greeted by extreme sorrow which, "to behold and heare their throbbing sobs and deepe-fetcht sighes, their griefe-wrung hands, and teare-bedewed cheekes, their dolefull cries, would draw teares from Adamantine eyes, that be but spectators of their mournefull Obsequies."[3] If sensitivity is

---

3. Wood, *New Englands Prospect,* 93; Morrell, *New England,* 20; John Smith, *True Relation of Virginia,* in Barbour, ed., *Jamestown Voyages,* I, 189, and *Map of Virginia, ibid.,* II, 364-365; Thomas Morton, *New English Canaan,* 1637, in Peter Force, comp., *Tracts Relating to the Colonies in North America* (1836; rpt. Gloucester, Mass., 1963), II, 19, 36; Ralph Lane, *An account of the men left in Virginia,* in Quinn, ed., *Roanoke Voyages,* I, 281.

one mark of the civilized person, then these extremes of sensitivity are worthy of note for English readers. Despite their fascination with the lavishness of the Indians' grief, the writers do not point out the superior consoling power of Christianity, either to the Indians or to the English audience.

One feature of Indian burials that is frequently remarked is the inclusion of the jewels, copper, and sometimes, the weapons of the dead person in the grave. Some writers specifically connect this practice to American belief in life after death. Wood explains that a "great Dogge" is at the entrance to paradise to keep out the unworthy. "Wherefore it is their custome, to bury with them their Bows and Arrows, and good store of their *Wampompeage* and *Mowhackies;* the one to affright that affronting Cerberus, the other to purchase more immense prerogatives in their Paradise." (Wood, 1634, 93; Va. Co., 1610b, 18; Smith, 1608, 189; and 1612a 364-365; Morrell, 1625; 20; Anon., 1635, 35; Archer, 1607a, 104)

John Smith reported that life after death was reserved for "Werowances and Priestes." These went "beyond the mountaines towardes the setting of the sun." There they would have fine clothes and all the beads, tobacco, hatchets, and copper they wanted. The common people do not live after death. (Smith, 1612a, 368-369) William Strachey used Smith's report, but added that the souls of the werowances and priests are eventually reincarnated, a belief which causes him to make another of those comparisons to classical cultures of which he is so fond. He says Indian belief in reincarnation reminds him of Pythagoras and he goes on: "Nor is this opinion more ridiculous or Savage, then was the Epicures long synce," who taught that the soul of man was nothing but "vitall power." (Strachey, 1953, 100) Other writers do not mention such a social distinction in immortality but do add a different complexity. They see a division between good and bad men, each of whom gets the afterlife he deserves. Paradise is variously described. Thomas Hariot called it "the habitacle of gods," a place of "perpetuall blisse and happinesse." (Hariot, 1588, 373) Others emphasized the gratification of all earthly desires. The torments of the wicked are equally variable. None of the writers compared this dual possiblity for life after death to the Christian doctrine of heaven and hell. William Wood compared the Indian paradise to that described in the Koran. He said Indian "enemies and loose livers" were "tortured according to the fictions of the ancient Heathen." (Wood, 1634, 93; Winslow, 1624, 52-53; Morton, 1637, 34-35; Morrell, 1625, 20; Anon., 1635, 40)

The John White who was a supporter of the Massachusetts Bay

Company felt that the creation story in which the Indians believed was a hopeful sign for their speedy conversion. It was one of the "footsteps" of religion that these lost Jews retained. (White, 1630, 7-8) As White pointed out, the various versions of Indian creation myths presented during the period are similar to the story in Genesis in important details. Several writers say the Indians believe the creation was performed by a supreme God who was himself uncreated, or existing from all eternity. God created one man and woman from whom all mankind is descended. They were commanded to live together and have children and were given dominion over all the animals. (Morrell, 1625, 22; Winslow, 1624, 52; Morton, 1637, 34-35) Hariot gives a complex description of the creation myth and shows how it varies from Christian belief. God first created lesser gods, including the sun, moon, and stars. These were to help in the creation and government of the world. Water was created next, out of which all creatures, "visible or invisible" were made. Finally, God created a woman, who "by the working of one of the goddes," had children who became the human race. (Hariot, 1588, 372-373)

William Strachey told of a charming encounter which took place at Christmastime in 1610. Capt. Argall and a company were out trading with Iapaseus, the brother of Powhatan. Since it was very cold, all the men were sitting around the fire and the chief became interested in the Bible which one of the Englishmen was reading. Capt. Argall turned to the picture of the creation of the world and asked Henry Spelman, who could speak the Indians' language well by then, to explain it to them, "which the king seemed to like well of." Iapaseus then offered to tell his peoples' creation story, "which was a pretty fabulous tale indeed." He said they had five gods, of whom the chief was a "mightie great Hare" and the others were the four winds. The Hare decided to create men and women and he kept them for a time in a bag to protect them from cannibal giants who were seeking them to eat them. Capt. Argall asked Spelman to question Iapaseus about what substance the men and women and the giants were made from, but the boy feared offending the chief by questioning him. The Great Hare next made the land and the water and placed a great deer on the land. The winds became envious and killed the deer and ate it. All that was left was the hair of the deer, so the Hare scattered it "with many powerfull wordes and charmes whereby every haire became a deare." He then placed the men and women on the earth, each couple in a different country. (Strachey, 1953, 101-103; Purchas, 1614, 767) This creation story enabled the Indians to explain how the entire world was peopled from a single creation, a problem which troubled the Europeans. Of all those who wrote about Indian ideas of the creation, only John White specifically made a comparison to Genesis.

The meaning of Indian religion was difficult for the English to determine. Most of the writers avoided comparisons to Christianity. Many, as we have seen, refused to consider it as anything but the inspiration of the devil. Equally difficult to many of the writers was the question of what religion meant to the Indians themselves. Despite the hopeful attitude struck by many of the writers and their assertion that the existence of Indian religion would make the American more easily converted to Christianity, there was a parallel and more difficult theme. Many of the writers appear to have grasped the fact that Indian religion was in fact central to Indian culture and that its existence was the greatest obstacle to the Europeanization of the American natives. The most blunt statement of this realization was credited to "Master Stockam, a Minister." He is represented as having said, "and till their Priests and Ancients have their throats cut, there is no hope to bring them to conversion." (Anon., 1619, 134-135)

Stockam's statement is horrifying in its ethnocentric disregard for the integrity of another culture as well as its contempt for human life. What he is saying, though, is interesting for our analysis. When he and other writers rail against the immense power of the Indian priests to delude and control their people, they are also testifying to the strength and integrity of Indian culture. Since they assume that Christianity and European culture are obviously superior to Indian religion and culture, they are faced with the necessity of explaining why the Indians are not being converted and civilized. The answer for them is that they are kept in "blindnesse" by their priests who have strong magical powers and are the society's doctors as well as their religious leaders. Only by eliminating the central pole around which Indian life is centered, its ceremonial and spiritual core, can the Indians be converted to the obviously superior Christianity.

George Percy testified in a different way to the vitality and importance of religion in Indian life: "It is a generall rule of these people when they swere by their God which is the Sunne, no Christian will keepe their Oath better upon this promise. (Percy, 1607, 417)

Indian society, like 17th century English society, was centered on its religious beliefs. Those writers who discussed Indian religion all recognized this, though they interpreted it variously. For many, the existence of complex religious beliefs in America provided hope for speedy assimilation of European beliefs. That the Indians saw the importance of religion was the key fact. These writers believed it would be a matter of small difficulty for them to substitute the obviously land needed nothing but "industrious men" and "engins" to make it among the most fruitful in the world.

There are two issues here which are of interest to us. One is the assumption which was universal among Englishmen that their technology was obviously superior to that of the Indians, a judgement continued by many historians. Every writer had schemes for developing the rich resources which he thought must be hidden in America. Even though their geographical knowledge slowly became more realistic as they realized that latitude was not the sole determinant of climate, they continued to believe that superior European technology would develop America in a way which the Indians never could.

What did English colonists say about the actual technological level of the Indians among whom they lived? This is the other issue which is raised by statements like those of Smith and Rosier. When this question is asked we again see the contrast between the rhetorical flourishes which occur in general statements and the reporting of detailed observations. Smith is a particularly outstanding example of this because, despite the denunciation just seen, he not only refers again and again to Indian agriculture, but he also makes no secret of the fact that he and all of the Jamestown colonists lived almost entirely on corn which they got from the Indians during the time he was in Virginia.

Agriculture was not just one form of technology among many. It was of prime importance, because it makes settled life possible. Just as the shepherd is superior to the hunter, so town life supported by agriculture is the highest form of human life for these writers. Mankind is meant to live gathered together in towns. We are not fully civil unless we live in this way. So towns and agriculture complete the picture begun by discussion of government and religion. Eyewitness evidence from America clearly placed the Indians on the side of civil humanity as town dwellers, not nomads ranging over the land hunting and gathering for their subsistence. Once the pictures of John White with Hariot's *Notes* were published in 1590, the "Towne of Secota" and the fortified "Towne of Pomeiooc" became familiar to readers all over Europe. So from the beginning the Indians were presented as town dwellers. The *Relation of Maryland* said their towns were "like Countrey Villages in England." (Anon., 1635, 36) Some reporters thought the Indians might be nomadic because they moved their place of habitation with the seasons. Thomas Morton ironically compared this practice to that of "the gentry of the Civilized natives," that is the English gentry, who move from town house to country seat seasonally. He also points out that if the Indians remained in one place the fuel would quickly be consumed. Moving shows they are provident, which is part of being civil. (Morton, 1637, 20) A large proportion of eyewitness writers about America mention Indian towns. Usually the towns were said to contain somewhere between 20 and 50 houses, but William Strachey said the town of Kecoughtan sometimes held 1000 people and 300 houses. (Strachey, 1953, 67; Winthrop, 1908, I, 188; Archer, 1607a, 103; Spelman, 1613, cvi) The overwhelming picture which the interested British public would have derived from eyewitness writings would have been of settled communities in native America, "very wel peopled and towned, though savagelie." (Lane, 1585, 208)

Alongside the towns in the typical picture of Indian life transmitted by eyewitness writers were the cornfields and gardens in which they grew their basic food of corn, pease, and pulses. DeBry's engraving of the town of Secota from John White's drawing shows fields of corn in three stages of growth, patches of tobacco, a group of sunflowers, a pumpkin patch, and a garden with unidentifiable vegetables. (Hulton and Quinn, 1964) Hunting was supplementary to the Indian basic diet of maize and beans. Neither of these two vegetables is a complete protein when eaten alone. That is, neither contains all of the eight amino acids which the human body cannot manufacture for itself. However, when eaten together, they do form superior complete proteins, increasing the protein content of the ingredients by fifty percent. (Lappe, 1971, 36, 195) Further, growing beans and corn together as the Indians did increases yield, because the beans, as legumes, fix nitrogen in the soil. Eyewitness reports from America refute the contention that the "colonials liked to regard the Indians as members of a nomadic hunting race with no fixed habitation, roaming over thousands of acres of virgin wilderness." (Jacobs, 1972, 111) Again and again writers from Virginia and New England refer to Indian corn and its cultivation. Several of the earliest writers actually presented several-page descriptions of methods of preparing the soil, cultivation, and storage and use of crops. (Hariot, 1588, 341-342; Barlow, 1584, 105; Smith, 1612a, 351-352; Spelman, 1613, cxi-cxii) Many writers make it clear that they have seen cornfields and gardens which extended to several hundred acres. The Indians are clearly people who are recognizable as fellow agriculturalists with the English. (Va. Co. Recs., IV, 450, 507-508; Strachey, 1953, 79, 118-119; Winthrop, 1908, I, 188; Archer, 1607c, 92-93)

When the Indians set out to clear a field, they did not cut down the trees and pull out their roots as the English did in order to plow in straight lines. The Indians killed the trees by girdling them or burning the roots, and then planted their crops in hills around and between the dead tree trunks. Both men and women worked on clearing new ground, but the tending of the crops was done by the women and children. Their method of clearing fields involved less work than the English method, but several writers remarked on the assiduousness with which the Indian women kept their fields free of weeds. William Wood said the fields looked more like gardens, the women "not suffering a choaking weede to advance his audacious head above their infant corne, or an undermining worme to spoile his spurnes." (Wood, 1634, 94-95; Hariot, 1588, 341-342; Smith, 1612a, 351; Strachey, 1953, 118-119)

Indian cultivation methods were portrayed as primitive, but English writers were extravagant in praise of the product, particularly the Indian corn, variously called maize or Turkey or Guinie wheat. It was commonly said to be superior to any European grain, mostly because of its larger yield and its greater variety of uses. For Hariot, its superiority came from the fact that the Indians had two harvests each year. He and the Plymouth colonists also remark on the beauty of its red, blue, yellow, and white kernels, "a very goodly sight." Several of the writers simply affirm that it is "good meat" and can be used in a variety of ways. One use for which some of the writers had great hopes was as a source of that precious commodity, sugar. The stalk was said to yield juice so sweet that Sir Thomas Gates says the colonists make a cordial of it. (Hariot, 1588, 338, 343; Va. Co., 1610a, 12; Bradford and Winslow, 1622, 6, 64; Anon., 1635, 27; Purchas, 1614, 734)

The most important attribute of maize was its great yield. English writers try various formulas to convey the fact that one grain of maize will produce a very large stalk which will have several large ears on it. Several writers simply affirmed that Indian corn is the best grain in the world. (Smith, 1620, 261; Waterhouse, 1622, 4) Some specifically say it is better than any English grain. Others try to give figures, such as Gabriel Archer, who says each grain of corn produces a large stalk with 2 or 3 stems each having an ear "above a spann longe. besett with cornes at the least 300 upon an eare for the most part 5, 6, & 700." The marginal note beside this statement puts it more simply: "infinit increase." (Archer, 1607b, 100; Lane, 1585, 207-208; Smith, 1612a, 351; Purchas, 1625 rpt. 1906, XIX, 209, 250; Va. Co., 1610a, 12; Morrell, 1625, 18; Fr. White, 1633, 10)

Not only was their grain superior, but some of the writers indicated that Indian cultivation methods were also superior. George Percy told of being conducted by Indians through "the goodliest Corne fieldes that ever was seene in any Countrey." (Percy, 1606, 411) Writers from all areas tell of the Indians instructing them in the planting and tending of Indian corn, but the Plymouth colonists complained that they still had smaller harvests than the Indians did. (Bradford and Winslow, 1622, 60; Winslow, 1624, 63; Bradford, 1953, 85, 112; Archer, 1607c, 89) One reason for poor yields in Plymouth colony was apparently their unwillingness to do the arduous work that the Indian women did in their fields. (Rutman, 1967, 10-11, 17, 46, 53-54) Lynn Ceci argues, though, that the most famous instance of instruction, that in which Squanto taught the Pilgrims to plant corn with fish, was not a transmission of an Indian trait. He had learned this technique, Ceci believes, from other Europeans with whom he had lived. (Ceci, 1975, 26-30) William Wood gave a vivid picture of all that was involved in Indian agriculture when he told of the instruction the colonists received:

Many wayes hath their advice and endeavour beene advantagious unto us; they being our first instructers for the planting of their Indian Corne, by teaching us to cull out the finest seede, to observe the fittest season, to keepe distance for holes, and fit measure for hills, to worme it, and weede it; to prune it, and dresse it as occasion shall require. (Wood, 1634, 70)

Care for the morrow was a principle attribute which distinguished civilized man from the brutes. Such providence was implicit in reports of Indian agriculture. Several of the writers carried the point further and wrote of the techniques by which the Indians stored their harvest for the winter. In fact most of the food grown was stored for winter use. (Swanton, 1946, 256) Many of the writers were self-contradictory when they wrote about the ways in which the Indians stored their wealth and food. This was because they admired many qualities about Indian life, or saw qualities in Indian life, which were themselves incompatible. They admired the fact that Indians seemed to share what they had with their fellows and that they were lavish in their hospitality. These were qualities which Englishmen of this period feared their own culture had lost. On the other hand, assuming the responsibility to provide for those dependent on you by your own labor was also a quality which the English admired. Providence and generosity, both important qualities, needed very careful balancing to exist together in the same person. Often when the writers are making general statements about Indian culture they emphasize the generosity of Indian life and say or imply that Indians have no care for the morrow, assuming that a bounteous nature will provide what they need. Later, in detailed descriptions of Indian life these same writers will show the Indians working and saving. John Smith told of the Indians drying fish and meat for winter storage, but says that for three-fourths of the year, the Indians "live of what the Country naturally affordeth from hand to mouth, &c." Capt. Smith gave the lie to his own assertions, however, by his repeated reports of the English commandeering large amounts of grain from the Indians all around Jamestown. It is probable that Indians who had formerly been able to live off their own harvest all winter were reduced to foraging because they had lost so much corn to the colonists. In an earlier report Smith had said that corn and food was "all there wealth." (Smith, 1608, 193; and 1612a, 352-353)

William Wood, who loved the Indian generosity and their disdain for coveting more than they needed, said of their hospitality:

wise Providence being a stranger to their wilder wayes: they be right Infidels, neither caring for the morrow, or providing for their owne families.

In another place, when he is describing Indian women and their agriculture, though, he described their ways of storing sun-dried corn in "their barnes" which were large holes in the ground lined with mats or bark in which the corn was stored in baskets. The holes were covered over with earth and the corn was not to be used except in necessity. Wood still maintained that the women had to keep these barns hidden from their husbands who would devour it all if they could. It is interesting to see what similes these practices called to mind. William Strachey compared the burying of corn and wealth to the practices of the ancient Romans, in one of those classical comparisons which enhanced his reputation for learning at the same time that it enhanced the picture of the American Indians. Thomas Morton compared the Indians to the one example from nature which was really congenial to the 16th and 17th century Englishman, the civilized Ant and Bee. (Wood, 1634, 67-68, 95; Strachey, 1953, 115; Morrell, 1625, 20; Morton, 1637, 30)

Agriculture was the base on which society was built. Reports of Indian agriculture were also important because they indicated that the country was fruitful and would be good for Englishmen who went there to live. Beyond this, many eyewitnesses assumed the role of ethnographers and endeavored to give a detailed picture of Indian life. The wealth of information was designed to enable the reader to picture the Indians and the environment they created. It was the details of daily life, the Indians in their houses, at meals, and at their occupations, which constituted a good ethnographic record for these writers and their audience. They generally attempted to give their readers a mental picture by comparing American things or practices to familiar ones, to bring them home. These descriptions were not characterized by disgust or scorn as many historians allege. The immense detail and the analytical tool of comparison of Indian practices to European ones both testify to the interest of the eyewitnesses in the Indians as human beings, not to an attitude of contemptuous dismissal.

Though all the writers clearly assumed that European technology was superior to Indian, they took great pains to affirm that the Indians were extraordinarily competent in their own relationship to their environment. Thomas Hariot, in the earliest eyewitness description of North American Indians, stressed their ingenuity and "excellencie of wit." (Hariot, 1588, 371) Affirmations of the Indians' skill and intelligence come from all areas and throughout the period. Frequently writers say they are trying to overcome the opinion in England that the Indians are, as Morton says, "dull, or slender witted people." Hariot's praise of their ingenuity is frequently echoed. The other qualities most often praised are their ability to learn quickly and their dexterity. Alexander Whitaker of Jamestown offered, in refutation of the opinion that the Indians are "simple," this description:

they are a very understanding generation, quicke of apprehension, suddaine in their dispatches, subtile in their dealings, exquisite in their inventions, and industrious in their labour. (Whitaker, 1613, 25)

"Subtile" was not always a praise word in this period. It can mean crafty, and smacks of sharp practice. Still, the picture communicated here is of intelligent and competent people. Their very subtlety means that the English will have to be careful in dealing with them.[1] Colonists back up this picture of intelligent and skilful Indians with detailed pictures of the Indians in their daily lives, working, hunting, cooking, and playing, and this included a description of the environment they created for themselves.

Thomas Hariot was the first writer to describe a North American Indian house and his description became accepted as absolutely standard by writers in all regions throughout the period. He described houses made of small poles or saplings driven into the ground and bound together at the top to make a rounded roof. The frame was then covered with bark or woven mats. Hariot says they are usually twice as long as they are wide, and that the length varies from 12 to 24 yards.

---

1. Morton, *New English Canaan*, in Force, *Tracts*, II, 31-33; Wood, *New Englands Prospect*, 78; Philip Vincent, *A True Relation of the Late Battel* (London, 1637), 13; Richard Whitbourne, *A Discourse and Discovery of New-found-land* (1620; rpt. London, 1622), 5; Edward Winslow, *Good Newes from New-England* (London, 1624), 60; William Bradford and Edward Winslow, *A Relation or Journall of the English Plantation setled at Plimoth in New England* (London, 1622), known as *Mourt's Relation*, 61-62.

The basic form is virtually the same for all writers, but estimates of the size of Indian houses vary from as little as 20 feet to 100 feet long. Doors are covered with mats which provide ventilation or protection as they are rolled up or down. A fire burns in the center of the floor and a hole in the center of the roof lets out the smoke. The Indians sleep on mats on a raised platform around the outer edge. The interior was described as being smoky but warm. Fr. White reminded his readers that the great halls of England had been built with fires in the center and smoke holes above. (Fr. White, 1634, 44) Hariot compared these houses to "many arbories in our gardens of England," and this comparison, like his description, was used again and again in the colonists' writings. Comparing them to garden arbors made them recognizable and less exotic. It reinforced the idea that these houses were "homely" as Francis Higginson called them. (Hariot, 1588, 370; Higginson, 1630, 13; Anon., 1635, 37; Morton, 1637, 19-20; Wood, 1634, 94; Strachey, 1953, 78-9; Archer, 1607a, 103)

Descriptions of Indian houses were usually presented simply, without praise or criticism. Only Edward Waterhouse, who, as Secretary of the Virginia Company, presented the official description and explanation of the massacre of 1622, was contemptuous of chief Opechancanough's "denne or Hog-stye." Waterhouse did not go to Virginia himself. His description of the massacre was reprinted by Purchas and John Smith. Smith, the only eyewitness of the three, omitted that phrase. (Waterhouse, 1622, 16; Purchas, 1625 rpt. 1906, XIX, 160; Smith, 1624, 574)

Imitation as a form of praise went both ways in the early colonial period. The Indians are reported to have admired English building styles, and occasionally colonists built an English house for a chief as a mark of favor. Englishmen, though, can also be found copying Indian styles. Two reports from Jamestown say that now that the colonists have taken to covering their houses with mats and bark in the Indian style, they are warm in winter and cool in summer, and are as well protected as by the "best Tyle." (Va.Co., 1610a, 20; Strachey, 1610, 57) William Wood says the Indian houses are "very strong and handsome, covered with close-wrought mats of their owne weaving, which deny entrance to any drop of raine, though it come both fierce and long, neither can the piercing North winde finde a crannie, through which he can conveigh his cooling breath, they be warmer than our *English* houses." (Wood, 1634, 94) Henry Spelman also pointed out that they were portable and suited to the Indians' style of life. (Spelman, 1613, cvi)

Indian food was a subject of great interest. Though there was such widespread interest in native agriculture, especially Indian corn culture and use, the reports of Indian hunting, fishing, and other food gathering are rarer. John White painted Indians fishing against a background of weirs. Hariot's note says of the design of these weirs: "Ther was never seene amonge us soe cunninge a way to take fish withall." (Hariot, 1590, 434-435; Smith, 1612a, 358-359) William Strachey described the weirs as being enclosures made of reeds "and framed in the fashion of a Labourinth or Maze." (Strachey, 1953, 75) Ralph Lane, the commander of Roanoke colony said his men tried to make weirs like the Indians', but they had not the skill. He lived in fear that the Indians might deliberately break those they had built for the colonists because the English could not even repair them. (Lane, 1586, 276, 282) Indians are also said to fish with hooks and lines, with spears, and with nets. Hariot praises their ingenuity in using a crab's tail for a hook in place of the metal they lack. Wood stresses that their fishing is successful because they study their prey and know its habits. They know the best fish and techniques for each season. Squanto, the Indian who befriended the Pilgrims at Plymouth, could catch eels in the mud with his bare hands. (Wood, 1634, 89-90, 95; Bradford and Winslow, 1622, 39; Strachey, 1953, 82)

John Smith's *Map of Virginia* has the entire Indian village going off to hunt, warriors followed by their women carrying mats and equipment to make camp houses and their household tools on their backs, and this is a typical picture. Writers from north and south show the Indians hunting in large groups, sometimes with several hundred men. The method is to surround the deer in a huge circle and then for the warriors to slowly move closer together, drawing the circle tighter and tighter. Sometimes they use torches or fire to help run the deer into the narrow space. Sometimes they can take an entire herd in this manner. If a single Indian is hunting, Smith says he puts a deer skin over his arm and fist, shielding his body under the skin. This enables him to get close to the animal hunted. In either method the deer is usually only wounded, and then the hunters track it until they can take it. In hunting even more than in fishing, William Wood maintained that the most important ingredient in the Indians' skill was their knowledge of the animals and their habits. Wood says the English cannot hunt beaver successfully because "these beasts are too cunning for the English, who seldome or never catch any of them, therefore we leave them to those skilfull hunters whose time is not so precious, whose experience bought-skill hath made them practicall and usefull in that particular." New England Indians also used spring traps of rope. (Smith, 1612a,

359-360; Wood, 1634, 88-89; Strachey, 1953, 82-83; Spelman, 1613, cvii)

As modern concern for the interaction between man and the environment grows, some writers have asserted that the first in a long chain of ecological disasters occurred with the entrance of Europeans into America. The "first ecologist" as Wilcomb Washburn calls the Indian, was, according to these authors, replaced on America's eastern coast by the European who thought in terms of exploiting nature, and of using her resources to make up for European deficiencies. The Indians, by contrast, according to Wilbur Jacobs, had "respect for animal life and reverence for the land." (Washburn, 1975, 11, 56; Jacobs, 1972, 19-30, 126-127, 159-160) The ecological concern of the American natives was most clearly seen in the care they took in hunting to harvest just enough animals for their needs, never endangering the herd by over-hunting. This care is contrasted with the ruthless depletion of beaver in the later 17th century by Indian hunters who hunted for Englishmen.[2]

It is undeniable that English writers of this period thought of the natural world as given to man by God for man's use. Not to develop nature's resources was seen by them as sinful. Nature, to 17th century Englishmen, represented potential. That is, all nature is the raw material from which man can make products necessary and useful for life. For this reason, the products of man and nature in combination were considered superior to nature alone. George Withers wrote that New England was a "rude Garden" in which it would be necessary to "order Nature's fruitfulnesse." John Brereton wrote that to be "artificiall" was above the powers of nature. (George Withers in Smith, 1616, 183; Brereton, 1602, 8) Artificial was a word of high praise, while natural meant simple, or simple-minded. John Smith was clearly in this tradition when, after discussing the greatest countries in the world, he said they were not naturally superior to New England: "They are beautified by the long labor and dilligence of industrious people and Art. This is onely as God made it . . ." (Smith, 1616, 197)

Seventeenth century writers, then, celebrated man's exploitation of nature. They did not see man as taking from nature and spoiling it in the process. Rather, they saw man as part of nature, as having a crucial and God-designed role in the development of nature's potential. God could have created the world with all species developed to perfection. He chose, instead, to create the possibility and the agent of perfection,

---

2. For a different treatment of this issue see Calvin Martin, *Keepers of the Game: Indian-Animal Relationships and the Fur Trade* (Berkeley, 1978).

man. George Hakewill presented this assumption clearly in his *Apology of the Power and Providence of God:*

It seemes by this, that all things by labour and industry may bee made better than Nature produces them. And it is certaine that God so ordained it, that the industry of man should in all things concurre with the workes of Nature, both for the bringing of them to their perfection, and for the keeping of them therein being brought unto it.

He went on to say that species will degenerate if not tended by man. (Hakewill, 1635, V, 156-157) Just as the bee in its exploitation of the flower performs a crucial role in the transmission of life, so man was equally part of nature and equally important in his exploitation. Seventeenth century writers would not have distinguished between a dam built by beavers and one built by man. Both would have been artificial and both natural.

This belief about man's function was often expressed in the form of an analogy with sexual reproduction. The name Virginia is the best-known example. Thomas Morton developed this imagery for New England when he compared New England to a "faire virgin" on her wedding night when English technology, "art and industry," will bring her potential to fruition. If the English do not take up this masculine role, then the virgin's womb will instead become a "glorious tombe." (Morton, 1637, 10)

The English did not think of exploitation of nature in terms of ruthless depletion of resources. English writers exhibited real concern for the development and conservation of resources. Furthermore, they were sometimes critical of observed Indian practices as wasteful. One such practice was the annual or semi-annual burning of the woods. Many of the early writers remark on the open parklike quality of American woods, and the great open areas. They say that thick underbrush is seen only in swampy areas. Reports from Virginia and New England claim that a man can ride a horse at a gallop through the woods. In fact, it seems likely that, because pre-contact Indians burned the woods every year, wooded areas in present day eastern North America are thicker and more tangled with underbrush, more like people's idea of the forest primeval, than those seen by the early colonists. (Wood, 1634, 15; Pringe, 1603, 329; Smith, 1612a, 356; and 1624, 427) Burning was a beneficial practice. Not only did it facilitate movement and hunting, but it also made possible the growth of a great variety of food-producing plants—fruits, berries, and nuts—and attracted animals, such as deer, elk, and buffalo, which would not live in a dense forest. Finally, the burning also drove away some unwelcome animals, such as reptiles. (Morgan, 1975, 55-56; Carl O. Sauer quoted in Jacobs, 1972, 127; Day, 1953, 334-339)

The burning generally destroyed underbrush, but not large trees. It could not, however, be controlled. Thomas Morton pointed out how dangerous the fires were. He says the timber in the high ground in New England has all been spoiled, so good trees must be sought in the low wetlands. He also describes his own practice of carefully burning the land around his own house so that, if the Indian fires come near, the house will not be in danger. "For when the fire is once kindled, it dilates and spreads it selfe as well against, as with the winde; burning continually night and day, untill a shower of raine falls to quench it." (Morton, 1637, 37; Hoskins, 1622, 14)

More of a problem is Indian treatment of animals. Did the Indian as the "first ecologist" carefully harvest the deer according to his need alone? Several of the early English writers were concerned about this issue. Thomas Hariot was concerned over the impact of English desire for deer skins on the deer population. He reassures his readers that they can trade for thousands of skins yearly and cause no more to be killed than is done already. (Hariot, 1588, 331; Spelman, 1613, cvi) Ralph Hamor believed that the fecundity of America was an example of the special providence of God. Were it not for this extraordinary fruitfulness, "the Naturalls would assuredly starve." Hamor was shocked by Indian hunting practices, as he said they kill deer "all the yeer long, neither sparing yong nor olde, no not the Does readie to fawne, not the yong fawnes, if but two daies ould." (Hamor, 1615, 20; Waterhouse, 1622, 23) New Englanders reported finding carcasses of deer which had had only the horns taken off. So many deer are killed at hunting time, according to Thomas Morton, that the Indians "have bestowed six or seaven at a time, upon one English man whome they have borne affection to." (Morton, 1637, 51; Bradford and Winslow, 1622, 30)

The evidence demonstrates that the Indians were not averse to making massive changes in the natural world, as in their burning, when they felt the result would favor their livelihood. It does not prove that the English were superior in their ecological concerns. What the evidence does demonstrate is that neither side had a unique grasp of the complexities and responsibilities in man's relationship to the natural environment. At least some 16th and early 17th century Englishmen were very concerned about establishing a responsible relationship to this environment.

Enjoying one's food was a great virtue for Englishmen of this time. Often writers commending the American climate offer the good appetites of the colonists as the best proof of its healthfulness. They were glad to note that the Indians ate happily and well. Several writers claimed that the Indians ate almost continuously and in huge amounts. William Strachey said that Indian laborers in Jamestown were given portions twice as large as those which the English ate. (Strachey, 1953, 84; Archer, 1607a, 103; Morton, 1637, 20; Barlowe, 1584, 109) William Wood agreed that they eat with relish, but said they eat enormous amounts "till their bellies stand south, ready to split with fulnesse," and then do not eat for two or three days. When they do eat, they are so hungry that they eat greedily without "trenchers, napkins, or knives" on the "verdent carpet of the earth which Nature spreads them." (Wood, 1634, 67) The *Relation of Maryland* gave a quite different picture. This writer wrote of a great feast of 200 guests in which every man was served with his own individual bowl. (Anon., 1637, 38)

The basic Indian diet, as described by colonists, was maize, supplemented by peas, beans, and sunflower seeds, and the meat of animals and fish. Many of the writers were interested in preparation of meals. One part of this was interest in how the Indians produced fire, a subject on which a great many writers offered information. Some said the Indians rubbed a pointed stick against a block of wood until sufficient heat was produced to cause bits of moss or dry leaves to catch fire. (Ingram, 1582, 288; Smith, 1612a, 357; Strachey, 1953, 115) Others said the natives wore special leather bags in which they carried special stones and soft wood for producing and catching sparks. (Archer, 1602, 312; Morton, 1637, 22, 37; Brereton, 1602, 10) Two basic methods for preparation of meat and fish were discussed by colonists. James Rosier, probably with one of the attributes of the medieval Wild Man in mind, specifically asserted that the Indians "eat nothing raw," either of fish or flesh. (Rosier, 1605, B3v) Reports from all areas presented fish and meat as being roasted or broiled on racks or spits over or by the fire. Meat and fish were also dried in this way for winter use. (Hariot, 1590, 436-437; Smith, 1612a, 351-352; Morton, 1637, 20; Wood, 1634, 67) Even more popular among the Indians was a sort of stew made by boiling some combination of fish, flesh, grains, and vegetables together. Indian corn is frequently described as being "seethed" or "sodden" in this way. Some writers like this "sweete, and savorie" stew, but William Wood complained that the Americans insisted that everyone partake of their "high-conceited delicates" in which "some remaining raw, the rest converted by over-much seething to a loathed mash, not halfe so good as Irish Boniclapper." (Wood, 1634, 68; Hariot, 1590, 430, 438; Fr. White, 1634, 44) Maize was sometimes eaten fresh or, if the grain was old or very mature, made into bread or cakes. Several writers described the making of corn bread, some emphasizing the meticulous cleanliness of the Indian women when making it. The Maryland colonists got instruction in making cornbread so their own servants could make it for them. (Anon., 1635, 13; Smith, 1612a, 351-352; Rosier, 1605, E3; Percy, 1607, 415; Hariot, 1588, 341; Strachey, 1953, 80-81; Archer, 1607a, & 1607c, 90, 104)

When Indians traveled, their reported diet became much simpler. They carried a powdered dried corn which they mixed with water as they found it. William Wood thought this *Nocake* even less palatable than Indian stew:

they take thrice three spoonefulls a day, dividing it into three meales. If it be in Winter, and Snow be on the ground, they can eate when they please, stopping Snow after their dusty victuals, which otherwise would feed them little better than a Tiburne halter. In summer they must stay till they meete with a Spring or Brooke, where they may have water to prevent the imminent danger of choaking. (Wood, 1634, 68; Bradford and Winslow, 1622, 34)

Some writers mention unusual foods or flavoring. James Rosier, for instance, is unique in asserting that the Indians make cheese from the milk of deer which they keep as the English keep cows. Both the making of cheese and the keeping of domesticated animals are found only in this source. Rosier says they hang whale meat in their houses and use the fat for flavoring their pulses, pease, and maize. (Rosier, 1605, E3-E3v) Thomas Hariot records that the Indians taught the colonists to make oil from acorns. Gordon of Lochinvar also mentions acorn oil. Oils, of course, were one of the Mediterranean products which England hoped to get from America, thus lessening her dependence on foreign countries. (Hariot, 1588, 330; Gordon of Lochinvar, 1625, C4) Oil was an essential ingredient in English textile manufacturing, so any mention of sources of oil might be important. Richard Whitbourne learned that the Indians dried egg yolk and used it in cooking, "as Sugar is used in some meates." (Whitbourne, 1620 rpt. 1622, R3v-R4) Salt was another product that would be important for developing America's resources. Fishing was clearly seen as a major industry for England in America; in fact it was the only industry that was already established at the time the colonies were being founded. Salt to preserve the fish would be necessary if the fishing industry was to expand. Therefore, it was a disappointment to find that the Indians did not know the use of salt. Thomas Morton says his native friends "would begge Salte of mee." (Morton, 1637, 31) Thomas Hariot found that the

Roanoke area Indians did have a salt-like herb which was burned to ashes and then used to flavor food. Presumbaly it could not be used to preserve food. (Hariot, 1588, 340)

Many writers were enthusiastic over the strength and versatility of Indian pottery which, though the walls were as thin as iron pots, could be used over an open fire because of the "special Cunninge" with which they were made. John White painted a picture of one of these pots being used on a wood fire. Colonists also saw vessels made of wood and of bark in use among the Indians.[3] Reports from New England reinforce the picture of a thriving trade network among the Indians by asserting that different designs of pottery and wooden bowls are made exclusively by different tribes and then are bought and sold. (Wood, 1634, 61-62; Morton, 1637, 30) William Wood hinted at the disastrous effect of European trade goods on Indian culture when he remarked that, despite the quality of their own pottery, they now prefer European metal kettles. (Wood, 1634, 62, 67; Winslow, 1624, 29)

The prevailing idea among the English was that the Indians lacked "Arts and Science." Certainly the reports of Indian life concentrated on the practical details of daily life. To a large extent, this probably reflects the interests of the English, their desire to present a picture of what Indian life looked like as well as to find out about products native to America which would be useful to English colonists and their backers.

There was some purely aesthetic interest in Indian work, especially weaving and embroidery. Indian baskets and mats were particularly praised for their fine designs, which William Wood thought must show evidence of their having been in contact with the ancient classical world. Their decoration of leather with painting and embroidery was similarly praised. John Smith was especially taken with a feather mantle he saw, "so prettily wrought and woven with threeds that nothing could bee discerned but the feathers."[4] William Strachey offered a peculiarly convincing form of praise for Indian weaving in grasses:

A delicate wrought fine kinde of Mat the Indians make, with which (as they can be trucked for, or snatched up) our people do dresse their chambers and

---

3. Barlowe, *first voyage to the coastes of America*, in Quinn, ed., *Roanoke Voyages*, I, 109; Thomas Hariot, *Notes* to the paintings of John White, *ibid.*, 436; Bradford and Winslow, *Mourt's Relation*, 12; Whitbourne, *Discourse and Discovery*, R3v-R4; James Rosier, *A True Relation of the voyage by Waymouth* (London, 1605), C3.

4. John Underhill, *Newes From America* (London, 1638), 8; Wood, *New Englands Prospect*, 90, 96; Smith, *Map of Virginia*, in Barbour, ed., *Jamestown Voyages*, II, 355; Morrell, *New England*, 21; Anon., *Relation of Maryland*, ed. Hawks, 34; Bradford and Winslow, *Mourt's Relation*, 12.

inward roomes, which make their houses so much the more handsome. (Strachey, 1610, 57, 63; and 1953, 75)

A few writers mentioned music among the Indians. John Smith said they have a pipe like a recorder, and a drum, "But their chiefe instruments are Rattels made of small gourds or Pumpions shels. Of these they have Base, Tenor, Countertenor, Meane and Trible." (Smith, 1612a, 363) William Wood commends the beautiful singing of Indian women. "To heare one of these Indians unseene, a good eare might easily mistake their untaught voyce for the warbling of a well tuned instrument." (Wood, 1634, 96; Strachey; 1953, 71) Strachey put in the words to a "kynd of angry song against us in their homely rymes" which included hopes of vanquishing the English. (Strachey, 1953, 85-86)

Though the Indians had no written language, there are several indications that they did keep records. The passage of time was noted in terms of winters and summers and by the moon. Samuel Purchas attributed stories of the great age which some Indians claimed to their counting each spring and fall as separate years. (Winslow, 1624, 60; Morrell, 1625, 23; Purchas, 1625 rpt. 1906, XIX, 118-119) Indians recorded their promises with little sticks "as by a tally." When Tomocomo accompanied Pocahontas to England, he tried to make a record of the number of people he saw to report back to Powhatan. His method was to make notches in a stick he carried. (Smith, 1624, 570; Purchas, 1625 rpt. 1906, 119) Edward Winslow testified to Indian interest in their own history:

Instead of records and chronicles, they take this course. Where any remarkable act is done, in memory of it, either in the place, or by some pathway near adjoining, they make a round hold in the ground, about a foot deep, and as much over; which when others passing by behold, they inquire the cause and occasion of the same, which being once known, they are careful to acquaint all men, as occasion serveth, therewith; and lest such holes should be filled or grown up by any accident, as men pass by, they will oft renew the same; by which means many things of great antiquity are fresh in memory. So that as a man travelleth, if he can understand his guide, his journey will be the less tedious, by reason of the many historical discourses will be related unto him. (Winslow, 1624, 61)

Regarding various natural phenomena, as Edward Winslow says, the Indians are "very ingenious and observative." Reports from New England and Virginia say they concur with Europeans in naming the constellation the Bear and that they know many of the fixed stars. Winslow says they also name the winds and can "guess very well at the wind and weather beforehand, by observations in the heavens." They actually claim that they can control the weather and use it against their enemies. (Winslow, 1624, 60; Rosier, 1605, E3; Va. Co. Recs., III, 584)

Reports of Indian technology, then, centered on providing a picture of Indian daily life. There was another type of technology that was almost equally interesting, and this consisted of Indian techniques or knowledge that might be useful to the English. Some of these techniques were practices which would help in coping with the wilderness, others were resources for possible export. No secret was made of the fact that the colonists relied almost entirely on Indian information to learn about the geography and natural resources of America. For example, John Brereton said of the hoped-for passage to the South Sea that it will never be found, "unlesse we plant first; whereby we shall learne as much by inquisition of the naturall inhabitants, as by our owne navigations." (Brereton, 1602, 21; Levett, 1624, 7, 11; Strachey, 1953, 51; Archer, 1607 b & c, 83, 87, 99)

Jewels and precious metals were what everyone hoped for. No precious stones were seen, except in the fantastic reports of David Ingram, but the Indians were reported to wear pearls as jewelry. (Ingram, 1582, 284-285, 288; Hakluyt, 1609, 500-501; Hariot, 1590, 424, 438-441) Many writers said the Indian pearls were now worthless, but that was because they were discolored and "spoyled with burning the Oysters in the fire, and the rude boaring of them." There was also hope that deep water pearls would be whiter than the shallow water ones which the Indians commonly wore. (Lane, 1586, 260-261; Anon., 1635, 39; Va. Co., 1610b, 18; Archer, 1607c, 93)

Copper was the only valuable metal which the writers were confident they had seen. Reports of the Indians wearing copper jewelry came from a variety of sources, but the source of the copper was never determined. In fact, it probably came from a great distance, some from the Appalachian Mountains, but most from the Lake Superior region. (Quinn, ed., 1955, I, 269) Roanoke colonists wrote of copper use and treatment. Thomas Hariot says they esteeme their copper jewelry "more then golde or silver." (Hariot, 1590, 424-425, 438-441) Ralph Lane transmitted reports of "a marveilous and most strange Minerall" that the Roanoke Indians knew of and which came from the country of Chaunis Temoatan. They were able to describe in detail the equipment and process of panning for the metal, called Wassador, which was said to be softer and paler than English copper. They also described the purifying of the metal over the fire. Lane's informant, a king's son whom he had taken prisoner, had never seen the process himself, because the land of Chaunis Temoatan was more than 20 days' journey to the west. Lane's efforts to reach this country ended in failure. (Lane, 1586, 268-270)

Reports from Jamestown speak of copper which the Indians say is gathered from the foothills of the mountains. They melt the copper in a hole in the ground over which they build a great fire. This makes it malleable and "causeth it to runne into a masse." Their only tools for working with the copper are smooth stones. Gabriel Archer marveled at its flexibility. (Archer, 1607 b & c, 93, 102; Purchas, 1625 rpt. 1906, XIX, 153-154) John Brereton's account of New England included praise for the abundance and fineness of Indian work in copper. Their chains are made of hollow pieces the size of a reed and the length of a man's finger. Their collars and bandoliers are made of many smaller pieces, all hollow. They also have large drinking cups and thin plates of copper. The metal varies in color from very red to very pale. It is so abundant that no one is without jewelry of copper. Brereton was very anxious to know the source of the metal, though he was careful to seem "little to regard it." When he asked the source, an Indian friend "taking a piece of Copper in his hand, made a hole with his finger in the ground, and withall pointed to the maine from whence they came.[5] (Brereton, 1602, 9-10)

John Smith reported that the Virginia Indians mined a mineral like antimony with shells and hatchets. This, after it was purified by washing in a stream, they sold all over the country in little bags. It was used for dusting all over themselves and their idols. William Strachey also heard of possible alum mines. (Smith, 1624, 418; Strachey, 1953, 40)

The use of roots and herbs for dyes and medicines were other areas in which America was expected to contribute to the English economy. Many ships were sent back freighted with sassafras, which was considered to be a cure for syphilis. The colonists were expected to find other natural products and to learn their use from the Indians. Knowledge of herbal remedies was sketchy, but interest was high. The writer of the *Relation of Maryland* is convinced that Indian herbal remedies will be valuable, but their "perfect use" the English "cannot yet learne from the Natives." He knows they have a poison antidote, which the colonists call snake-root. He also knows they have many other cures for all kinds of wounds. An Englishman was cured of the pain of a toothache when

---

5. Despite these references to fires, D. B. Quinn asserts that copper ore was not smelted in any part of North America before the arrival of Europeans. Quinn, ed., *Roanoke Voyages*, I, 269 fn.

he put a root given him by an Indian into his mouth. The Indians also have "Saxafras, Gummes, and Balsum." (Anon., 1635, 21-22)

Thomas Hariot says the Indians use a clay which they call "Wapeih" and which is similar to English *terra sigillata*. The natives use it to cure all sorts of wounds, as it is very plentiful. Hariot also mentions Indian use of blood-letting as a medical practice. (Hariot, 1588, 328; and 1590, 441) Purchas quotes George Percy on the herb "Weysake, like Liverwort which they chew and spit into poisoned wounds, that are thereby healed in foure and twenty houres." When they gather this root, "six of them hold together by the armes, and so go singing, and withall searching: and when they have found it, sit downe singing, crossing the roote with their hands for a good space, then gather, chew, and spit." (Purchas, 1614, 768)

John Smith describes a variety of medical practices, some of which would be unfamiliar to Europeans. He says they take a powerful spring purge with a root they call "wighsacan" and water.[6] It takes them three or four days to recover their former health. If they have swellings or dropsy, they sweat the patient "extreamely" in a specially built small "dovehouse" with a "few coales and therein covered with a pot," or they treat swellings with small sticks of touchwood and sucking. "Wighsacan" is used to heal "greene wounds," but any larger surgery is done with stone splinters. "Old ulcers or putrified hurtes are seldome seene cured amongst them." Smith goes on to speak of the charms and conjurations of their "professed Phisitions" and their belief that English doctors were superior in power. (Smith, 1612a, 363-364) This interest in the magical aspects of Indian religion and confusion over how much it contributed to cures is seen clearly in Morrell and Wood. Morrell talks of the medicine man's skill with "herbes, and rootes, and plants," but says they cure by "their curst magicke." (Morrell, 1625, 19) William Wood, in writing of the hardiness of the Indians, says they survive as nothing wounds which would be "suddaine death to an English man." He describes a variety of "desperate wounds" he knows they have suffered, "which eyther by their rare skill in the use of vegitatives, or diabolicall charmes they cure in short time." (Wood, 1634, 75)

Clearly the promise of America as a land of useful products and of the Indians as the key to those products was still tantalizingly unknown but definitely hoped for. Pitch and tar for naval stores was another hoped-for product. Francis Higginson gives an indication that both will be plentiful. The Indians burn pine splinters instead of candles, "which

---

6. "Wighsacan" and "Weysake" were probably different renditions of the same name. See Barbour, ed., *Jamestown Voyages*, I, 146 fn.

are so full of the moysture of Turpentine and Pitch, that they burne as cleere as a Torch." Higginson sent some home for his friend to test. (Higginson, 1630, 11)

Leather and animal skins was another hoped-for commodity group, though it certainly was not realized that these would become the major export of the northern colonies. The writers clearly assumed that Indian hunters would provide the skins, and many writers wrote about Indian methods of tanning and processing leather obviously hoping that they could rely on native dressing as well.

Fibers constituted another class of commodities which the promoters hoped to export from America. Arguing from their idea that climate is constant in a given latitude around the globe, they believed that silk culture could be sustained, at least in Virginia. Thomas Hariot reported that he had seen silk worms in the Roanoke area, and he had also found a "grasse Silke" which would make a good silk. Though he found little hemp or flax, he believed they would grow easily in that area. Despite these expectations, colonists seem to have been surprised and delighted by the variety and skill of native work in fibers. Many writers remarked on the strength of Indian rope and cord. William Wood found it superior to the European product, both in strength and texture. He said it "lookes more like silke than hempe." As in his discussion of pottery, Wood once again pointed to the destructive effect of the introduction of European technology on the integrity of Indian culture. He says the Indians have ceased to make their rope, preferring the inferior English cord. The cause of this preference, he thinks, is laziness. (Hariot, 1588, 325-327; Smith, 1616, 207; Rosier, 1605, E3; Wood, 1634, 89)

Some New England colonists testified to the strength of Indian rope in another way. They described the deer traps made of rope and young trees which were uncommonly strong. Wood told how an English mare stumbled into one and was found "hanging her like mahomets tombe, betwixt earth and heaven." When the Indians found this horse:

praunce in their Merritotter, [see-saw] they bade her good morrow, crying out, what cheere what cheere Englishmen's squaw horse; having no better epithite than to call her a woman horse, but being loath to kill her, and as fearfull to approach neere the friscadoes of her Iron heeles, they posted to the English to tell how the case stood or hung with their Squaw horse . . . (Wood, 1634, 89; Morton, 1637, 52)

William Bradford and Edward Winslow's *Relation of the English Plantation at New Plimoth,* known as *Mourt's Relation* after its editor, described an episode when a party was examining one of these Indian traps. As Bradford moved around the trap, "it gave a sodaine jerk up, and he was immediately caught by the leg." The *Relation* graciously goes on to praise the trap's construction: "It was a very pretie devise made with a rope of their owne making, and having a noose as artifically made as any roper in England can make, and as like ours as can be." (Bradford and Winslow, 1622, 8)

Another highly praised Indian product was their tobacco pipes made of clay or stone and some partly of copper. Several writers remark on the large size of the pipes, Brereton being particularly glad of this because the tobacco was "better than any I have tasted in England." William Wood expected a good sale in England for Indian pipes because of "their rarity, strength, handsomnesse, and coolnesse." (Brereton, 1602, 6; Wood, 1634, 62; Percy, 1607, 410; Rosier, 1605, C2v; Strachey, 1953, 123) Despite strenuous efforts of many people in authority to discourage its use, including a tract written by King James, tobacco smoking became very popular in England very quickly. People who had been to America often became addicted to tobacco. Thomas Hariot was a constant smoker and his death resulted from the first documented case of smoking-related cancer. (R. H. C. Tanner in Shirley, ed., 1974, 93-94)

In all the discussion of Indian technology thus far, we have been looking at those products which the English thought could be useful to them. There was another category of Indian products which was at least as important to them. Discussion of the technological level of the Indians included the question of what the English had to fear from them. How effective could hostile Americans be in fighting European arms? The best weapon in the American arsenal, as will be shown later, was simply withdrawing from the English, refusing to have any contact with them. The earliest colonists in all areas, despite their claims of technological superiority, were extremely dependent on Indian help in coping with the environment, particularly for food. The writers usually do not attempt to disguise this dependence. Some go as far as to speak of the Indians making war upon them by withdrawing. (Va. Co., 1610b, 11; Lane, 1586, 265-267, 270) When the writers speak of the ability of the Indians to wage war, however, they usually are thinking of active war and the effectiveness of Indian weapons.

Most writers assured their readers that Indian weapons were inferior. Thomas Hariot said Indian weapons were inadequate "to offend us withall," and he made the ominous additional comment that they have poor means of defense as well. William Symonds who stayed in England contrasts the fear of the Israelites entering Canaan with the ease of entering North America:

But wee should be worse then mad, to bee discouraged by any such imaginations of this place. There are but poore Arbors for Castles, base and homely sheds for walled townes. A mat is their strongest Portcullis, a naked brest their Target [shield] of best proofe: an arrow of reede, on which is no iron, their most fearefull weapon of offence, heere is no feare of nine hundreth iron charets. (Symonds, 1609, 25)

The main source of English confidence was the fact that the American natives did not know the use of iron and steel, and it was taken for granted that Indian arrows, without metal tips, would be ineffective. (Hariot, 1588, 369; Gordon of Lochinvar, 1625, Dv; Levett, 1625, 21)

There was, however, a good deal of interest in Indian weapons. John White put weapons in the hands of two of the Indian men he painted. In addition to the traditional bows and arrows, many writers referred to hatchets or tomahawks, javelins, knives, and swords, as well as targets, by which they meant shields. Moreover many writers stressed that, though Indian fletchers lack iron and steel, they do not lack ingenuity in finding things to tip their arrows with. They are described as using sharp pieces of rock or animal bone or horn, the claws and bills of large birds and sometimes copper or brass. The points and feathers are glued on to the arrows with a glue made by boiling deer horns. (Smith, 1612a, 358; Pringe, 1603, 325; Strachey, 1953, 108-9)

Not only are Indian arrows artfully made, but the bows are affirmed by several writers to have great power, and the bowmen to be extremely skilled. George Percy reported an incident where the English invited an Indian to shoot at a shield which a pistol could not penetrate. He drew his bow and shot the shield a foot through. (Percy, 1607, 414) Alexander Whitaker gave a graphic description of Indian skill:

I suppose the world hath no better marke-men with their bow and arrowes then they be; they will kill birds flying, fishes swimming, and beasts running: they shoote also with mervailous strength, they shot one of our men being unarmed quite through the bodie, and nailed both his armes to his bodie with one arrow.[7] (Whitaker, 1613, 25; Rosier, 1605, C-Cv; Smith, 1612a, 359; Va.Co.Recs., IV, 67)

One of the most intriguing questions is whether the matchlocks and

7. See Fr. Andrew White, *A Briefe Relation of the Voyage unto Maryland*, 1634, in C. C. Hall, ed., *Narratives of Early Maryland, 1633-1684* (New York, 1910), 43 for the opposite opinion.

muskets of the colonists were actually better weapons than the bows and arrows of the Indians. Certainly this was the universal assumption at the time. It is undeniable that the Indians were impressed by the colonists' guns and wanted them for themselves. Further, those Indians who had guns were thought to have an advantage over tribes to the west who lacked them. The English repeatedly passed laws prohibiting trade in guns, laws which were unsuccessfully enforced.

There is another side to this picture of relative technologies. A bowman could shoot a dozen arrows a minute, while the 17th century gun could shoot only about two balls in that time, and the range and accuracy of the guns were not greater. If a surprise attack by a small group was the goal, then the bow and arrow might be superior. The early colonists' guns required that a member of the company carry a lighted wick at all times with which to fire the guns. William Strachey transmitted a story from an early New England expedition which illustrates the problem clearly. An exploring party and a group of Indians were in a tense, but nominally friendly confrontation. One of the Indians came aboard the explorers' boat and picked up their firebrand as if to light his pipe. As soon as he had it, he threw it in the water and extinguished it and then he leaped back on shore. The Indians repelled English attempts to get fire from their camp. In the end the English simply rowed away, neither side having opened fire. (Strachey, 1953, 171) In addition the guns frequently misfired, which could be dangerous to the man firing. John Smith reported that the president of Jamestown "split his hand" when his gun misfired. (Smith, 1608, 199; Russell, 1962, 5-6; Craven, 1971, 45; Driver, 1969, 310) The inaccuracy of the colonists' guns was not a problem when they were shooting at massed targets, but could be a problem in frontier warfare. This was clearly on Hakluyt's mind when he urged the Jamestown colonists to let the Indians see only their best marksmen shoot, "for if they See Your Learners miss what they aim at they will think the Weapon not so terrible and thereby will be bould to Assaillt You." (Va. Co., 1606, 52) When John Smith, in his captivity, was asked to demonstrate his pistol on a target which the Indians had set up, he broke the cock on the gun to avoid having to shoot in those circumstances. Clearly he did not feel safe relying on his pistol's accuracy. (Smith, 1608, 184)

The single most popular product of Indian technology was the canoe. Many writers described the wonderful boats, and frequently they gave long descriptions of their manufacture as well. The canoes were of two types. The earliest descriptions, those from Virginia territory, were of dugout canoes. John White painted a picture of one of these being made. Hariot began his note to this picture: "The manner of makinge their boates in Virginia is verye wonderfull." He was concerned to demonstrate that it is possible to make such a canoe without iron tools. The method he described, that of alternately burning out the center and scraping it with sea shells, proved to his satisfaction that "god indueth thise savage people with sufficient reason to make thinges necessarie to serve their turnes." Hariot and Barlowe say these canoes can carry up to 20 men, but John Smith says some of them have a capacity of 40 though he admits the smaller ones are more common. (Hariot, 1588, 363-364; and 1590, 432-433; Barlowe, 1584, 104-105; Smith, 1612a, 358; Percy, 1607, 408; Hamor, 1615, 38; Strachey, 1953, 82) Only William Wood of New England mentioned dugouts. (Wood, 1634, 43, 91)

It was the birchbark canoes which were seen as most marvelous. Martin Pringe offered the first and one of the best descriptions of their manufacture. The canoes he saw, one of which was brought back to Bristol, were 17 feet long and 4 feet wide:

made of the Barke of a Birch-tree, farre exceeding in bignesse those of England: it was sowed together with strong and tough Oziers or twigs, and the seames covered over with Rozen or Turpentine little inferiour in sweetnesse to Frankincense, as we made triall by burning a little thereof on the coales at sundry times after our comming home: it was also open like a Wherrie, and sharpe at both ends, saving that the beake was a little bending roundly upward. And though it carried nine men standing upright, yet it weighed not at the most above sixtie pounds in weight, a thing almost incredible in regard of the largenesse and capacitie thereof. (Pringe, 1603, 326)

John Winthrop said the canoes of the Long Island Indians could hold 80 men. (Winthrop, 1908, I, 109)

The most startling characteristic of the canoe was its lightness for its size and capacity. Thomas Morton says that two men can carry a canoe that will hold ten to twelve men. (Morton, 1637, 45) William Wood says one man can carry a canoe a mile, and he points out that this is what makes canoes well-suited to the environment, that they can be carried overland from stream to stream. (Wood, 1634, 91) As John Guy says, ". . . every place is to them a harborough; where they can goe ashoare themselves, they take aland with them their Canoa." (Guy, 1612, 422-23) Allied with this lightness was the marvelous swiftness of the canoe. James Rosier recounted an incident in which "they in their Canoa with three oares, would at their will go ahead of us and about us, when we rowed with eight oares strong; such was their swiftnesse, by reason of the lightnesse and artificiall composition of their Canoa and oares." (Rosier, 1605, C3v)

There is a theme running through all English discussions of Indian technology which emerges most clearly in descriptions of the canoe. This is the belief that the Indians were better adapted to life in America than the English were. Though the writers believed in the general superiority of English technology, they were clearly aware of the fact that they would have to learn from the Indian in order to survive. Not only did they realize this, they made no attempt to disguise it from their English audience. Concerning the canoe, they not only demonstrated that it was a faster craft than their small boats, but they also showed that it was more useful in America, because it could go where their small boats could not go, and was more flexible to use. William Wood gives a vivid picture of the relative clumsiness of the Englishman and his boat:

In these cockling fly-boates, wherein an English man can scarce sit without a fearefull tottering, they will venture to Sea, when an English Shallope dare not beare a knot of sayle; scudding over the overgrowne waves as fast as a winde-driven Ship, being driven by their padles; being much like battle doores; if a crosse wave (as is seldome) turn her keele up-side downe, they by swimming free her, and scramble into her againe. (Wood, 1634, 91)

Indian canoes easily navigated the rocky and swift-moving rivers for which English boats were useless and they could easily be carried around obstacles. John Smith was scornful of the equipment sent to Jamestown by the Virginia Company. He wrote them specifically about a boat in four pieces which they sent to be carried in pieces above the fall line and then assembled and used for exploring the river. Smith explained the difficulty: "If he had burnt her to ashes, one might have carried her in a bag; but as she is, five hundred cannot, to a navigable place above the Falles." (Smith, 1624, 349, 443; Anon., 1635, 19) American conditions were going to require adaptation.

Not only is the Indian's technology better suited to the American environment, but Thomas Morton says the Indian himself is. Their senses are so perfected beyond the capacities of the English that, if it were not for the corroboration of French accounts from Nova Francia, he would have been reluctant to say what he has seen, "which is a thinge that I should not easily have bin induced, to beleeve, if I my selfe, had not bin an eie witnesse, of what I shall relate." He says Indians can sight a ship at sea one to two hours before an English man watching for the ship can see it. Their "sight is so excellent" that Morton says "one would allmost beleeve they had intelligence of the Devill, sometimes." He attributes this to the blackness of their eyes. "And as they excell us in this particular so much noted, so I thinke they excell us in all the rest." He has heard from French sources that they can distinguish between a Frenchman and a Spaniard just by the smell of their hands, and Morton has personally accompanied an Indian who tracked a deer and distinguished old from new tracks just by sight and smell, "and I did eate part of it with him: such is their perfection in these two sences." In none of this discussion does Morton, even implicitly, make a comparison to the keener sense of smell of animals. His attitude is wholly one of admiration. (Morton, 1637, 33-34)

George Hakewill in the 3rd edition of the *Apologie of the Power and Providence of God,* offered a philosophical justification for this phenomenon. He asserted that knowledge is of three sorts and that the possessor of one sort may not necessarily be superior in all situations to the possessor of another sort:

A beast is guided by his sence, a man by reason, a Christian by religion, and looke how much a man is beyond a beast, so much is a Christian beyond a meere man; and as a beast is able to judge of those things which belong to his sence, as his meate and drinke, better then some men indewed with reason, though of human affayres as the government of kingdomes hee cannot judge: so the meere naturall man by the light of reason can many times judge of humane affayres or things meerely naturall or morall, better then the most illuminated and sanctified Christian. (Hakewill, 1635, Bk. V, 84)

There was no philosophical bar to learning from the Indians how to cope with the American environment, just as the enthnocentrism of the colonists did not prevent them from appreciating the technological competence of the Indians. More importantly, their ethnocentrism did not prevent their being interested in Indian life as it was actually carried on. This reflected the interest of the English reading public who wanted to be able to picture Indian life. The writers wrote to satisfy this consumer demand. They responded to the interest of the English audience in how Indian society functioned, particularly in maintaining order and distinctions between people, the maintenance of which were also the main functions of European society. As ethnographers, they were consciously describing another society, one which was strikingly different from their own, but which was understandable and recognizable as a society by their own definition. Their reports constitute, even today, the major ethnographical resource for information about the coastal Algonquians of the 16th and 17th centuries.

Just how real this accomplishment is can be judged by comparing eyewitness writers to those who remained in England. Most of the people who wrote about America without seeing it continued the tradition of the medieval cosmologies and wrote about the Indians in a rhetorical way.[8] It is these writers who dismissed Indian culture with phrases about their being brutish or beastlike. It is only writers who stayed in England who assign the Indians to a place outside the ranks of full humanity. Historians who say that the English rejected the Indians and their culture out of hand on first sight overwhelmingly rely on non-eyewitnesses to prove their point.[9] When the crucial distinction between eyewitnesses and non-eyewitnesses is made, the balance and objectivity of eyewitnesses becomes clear. Not all eyewitnesses admired Indian culture, many were strongly hostile to it, but they did not place the Americans outside the ranks of civil men. They manifestly did not consider the "savages" to be sub-human or brutish. As we will see in the second half of this book, the early colonists were dependent on Indian aid in so many ways and were so vulnerable that they could not afford to be contemptuous of native accomplishments. Writers in England could romanticize about savage men who ran in herds like deer, but actual colonists could not. John Smith himself pointed to the importance of distinguishing eyewitnesses from others:

...there is a great difference, betwixt the directions and judgement of experimentall knowledge, and the superficiall conjecture of variable relation: wherein rumor, humor, or misprison have such power, that oft times one is enough to beguile twentie, but twentie, not sufficient to keep one from being deceived. Therefore I know no reason but to beleeve my own eies, before any mans imagination, that is but wrested from the conceits of my owne projects, and indeavours. (Smith, 1616, 218-219)

---

8. See for example Robert Johnson, *Nova Brittania* in Force, *Tracts*, I, 11; Robert Tynley, *Two Learned Sermons* (London, 1609), 67; Richard Crakanthorpe, *A Sermon at the Inauguration of King James* (London, 1609), D2v; Robert Gray, *A Good Speed to Virginia* (London, 1609), C2v; William Crashaw, *A Sermon Preached in London* (London, 1610), 31; William Symonds, *Virginia. A Sermon* (London, 1609), 15; William Alexander, Earl of Stirling, *The Mapp and Description of New-England* (London, 1630), 37-38, 44; Richard Eburne, *A Plain Pathway to Plantations*, ed. Louis B. Wright (1624; rpt. Ithaca, N.Y., 1962); 89, 102; Samuel Purchas, *Virginia's Verger* in *Hakluytus Posthumus or Purchas His Pilgrimes* (1625; rpt. Glasgow, 1906), XIX, 222-224, 231.

9. See for example Hodgen, *Early Anthropology*, 362-364, 409; Nash, *Red, White, and Black*, 38-42; Pearce, *Savages of America*, 5-7; Jennings, *Invasion of America*, 74. For a more detailed discussion of this issue see Karen Ordahl Kupperman, "British Attitudes Toward the American Indian 1580-1640," unpub. PhD diss., Cambridge University, 1978, 124-130.

6

Were the Indians Alien?

Michael Drayton was a fellow member of London's literary circles with George Sandys. When Sandys went off to Virginia Drayton wrote a poem to him encouraging him to go on with his translation of Ovid and also to write a report of the land and its products. He did not want to hear about the Indians:

But you may save your labour if you please,
To write to me ought of your Savages
As savage slaves be in great Britaine here,
As any one that you can shew me there. (Drayton, 1622 rpt. 1961, III, 208)

Drayton obviously differs from the audience most colonial literature was written for in that he was not interested in the Indians, but his reason for not wanting to know about them is highly interesting in itself. He clearly assumed that they would not be alien, in fact that they would not differ from the lowborn in England in any important way, and that they therefore would be no more interesting than humble English people. Though Drayton is atypical in his professed lack of interest in Indian culture, he is completely typical in his assumption that the Indians do not represent a fundamentally different race of people.

All the ethnographical reports we have been considering, interesting though they were to the English public, were only the starting point for a whole range of much more fundamental questions. This range can be summed up in the basic question: "Who are the Indians?" This naturally led on to the subject of how the Indians differed from Europeans and whether these differences were superficial or profound. In this chapter, we will first attack this set of questions directly, by looking at the ways in which English writers wrote about the origins and heritage of the American Indians. We will then approach the problem from a different direction, by comparing descriptions of different sorts of English people to descriptions of Indians. In this way we can see whether the differences between the two cultures were superficial and subject to change or whether they were so fundamental as forever to set the Indians apart from English people.

All British writers before 1640 took up the theologically orthodox position that all men, including the American Indians, must be descended from the same creation in Genesis. Philip Vincent impatiently brushed aside speculations on the subject:

It were needlesse curiosity to dispute their originall, or how they came hither. Their outsides say they are men, their actions say they are reasonable. As the thing is, so it operateth. Their correspondency of disposition with us, argueth all to be of the same constitution, & the sons of Adam, and that we had the same Maker, the same matter, the same mould. (Vincent, 1637, B; Whitaker, 1613, 24; Levett, 1624, 11; Rolfe, 1616 rpt. 1951, 40)

This conviction, simple enough in itself, created two further problems. The first was that since the Europeans themselves had only recently developed the "loadstone," the basis of the compass, and therefore the ability to sail out of sight of land, how did the ancestors of the Indians get to the new world? The second involved the identification of the Indians with some culture known to the ancient world. It was assumed that they must have come from a part of the world known to the ancients and that they would retain some characteristics of their original culture. Most writers found these questions fascinating, certainly not "needlesse curiosity."

Debate on the origins of the Indians was lively and there was widespread agreement about the kinds of evidence which would decide the question. Some writers pointed to Indian beliefs or customs, but most considered analysis of language to be the only really reliable source of information about the origins of a people. Writers assumed the Indians' language would still bear some resemblance to the known ancient language from which it developed. People who wrote about the Indians frequently included lists of Indians words and their translations so that scholars in England could study them and see what ancient language they resembled. William Wood included a "small Nomenclator" despite his fear that, because Indian words resemble many different languages, the language represented "some of the gleanings of all Nations." This fear was shared by other writers. (Wood, 1634, 91, 99) There was controversy, though, over how linguistic evidence should be interpreted. Morton ridiculed Wood's idea and said he erred because he listened to the sound of the words only. Anyone "of reasonable capacity" would think instead of "the sence and signification of the words . . . otherwise hee shall but runne rounde about a maze." (Morton, 1637, 17-18) Morton was in the minority. Most writers were interested in the sound, not the meaning, of Indian words. Such words as "penguin" provided the proof for those who believed that the Indians were Welsh, descendants of the Prince Madoc who was supposed to have discovered America in 1170. This theory was reinforced by Indian use of crosses and by the reported belief of the Mexicans that their kings were descended from bearded white men who came from far away. (Hakluyt, 1589c, II, 506-507; Ingram, 1582, 292; Peckham, 1583, 459-460; Strachey, 1953, 12) Morton himself believed that the Indian language was a mixture of Greek and Latin and that the Indians were descendants of the "scattered Trojans." He felt he had found linguistic evidence that they came from the region of the Tropic of Cancer and that they had once worshipped the god Pan. (Morton, 1637, 15-18)

Since Europeans had achieved the technology to navigate across the ocean comparatively recently, many writers wondered how the Indians could have gotten to America in ancient times. Purchas offered one solution, that the continent was peopled by ships blown off course. For John Donne and Edward Brerewood the presence of "ravenous and harmful beasts" ruled out the possibility that the ancient immigrants came by sea. They would never have included purely harmful animals in a ship's cargo. (Purchas, 1614, 726-728; Donne, 1626, 41; Brerewood, 1614, 97-98) Sir William Alexander pointed to the absence of "the most usefull kindes of tame Cattle" as well as the presence of harmful animals and he argued for the modern explanation of the peopling of America. There must be a "Narrow Sea towardes the North" which would freeze in the winter and allow people and animals to pass. (Alexander, 1630, 40-41) Brerewood, endorsed by Purchas, also argued that the Indians were descended from "those olde Tartars," pointing out that the two continents are very close together in the north. (Brerewood, 1614, 94-98; Purchas, 1614, 727) Thomas Morton, though he endorses many of Alexander's views, argues powerfully against the idea that people traveled to America over a frozen sea. A settled people will not move unless compelled to or unless they have the expectation of a better life in a new land. If the Tartars were compelled to move, "then by whome, or when?" Otherwise it is unlikely a people at ease:

Will of their one accord undertake to travayle over a Sea of Ice, considering how many difficulties they shall encounter with, as first whether there be any Land at the end of their unknowne way, no Land beinge in view, then want of Food to sustane life in the meane time upon that Sea of Ice, or how should they doe for Fuell, to keepe them at night from freezing to death, which will not bee had in such a place . . . (Morton, 1637, 16)

One reason why William Penn is sometimes seen as founder of a new tradition of respectful relations with the Indians in the last quarter of the 17th century is that Penn thought the Indians might be descended from the Ten Lost Tribes of Israel. (Nash in Dudley and Novak, 1972, 72) In this, as in his admiration for Indian character, physique, and language, Penn was not unique. Many writers throughout the period of this study found linguistic and cultural evidence of Jewish origins in the Indians; in fact this was the favorite answer to the question of who the Indians were. Some writers pointed to Indian religious practices as echoes or "foot-steps of the knowledge of God." (Whitaker, 1613, 27; White, 1630, 7-9; Fr. White, 1634; 45; Va.Co.Recs., III, 584) Other writers pointed to cultural practices, such as the separation of menstruating women, and some felt these must be reflections of Jewish taboos. (White, 1630, 7-9; Winslow, 1624, 59; Henry Spelman in Purchas, 1614, 757) The Puritan John White was convinced by these and by linguistic evidence. He was sorry that Massachusetts Bay settlers of the advance party had named their settlement Salem, because the former name *Nahum Keike* "prooves to bee perfect Hebrew," meaning "The bosome of consolation." (White, 1630, 7-9)

The idea that the Indians might be lost Jews was widely debated throughout Europe in the middle years of the 17th century. Roger Williams and John Eliot in America were convinced of the Indians' Jewish origins. The evidence was brought together and argued forcefully by Menassah ben Israel's *Spes Israelis* (1650), which was translated as *The Hope of Israel*. Thomas Thorowgood, in the same year, initiated a lively debate with publication of his *Jewes in America, or Probabilities that the Americans are of that Race*. It was answered by Hamon L'Estrange with his *Americans no Jewes, or, Improbabilities that the Americans are of that Race* in 1652. Thorowgood restated his case in *Jews in America, or, Probabilities that those Indians are Judaical* in 1660. (Huddleston, 1967, 128-134)

When the English distinguish themselves as a group from the Indians, they sometimes call themselves English, but usually they refer to themselves and all Europeans as Christians. None uses the word European. Anthony Parkhurst says he comes from "Kent and Christendome." (Parkhurst, 1578, 131) They did not come to grips with the general problem of how one designates Christian Indians. They clearly meant Christian to be synonymous with European, but since large-scale conversion was still a hope for the future by 1640, they probably would not have accepted the full legal distinction between Christian and converted Indian which Winthrop Jordan sees as set by the end of the century. (Jordan, 1969, 95) In the early period they still thought the Indians, when fully civilized and converted, would be similar to themselves. The status of those Indians who actually placed themselves with the English was indeterminate. John Smith says Pocahontas was "the first Christian ever of that Nation." (Smith, 1624, 532) Manteo, who helped White's Roanoke colonists against some enemy Indians was said to have "behaved himselfe toward us as a most faithfull English man." After this he was christened, but still as "our Savage Manteo." (White, 1587, 530-531) But when the Chickahominies became "King JAMES his subjects," they were no longer "Naturalls, of that place." They took the Indian name for Englishmen. (Hamor, 1615, 15) The ambiguous situation of such Indians is best illustrated by John Smith's report of his meeting with Mosco, the bearded Indian who was thought to have had a French father. He greeted the English party and was happy to "see so many of his Countrymen." Paradoxically, in the following sentence, Smith says Mosco got "divers of his Countreymen," that is, Indians, to help tow the English boat up the river. (Smith, 1624, 424)

Some of the writers were interested in Indian ideas of who the English were. Some colonists reported that the fact that the great sickness which was killing so many Indians did not attack the English gave them a semi-magical status. (Lane, 1586, 278; Hariot, 1588, 379-380) Many placed great hope in their conviction that the Indians viewed them and all Europeans as "Demy-Gods." (Va.Co, 1606, 52; Smith, 1612b, 388, 408; Hamor, 1615, 36) Another reason given for the Indians seeing Englishmen as especially loved of God and especially powerful was the scientific equipment which the English enjoyed demonstrating. Thomas Hariot wrote of how he showed the Indians near Roanoke "Mathematicall instruments, sea compasses, the vertue of the loadstone in drawing yron, a perspective glasse whereby was shrewed manie strange sightes, burning glasses, wildefire woorkes, gunnes, bookes, writing and reading, spring clocks that seeme to goe of themselves . . ." (Hariot, 1588, 375-376; Rosier, 1605, C; Smith, 1608, 181 and 1612b, 390, Purchas, 1614, 757)

"Savages" was the usual word for the Indians, though its meaning is not at all clear. Francis Jennings asserts that it originally meant only wild person, but that it changed its meaning under the impact of colonization. "The special development of 'savage' in English was a stress on beastly ferocity that displaced simple wildness as the dominant meaning of the word." (Jennings, 1975, 74-75) This is doubtless true of some writers, especially those who use the word only when they are writing of episodes of fighting between Indians and English. The view of the Indian implied by use of the word appears to be rather more complex and ambiguous for many other writers. There are writers throughout the entire period who avoid its use altogether. Hariot is one of these. Substitutes, which occur throughout the period, center around some variation of "naturalls" or natural inhabitants, as well as "Indian." In England the word natural meant a half-witted person as well as the native of a country, but this meaning does not seem to be in the minds of the writers. Though many remark favorably on the simplicity of Indian life, there is no indication that they saw the Americans as simple-minded. In much the same way, most of the writers who use the word savage seem to mean little more than we would by the word native. Often savage is used interchangeably with other words. The impression that savage normally meant the equivalent of the modern native is reinforced by several ambiguous discussions of the "savages," which clearly indicate that the word did not have an absolute meaning. Occasionally one finds the word savage used in conjunction with the word civil, as when John Smith wrote that the "Salvages" conquered by Cortez were "a civilized people." (Smith, 1612b, 409 and 1624, 600; Purchas, 1625 rpt. 1906, XIX, 168) Thomas Dermer wrote of "our Savage friends." (Dermer, 1619, 131) Late in the period Thomas Morton indulged in a rhetorical flourish: "but I have found the Massachusetts Indian more full of humanity, then the Christians, & have had much better quarter with them." He goes on to sum up his experiences: "the more Salvages the better quarter, the more Christians the worser quarter I found, as all the indifferent minded Planters can testifie." (Morton, 1637, 77-78; Percy, 1607, 411) For all these writers as for most the word savage was as neutral as the word Indian. James Rosier, after describing an encounter with Indians he designates "Salvages," writes of "the kinde civility we found in a people, where we little expected any sparke of humanity." (Rosier, 1605, B4)

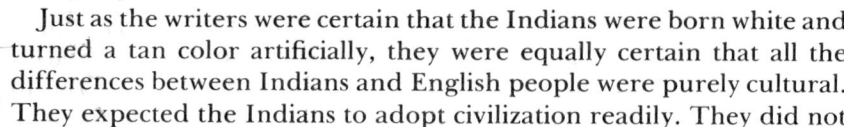Just as the writers were certain that the Indians were born white and turned a tan color artificially, they were equally certain that all the differences between Indians and English people were purely cultural. They expected the Indians to adopt civilization readily. They did not

regard "such a leap to be impossible or undesirable."[1] It was a commonplace that the English would perform for the Indians the same function as the Romans once performed for the English—the bringing of civilization and Christianity. They constantly play on the theme that the Indians are "our kinsmen and younger brethren." William Crashaw elaborated the point:

> Nor can it be denied that they (in this case) are our brethren: for the same God made them as well as us, of as good matter as he made us, gave them as perfect and good soules and bodies as to us, and the same Messiah & saviour is sent to them as to us . . . (Crashaw, 1610, c3-c3v; Johnson, 1612, 8, 18; Vaughan, 1626, III, 31; Jesuit Letters, 1639, 129)

Related to the idea that the Indians were younger brothers to the English was the argument, given by a wide variety of writers, that the English had once been "as Salvage, and as miserable as the most barbarous Salvage."[2] Not only had the English been culturally as savage as the Indians, but they had also looked like them. John White followed his paintings of the American Indians with drawings of ancient Picts and Britons who looked very much like his Indians, particularly in dress and body decorations. (Hulton and Quinn, 1964; Strachey, 1953, 70-71) The report of Sebastian Cabot's voyage in the *Divers Voyages* spoke of seeing Indians who ate raw flesh and lived like brute beasts. Later the speaker saw the same men in England in English clothes and found they were indistinguishable from Englishmen. The reverse happened to Ralph Hamor. He saw an Englishman who had spent three years living with the Indians. The man was like an Indian "in complexion and habite." (Hakluyt, 1582b, 23-24; Hamor, 1615, 44)

Not only do Europeans have no monopoly on humanity, but two writers even argued that the Americans might one day surpass

---

1. For the opposite view see Neal Salisbury, "Red Puritans: The 'Praying Indians' of Massachusetts Bay and John Eliot," *William and Mary Quarterly*, 3rd Ser., 31 (1974), 29 and Hodgen, *Early Anthropology*, 365.

2. John Smith, *A Description of New England*, 1616, in Arber and Bradley, eds., *Travels and Works*, I, 228, and *Advertisements For the unexperienced Planters of New-England, or any where*, 1613, *ibid.*, II, 934-5; Alexander Whitaker, *Good Newes from Virginia* (London, 1613), 24, 27; Whitbourne, *Discourse and Discovery*, 14; John White, *The Planters Plea*, 1630 in Force, comp., *Tracts*, II, 21-22; Symonds, *Virginia*, 19; Eburne, *Plain Pathway to Plantations*, ed. Wright, 56; Crashaw, *Sermon*, C4v; Gray, *Good Speed to Virginia*, C2; Vincent, *True Relation of the Late Battel*, Bv; John Rolfe, *A True Relation of the State of Virginia*, 1616 (New Haven, 1951), 40; George Donne, *Virginia Reviewed*, ed. T.H. Breen, *William and Mary Quarterly*, 3rd Ser., 30 (1973), 461; "Extracts from the Annual Letters of the English Province of the Society of Jesus," in Hall, ed., *Narratives of Early Maryland*, 127; Strachey, *Historie of Travell*, ed. Wright and Freund, 9; Nathaniel B. Shurtleff, ed., *Records of the Governor and Company of the Massachusetts Bay in New England*, I, 384.

Europeans in either civility or God's favor. George Hakewill offered a cyclical view of history:

> the most civill nations which now are, may againe in future ages become as barbarous as they, and the most barbarous bee civillized, or returne againe to that civility which perchance in former ages they practised, and by this meanes is the ballance of humane affaires kept upright. (Hakewill, 1635, V, 58)

Robert Cushman, who took a dark view of Indians and English alike, suggested that God may intend that "the kingdom of heaven be taken from them which now have it, and given to a people that shall bring forth the fruit of it" as a punishment for Christian Europe's "coldness, carnality, wanton abuse of the Gospel, contention." (Cushman, 1622, A2v)

 If we are really to understand how the English viewed the Indians, then we must not only analyze the way they described the Indians, but also how they saw their own culture and their fellow Europeans. We must attempt to make explicit the comparison which was implicit in all they wrote. This second dimension, the self-image and degree of sophistication of the English, is largely ignored by modern writers on the subject of the relations between English and Indians in the early years of contact. The result is that the English are assumed to have been more sophisticated and superior than they really were and than they themselves thought they were. We have eliminated the 19th century view of the native, but have largely retained the 19th century view of the colonist.[3] Daniel J. Boorstin offers a good example of this overdrawn contrast:

> Modern European civilisation, possessed of the achievements of Christendom, the liberalizing influence of Protestantism, the innovating spirit of the Renaissance, and the exploring vision of modern science, found itself in America suddenly on a scene of pre-history. When before had there been so intimate, so extensive, so vivid a confrontation of two such disparate stages in human development? (Boorstin, 1975a, 636)

 One subject on which historians assume an inappropriate degree of sophistication for the English is that of the interpretation of natural phenomena. Calvin Martin, contrasting what he calls the European abstract material culture with that of the Indians says: "The Indians' world was filled with superhuman and magical powers which controlled man's destiny and nature's course of events." (Martin, 1974, 12,

---

3. See Brian V. Street, *The Savage in Literature: Representations of "primitive" society in English fiction, 1858-1920* (London, 1975).

22-23) Precisely these same words describe the culture of the English. (Thomas, 1973) Often the English interpret difficult natural events no differently than the Indians do. There is considerable confusion and a great deal of credulity about cause and effect in sickness. Though many English writers realized that scurvy responds to eating fresh lemons and green vegetables, they also saw a moral element in contracting the disease. Scurvy is said to attack only lazy or morally inferior people. Reports from all colonies speaking of such people actually dying of laziness. (Kupperman, 1979a, 24, 34) Colonists were drawing on the traditional doctrine that nature always offers the cure for a new evil near the place where the evil was discovered when they endorsed the view that snakeweed cures snakebite. William Wood said the colonists always carried a piece with them, but never used it unless bitten. If it is tasted without being bitten by a rattlesnake, it is "ranck poyson." Further, "it is reported" that if the person bitten lives, the snake dies, but if he dies, the snake lives. (Wood, 1634, 45; Higginson, 1630, 12) It was on a similar principle of evils occurring together with their antidotes that sassafras was taken to be a cure for the new world disease, syphilis.

Indians all over North America were hit hard by European diseases to which they had no resistance. Because of the wave of "plague" that swept over the New England Indians periodically, the colonists there had only a fraction of the original population to confront. This plague represented a problem in interpretation to the colonists because it seemed to attack the Indians only, skipping over English families. Several writers reported that the Indians see this as a manifestation of the power of the English God and some indicated that they encouraged the Indians to believe this. But it is clear that these same people are unsure whether it in fact does represent a judgement of God against the Indians who have harmed Christians. Some are sure that the plague is God's "Minister" as Morton terms it. (Morton, 1637, 13, 18-19; Winslow, 1624, 10-11, 55; Smith, 1631, 933; Lane, 1586, 278) Thomas Hariot, the most scientific among the observers, was very concerned about this as an intellectual problem. The problem was complicated for him by the fact that the plague seemed only to attack Indians who had actually done harm to the English. He reported the Indian belief that the English are risen spirits and that some of them are still invisible. These spirits make the Indians sick by firing invisible bullets at them. Hariot thought the sickness was very probably a visitation of God, but "some Astrologers", he said, thought it might be related to two other phenomena, an eclipse and a comet, which the colonists have seen recently. Hariot says he has reasons, which he does not want to disclose, for excluding the comet and eclipse as causes. The entire question left him puzzled and unresolved.[4] Disease as punishment could also strike English people. Patrick Copland says "God's rod of mortallitie" was sent to punish the English who lived dissolutely at Jamestown. (Copland, 1622, 24)

English colonists also struggled with the intellectual problem presented by the powers of the Indians priests and medicine men. Some call them "divells" but the most frequent analogy was to "our English witches." (Whitaker, 1613, 24, 26; Levett, 1624, 19; Morrell, 1625, 19; Dudley, 1631, 69) The comparison to witches was an exact one, not a way of making the medicine men seem outlandish. Witches, wizards, and cunning men or women were frequently resorted to in 16th and 17th century England. At the opening of the 17th century it was widely accepted that every parish had its magical practitioner and that their numbers were roughly similar to the number of parish priests. (Thomas, 1973, 291-292) In America as in England, people were regularly accused of using supernatural powers wrongly against their fellows. (Macfarlane, 1970b; Winthrop, 1908, I, 126, 268; II, 8; Mins. Va. Council and Gen. Ct., 1924, 111-112, 114) Just as most people in the period believed that "our English witches" had supernatural powers, most of the colonists thought the Indian "powahs" were more than ordinarily powerful, though it was difficult to tell just what their powers were. Foretelling the future and curing the sick were the most commonly remarked, along with a variety of magical tricks. Some said the source of their power was the Indian god, who was not as powerful as the Christian God, but most believed that the "powahs" derived their power from the devil with the indulgence of God. Many writers say these Indian conjurors can make the devil appear or that the devil does appear to them in various shapes. These supernatural powers gave them power over their fellow Indians. Several writers, including Hariot, state clearly that the "powahs" are believed because they are successful. Their predictions come true. (Whitaker, 1613, 26; Winslow, 1624, 50, 60; Hariot, 1590, 431, 442-443; Levett, 1624, 19; Strachey, 1953, 76, 89; Winthrop, 1908, I, 297; Spelman, 1613, cv-cvii; Magnel, 1610, 154)

Thomas Morton affects disdain for the "Feats or jugling tricks (as I may right terme them)" of the powahs and calls them "weak witches," but he offers examples of their powers. One famous powah claimed the ability to swim a broad river under water in one breath, a thing Morton

---

4. Thomas Hariot, *A briefe and true report of the new found land of Virginia*, 1588, in Quinn, ed., *Roanoke Voyages*, I, 379-381. See John W. Shirley, ed., *Thomas Harriot: Renaissance Scientist* (Oxford, 1974) for estimates of his scientific contribution.

felt was impossible. He says the powah accomplished this to the satisfaction of his spectators only by "casting a mist before their eies" so they could not see between his entering and leaving the river. Not only has he done these things before Indian audiences, he has also been seen:

likewise by our English in the heat of all summer to make Ice appear in a bowle of faire water, first having the water set before him hee hath begunne his incantation according to their usuall accustome and before the same has bin ended a thick Clowde has darkned the aire and on a sodane a thunder clap hath bin heard that has amazed the natives, in an instant hee hath shewed a firme peece of Ice to flote in the middest of the bowle in the presence of the vulgar people.

Though he calls these feats "sleights and such like trivial things," he offers no explanation except that they are "doubtles . . . done by the agility of Satan his consort." (Morton, 1637, 25-26) William Wood has been told by Indians of "one Pissacannawa, that hee can make the water burne, the rocks move, the trees dance, metamorphize himselfe into a flaming man." In the middle of winter, he will produce a new green leaf from the ashes of a dead one and will allow his audience to handle the new leaf. Wood points out that even if it were sleight of hand there are no fresh green leaves in the winter. These and "stranger things" are affirmed by the Indians. Wood is willing to go further. "But to make manifest, that by Gods permission, thorough the Devils helpe, their charmes are of force to produce effects of wonderment; An honest Gentle-man related a storie to mee, being an eye-witness of the same." This gentleman told him of a man who had a stump through his foot. Since it was "past the cure of his ordinary Surgery," the powah "betooke himselfe to his charmes" and allowed the Englishman to watch. The stump was extracted "by his sucking charmes" and the foot was completely whole in a short time. The Indians survive wounds which "would be suddaine death to an English man." He attributes this either to "their rare skill in the use of vegitatives, or diabolicall charmes." (Wood, 1634, 75, 82-83) Descriptions of Indian medicine rarely mention the use of herbal medicine. The colonists overwhelmingly prefer to describe incantations and magical charms. There is also evidence that sick English colonists submitted to treatment by Indian medicine men. (Morton, 1637, 26; Lurie in Smith, ed., 1959, 58) Going to a doctor who used only herbs and charms would not be foreign to the Englishman's experience, nor would consulting a man who combined the functions of medicine man and priest. "In many country parishes after the Reformation the minister combined his religious functions with the practice of medicine, and his methods sometimes differed little from those employed by the folk healers of the day." (Thomas, 1973, 328-330) The activities of Indian medicine men and conjurors and the people's belief in them would not have made Indian society seem strange or particularly primitive to English colonists of the 16th and early 17th centuries. These were normal for their own society. In fact, the credulity of the English about the powahs' powers helps explain the fact that so many English writers advocated attacking the position of the priests first. Not only was the priest central to the society's culture as we have seen, but he possessed powers which the English feared. Though they believed their association with the Christian God would protect them, the colonists could not rest easily until the Indian medicine men no longer had power to use against the English.

How alien did Indians seem to English colonists who arrived during the first 60 years? Clearly Indian culture was very different from English, but the question is really whether these differences were seen as forever setting the Indians apart from English civilization. Were the Indians fundamentally alien? This question can be answered in many different ways. One is to look at the phenomenon of people crossing the line dividing Indian from English society. We have already seen that Henry Spelman was left with Indians near Jamestown in order to learn the language. He was one of many ship's boys who were so left, often in trade for Indians who were taken back to England. Captain Newport, who brought the settlers to Jamestown, left a boy, ironically named Thomas Savage, with Powhatan in return for Powhatan's "trusty servant" Namontacke. Since Newport told them Savage was his son, the Indians called him Thomas Newport. All the colonies, especially Jamestown during the starving time, were plagued by the problem of colonists who attempted to escape the hardships of colonial life by running away to live with Indians. The Indians could not have seemed so alien to these people. Some were specifically said to have fled the cruel martial law at Jamestown by "runninge to the Indians to gett reliefe." (Jl. of Va. Burgesses, 1915, 31)

Formal intermarriage is recorded only for John Rolfe and Pocahontas during this period. Some writers in England objected to the idea of intermarriage, generalizing from God's warning to Abraham not to "marry nor give in marriage to the heathen, that are uncircumsized." (Symonds, 1609, 35; Mass. Bay Recs., 1853, I, 140) Rolfe himself wrote a long difficult letter justifying his marriage. Rolfe felt his marriage would help save Pocahontas's soul and help the colony, but he was worried by the anger of God against Levi and Israel for marrying strange wives. Clearly these fears were overcome, not only by Rolfe, but by the Rev. Richard Buck who performed the ceremony. (Rolfe in Hamor, 1615, 64-66) Later writers refer respectfully to the couple and sometimes identify Rolfe simply as the husband of Pocahontas. Governor Sir Thomas Dale offered to marry another daughter of Powhatan to further cement relations between the colony and Powhatan's empire. (Hamor, 1615, 40-41) Sir William Alexander wrote praising the Rolfe-Pocahontas marriage precisely because he hoped intermarriage would erase distinctions and "by admitting equalitie remove contempt." (Alexander, 1630, 28) Not only did he not see an insuperable barrier between Indians and English, but he was anxious to erase the distinctions which did exist. The New England colonies punished fornication between the races in the same manner as that which occurred within the English community.

Manner of life was the only thing, besides Christianity, which surely distinguished Indians from English colonists, and yet English writers argued that the colonists could adopt some of the Indian life style during the initial period of colonization. Even in England the forest dwellers lived a life similar to that of the early English in North America. Edmund Morgan makes the point vividly:

> In the greater part of England and Wales, in most of the north and west and in the hilly parts of the south and east, where lands were only marginally fertile, men lived from a way of farming that occupied a good deal less than half their time . . . they tended little gardens of an acre or two and supplemented their diets, as the Indians did, by gathering roots and nuts and berries from the wilds. In some places they shifted their gardens from time to time, like the Indians, allowing the land to return to forest or waste for a long fallow period. They did not grow enough grain even for their own bread. Their only advantage over the Indians in food production came from the domestic animals . . . which they kept. Turned into woods or pastures to forage for themselves in the warmer months, the animals required only a little more care than it took to hunt deer in Virginia. . . . (Morgan, 1975, 64; Kerridge, 1973, 60)

In fact Thomas Morton specifically denied that the Indians lived as poorly as "our beggars in England." (Morton, 1637, 38) Gentlemen who lived in London and its neighboring counties sometimes wrote about these inhabitants of the north and west of England in exactly the same terms which they used for the Indians, often comparing British people from the "dark corners of the land" to the American Indians.

They also lived barbarous lives in a "howling wilderness" and in ignorance of true Christianity. (Hill, 1975, 19-20, 25, 27-28)

Colonists told themselves they could live off the land, eating what the Indians ate when necessary. They could wear the skins of animals as their forefathers had done and they could live in tents or copy Indian houses. Richard Eburne reminded his readers that God himself lived in a tent "in the midst of Israel."[5] Wilcomb Washburn has argued that it was the Indians in Virginia who lived in settled communities and the English, spread out along both sides of the James River for 70 miles, who were the straggling, dispersed inhabitants in 1622. (Washburn in Smith, ed., 1959, 23-24) Whereas English houses in early Jamestown were described by the General Assembly as "meane and poore," John Smith bought the Indian village of Powhatan from the emperor's son and used it as a fort. There was "no place so strong, so pleasant and delightful in Virginia, for which we called it Nonsuch." (Smith, 1612b, 455) American Indian culture even had an impact on English fashion. Though Purchas expressed horror at the "Devill-lock at the left eare" worn by an Indian who accompanied Pocahontas to England, Francis Higginson reported that dandies in England had adopted the fashion of wearing one lock of hair longer than the rest, "which fashion I thinke came from hence into England." (Purchas, 1625 rpt. 1906, XIX, 118; Higginson, 1630, 12)

The question of whether English people saw the Indians as alien can also be answered by looking at the ways they described the collective personality of the Indians, and comparing it to the way they described their fellow English. Were there character traits which were specific to the Indians? Was the "savage" quite different from the civilized European? How willing were the writers to take account of individual differences between Indians? Did they see differences between English people, or did they assume that the virtues and vices of the civilized European were quite distinct from those of the "savage" Indian?

English observers in North America before 1640 found much to praise in the character of the Indians. They were a cheerful people, sharing what they possessed with each other, and they were especially loving as parents. They regarded churlishness as one of the greatest crimes. They were often said to be trustworthy. Above all, they were dignified and courteous; their chief men were grave and wise. In fact, even the most hostile critic allowed the dignity of the Indian, and

---

5. Hariot, *Briefe and true report*, in Quinn, ed., *Roanoke Voyages*, I, 337; Eburne, *Plain Pathway to Plantations*, ed. Wright, 46; Ralph Hamor, *A True Discourse of the Present Estate of Virginia* (London, 1615), 23-24; Virginia Company, *A True Declaration of the estate of the Colonie in Virginia*, 1610, in Force, comp., *Tracts*, III, 20.

dignity was an extremely important quality to these writers. Agreement on the praiseworthy traits of the Indian was virtually universal, the same ones appearing in most writers and throughout the period. Moreover, the praise continued from all other colonies after the massacre of 1622 temporarily ended the favorable attitude in Virginia. The picture of the Indians varies in detail from writer to writer, but the most basic elements are the same throughout the period, regardless of the colony represented or the background and beliefs of the writer. Puritans, such as Wood, and soldiers, such as Percy, agreed remarkably well about the traits they found praiseworthy in the Indians. The least praise came from writers who had least contact with the Indians. When the two cultures had prolonged contact, there was agreement on the admirable nature of the Indians. William Wood, writing of New England in 1634, offered a good summing up. He says the Indians "be wise in their carriage, subtle in their dealings, true in their promise, honest in defraying of their debts . . . constant in friendship, merrily conceited in discourse, not luxuriously abounding in youth nor dotingly froward in old age . . ." (Wood, 1634, 78-79)

There is even greater agreement on the Indians' bad qualities. English writers accused American Indians of being a prey to a great many character defects and vices, ranging from improvidence, vengefulness, treachery, thievery, sexual promiscuity, all the way up to cannibalism. The men are often said to be lazy, sometimes cowardly. What is important for our purposes is to see how these allegations occur. Some of the writers use all the praise and blame terms in their accounts, depending on the changes in theme in their stories. Some are full of praise when recounting events in which Indian steadfastness, courage, or honesty has been helpful, but give a formula lower estimate of Indian character when making a formal, abstract statement. It seems likely that, in telling of events, the writer is thinking of individual Indians whom he knows relatively well, but that the formal analysis of the native character calls forth the writers' preconceptions. Sometimes writers contradict themselves. Richard Whitbourne, for instance, says Indians are thieves, but elsewhere remarks that returning fishing fleets find all their equipment just as they left it. (Whitbourne, 1620 rpt. 1622, 4, 32) Some contradiction is inevitable. For instance, native generosity is highly praised, but its associated profligacy is criticized. Often a writer will praise the former and then criticize Indian lack of care for the morrow a few pages later without recognizing the contradiction. This conflict reflects conflict in English social ideals. They value social attributes which are, in themselves, contradictory.

Discussion of the Indian character is complicated by the assumption that there was a native hereditary class system. The praise of Indian courtesy, dignity, and trustworthiness was often restricted to the Indian nobility. The writers would have made the same distinction when writing of English society, where noble virtues resided in the "better sort." Study of colonial legislative and judicial records shows that colonial authorities were overwhelmingly concerned about the maintenance of social control, with regulating the activities of the "meaner sort." It seems plain that an Englishman of gentry status or above saw English people of low status in roughly the same terms as he saw the rank and file Indians. Conversely Indians of the "better sort" were described as having qualities which Englishmen of lower status could not aspire to.

What all this means is that status, not race, was the category which counted for English people of the early years of colonization. Put in its most direct form this means that it was not the case that the "savage" was forever set apart from civilized mankind by qualities which were peculiar to him. The "meaner sort," the low-born, whether Indians or English, were set apart by qualities peculiar to them. This can be seen by looking in some detail at the kinds of vices and defects which were attributed to ordinary Indians and comparing these descriptions to descriptions of humble Englishmen. Sometimes these character defects were seen as peculiar to the "meaner sort." Sometimes they were vices which all men, given the right set of circumstances, might exhibit. Concern over such traits and their attendant disorder was dominant in English thinking whether in England itself or in the colonies. Social control, keeping the categories of mankind straight, and keeping the duties and rights of each category clear, was the theme of writings on society of people involved in the early years of colonization.

Concern for social control was increased by the fact that the colonies, as all observers complained, usually did not attract the most responsible people. The disorders of Jamestown colony and of Morton's Merrymount were widely analyzed in the published literature. Jamestown's troubles were frequently attributed to the fact that the colonists were the "very scumme of the land," and to the lack of proper government.[6] John Smith wrote that many who were sent to him at Jamestown were worse than the "savages" and in another place he says of the Indians:

---

6. Edward Hayes, *A report of the voyage by sir Humfrey Gilbert knight*, 1583, in Quinn, ed., *Gilbert Voyages*, II, 399, 409; Patrick Copland, *Virginia's God be Thanked* (London, 1622), 24; John Smith, *The Generall Historie of Virginia, New-England, and the Summer Isles*, 1624, in Arber and Bradley, eds., *Travels and Works*, II, 606, 611, 615; Robert Johnson, *The New Life of Virginea*, 1612, in Force, comp., *Tracts*, I, 10; Crashaw, *Sermon*, E4v and "Dedication" to Whitaker, *Good Newes from Virginia*, B2v-B3; Dale in Hamor, *True Discourse*, 58; *Purchas His Pilgrimes*, XIX, 3.

"(of whom there was more hope to make better christians and good subjects then, the one halfe of those that counterfeited themselves both.)" (Smith, 1612b, 448; Whitaker, 1613, 22) Such reports came from New England also. Edward Winslow of Plymouth said some of the men sent to New England were "rather the image of men endued with bestial, yea, diabolical affections, than the image of God, endued with reason, understanding, and holiness. (Winslow, 1624, A3; Gorges, 1622, B3-B3v) Robert Cushman said that even in England "where the Gospell hath beene so long and plentifully taught, they are yet frequent in such vices as the Heathen would shame to speake of . . ." (Cushman in Bradford and Winslow, 1622, 72) Colonial records reveal that every colony spent enormous percentages of its official time worrying about the disorders of the "prophane and dissolute." The Virginia Company attempted to cure the problems at Jamestown by instituting a harsh military government. The New England colonies built houses of correction to deal with what the Connecticut records refer to as the "many stubborne & refractory Persons" in the colony. (*Mass. Bay Recs.*, I, 48, 77, 100, 170, 232-233; *Plymouth Recs.*, 75, 115; *Conn. Recs.*, 47) The crime of drunkeness was particularly worrying because it led to other crimes and because spending money on drink drove up prices generally.

It is instructive to compare the kinds of accusations which are made against Indians with those which are directed at English people in the same writings. Laziness was a charge frequently made against Indian men, but it is never made so strongly as when John Smith asserted that the Jamestown colonists "would rather starve and rot with idlenes, then be perswaded to do anything for their owne reliefe without constraint." Smith and other writers expressed contempt for the "bestiall slouth of the common sort." In one famous passage, Ralph Hamor wrote of Governor Dale arriving in Virginia to find the starving colonists at their "daily and usuall workes, bowling in the streets."[7] In fact work patterns in England and in the American colonies at their most controlled called for 4 to 6 hours work per day. (Smith, 1612b, 440; Va. Co., 1610a, 20; Strachey, ed., 1612, 45; Rabb, 1974, 683-684) Spending most of the day in idleness or at least in pursuits other than work was normal in the

---

7. Smith, *True Relation*, in Barbour, ed., *Jamestown Voyages*, I, 174, and *Map of Virginia*, ibid., II, 374, and *Description of New England*, in Arber and Bradley, eds., *Travels and Works*, I, 215, and *Generall Historie*, ibid., II, 606, 611, 615; Virginia Company, *A True and Sincere declaration of the Plantation begun in Virginia* (London, 1610), 10 and *True Declaration of Estate*, in Force, comp., *Tracts*, III, 14-20; Johnson, *New Life of Virginea*, ibid., I, 10-11; Whitaker, *Good Newes from Virginia*, 22; Hamor, *True Discourse*, 2, 26; Eburne, *Plain Pathway to Plantations*, ed. Wright, 48-49; Winslow, *Good Newes From New-England*, A4; Crashaw, *Sermon*, F2.

chronic underemployment of late 16th and early 17th century England.

Improvidence is related to laziness. Since lack of care for the morrow was supposed to be a mark of the savage, it is important that English writers accused each other of it so frequently, one even saying that improvidence is a peculiarly English quality. (Gray, 1609, Bv, D3v) In fact the steady stream of expeditions to get corn from the Indians showed the lack of provident behavior on the part of the colonists just as it demonstrated that the Indians did in fact store corn. Hamor made the point vividly when he described the colonists as being "no more sensible then beasts, would rather starve in idlenesse (witnesse their former proceedings) then feast in labour." He was indignant that they were "not so provident, though once before bitten with hunger and pennury, as to put corne into the gound [sic] for their winters bread." (Hamor, 1615, 2, 26) Some writers pictured the English as being so lazy and improvident that they either ate their fish raw or else tore up their fort rather than go into the woods to get firewood. John Smith's *Map of Virginia, Part II*, reported that the soldiers were reduced to eating food that was so rotten and infested with parasites "as the hogs would scarcely eat it." Smith believed that if he had not forced the colonists to go out and gather wild food, they would rather "all have starved, and have eaten one another." (Smith, 1612b, 440, 446-447 and 1608, 174-177; Va.Co., 1610a, 14-20; Strachey, 1610, 46-47)

Factions in the Virginia Company both in Virginia and in London accused each other of all kinds of stealing. Officials in Virginia were said to have enriched themselves by manipulating the sale of necessities and other forms of extortion.[8] Virginia Company officials in London were similarly accused of enriching themselves by defrauding the company and exploiting the colonists. Money collected for the support of the colony was diverted into the pockets of these "sinister and greedy men" either through the high salaries they voted themselves or through less public means.[9]

Stealing was a major problem in the early colonies and the Indians were clearly not the only Americans who needed watching. Published works and the colonial records abound in accusations of stealing and

---

8. John Smith, *The Proceedings of the English Colonie in Virginia*, 1612, known as *Map of Virginia, Part II*, in Barbour, ed., *Jamestown Voyages*, II, 384, 441; Kingsbury, ed., *Virginia Company Records*, I, 239, 333, 344, 397; II, 350, 375; III, 69, 504, 517-8, 519, 522-3, 605-6, 608; IV, 32-3, 69, 76, 94, 177, 217, 230-1, 261, 277. A denial of the charge occurs in H.R. McIlwaine, ed., *Journals of the House of Burgesses of Virginia, 1619-1658/59* (Richmond, 1915), 24.

9. Kingsbury, ed., *Virginia Company Records*, II, 169-177, 181-6, 187-195, 219-221, 223, 240, 308, 394, 401-4, 528; IV, 81, 117, 174, 208, 223, 521; *Jls. Virginia Burgesses*, 28.

prosecutions for that crime. The mariners on whom the colonists relied were assumed to be ready to steal whatever they could get their hands on. They were accused of stealing the supplies which were sent to the colonists and then selling them at very high prices. John Smith wrote that those colonists who could afford to visit one ship bought food at "15 times the valew" at "this removing tavern." The mariners were also accused of cheating the colonists in the sale of their tobacco in Europe. Masters were accused of overloading their ships out of greed thereby causing the deaths of many passengers. (Smith, 1612b, 393, 417 and 1631, 930; Va. Co., 1610a, 17) Ordinary stealing between colonists also went on in all colonies, as well as stealing from the Indians.[10] Much official time was taken up with prosecutions for stealing. When the Adventurers in London asked William Bradford about reports that there was much stealing in Plymouth colony, he answered that stealing occurred because New England mirrored Old: "Would London had been free from that crime, then we should not have been troubled with these here." (Bradford, 1953, 143-144)

A strange form of stealing found throughout the period involved the desecration of Indian graves. Richard Hakluyt and the Virginia Company recommended it as a way to riches. (Hakluyt, 1609, 501; Va.C., 1610b, 18) The Plymouth colonists, when they first uncovered graves, reported their sensibility that "it would be odious unto them to ransacke their Sepulchers," but later they again dug up graves and "we brought sundry of the pretiest things away with us, and covered the Corps up againe." This particular form of stealing is always reported straightforwardly, not as if they thought it required any special justification. Only Thomas Morton wrote indignantly against it. Desecrations have caused the Indians, he said, to speak of the Plymouth colonists as "this theevish people." (Morton, 1637, 36, 73, 76; Bradford and Winslow, 1622, 6, 11)

10. John Smith, *New Englands Trials*, 1620, in *Travels and Works*, ed. Arber and Bradley, I, 264, and *Advertisements, ibid.*, II, 930, and *Map of Virginia, Part II*, in *Jamestown Voyages*, ed. Barbour, II, 393, 417, 445; Virginia Company, *True Declaration of Estate*, in Force, comp., *Tracts*, III, 16; Winslow, *Good Newes from New-England*, 14, 35; Bradford and Winslow, *Mourt's Relation*, 6-8, 13; Levett, *Voyage into New England*, 10-11; William Bradford, *Of Plymouth Plantation, 1620-1647*, ed. Samuel Eliot Morison (New York, 1953), 78, 112, 269; John Winthrop, *Winthrop's Journal: The History of New England, 1630-1649*, ed. James Kendall Hosmer (New York, 1908), I, 102, 158, 175, 322; H.R. McIlwaine, ed., *Minutes of the Council and General Court of Colonial Virginia, 1622-1632, 1670-1676* (Richmond, 1924), 4, 15-6, 18-9, 66-8, 94-5, 104, 110, 159, 162-4, 168, 200; Kingsbury, ed., *Virginia Company Records*, II, 113; III, 90; IV, 5-6, 59, 150, 233, 266, 271-2, 466-7; Shurtleff, ed., *Massachusetts Bay Records*, I, 75, 82, 86, 88, 100, 104, 144, 162-3, 172, 184, 194, 203, 241, 266, 268, 282, 295, 306, 309; Nathaniel B. Shurtleff, ed., *Records of the Colony of New Plymouth in New England* (Boston, 1855), I, 68, 74, 85, 97; Charles J. Hoadly, ed., *Records of the Colony and Plantation of New Haven, From 1638 to 1649* (Hartford, 1857), 24, 26, 28.

Vengefulness and cowardice were widely attributed to the Indians but these were not specific to them. There was profound ambivalence about vengeance in English culture of this period. While the writers criticized the Indians as vengeful, they felt it was absolutely necessary that they demonstrate their own strength and determination by always exacting full vengeance for any advances made by Indians. Some colonists and virtually all the Indians were horrified at the degree of vengeance which the colonists exacted, as Hariot put it, "upon causes that on our part, might easily enough have bene borne withall." (Hariot, 1588, 381; Va. Co., 1610a, 7; Hakluyt, 1589d, 478; Lurie in Smith, ed., 1959, 50) John Underhill reported that Indian allies of the English were horrified at the vengeful treatment of the defeated Pequots. Though they "rejoyced at our victories," they "cried *mach it, mach it;* that is, it is naught, it is naught, because it is too furious, and slaies too many men." (Underhill, 1638, 42-43; Vincent, 1637, 20) Not only was vengeance seen as good policy in the colonial situation, but it was also fundamentally important. The taking of vengeance, "the inalienable right to exact retribution," was seen as a virtue, an ingredient in nobility, in courtly circles in Renaissance England. The Virginia Company justified it by an appeal to St. Augustine. (Kermode, ed., 1972, liii; Broude, 1975, 46-47; Va. Co., 1610a, 7)

The Indians were sometimes said to deviate from European standards of morality in their sexual practices, most notably in the alleged practice of polygamy. Colonial records show more prosecutions of English people for fornication of various types, including forms of sexual deviance, than for any other type of crime. Massachusetts Bay legislated the death penalty for adultery, so serious was this form of disorder in their eyes. (Kupperman, 1978, 39-40) It now appears that Governor Dale's wife, Elizabeth Throckmorton, was actually in Jamestown with him when he asked for Powhatan's daughter to be his "neerest companion, wife, and bedfellow." (Hamor, 1615, 40-41; Barbour, 1969, 269 fn) Jamestown continued to have some cases of bigamy, mostly because of the shortage of women. In 1624 the Assembly enacted that bigamy should be punished according to the quality of the offender. (Va. Co. Recs., IV, 218-220, 487)

Torture, as a uniquely barbaric element in Indian savagery continues to be assumed by historians. J. H. Parry speaks of the Indians' "naturally barbarous methods of fighting, and of torturing prisoners." Francis Jennings argues that not only was European warfare in the 16th and 17th centuries as barbarous as Indian, but there is some evidence that torture was not used among the Indians of the Northeast before the English came. (Parry, 1969, 132; Jennings, 1975, 160-161)

The English acknowledged incidents of torture of captives by Englismen during the Pequot War. (Vincent, 1637, B4; Winthrop, 1908, I, 219) In fact, of course, normal judicial punishments in 16th and 17th century England were barbaric by modern standards. The colonists were used to those in authority inflicting great pain. The extreme methods used by Governor Dale in bringing order to Jamestown colony were defended by Ralph Hamor and Alexander Whitaker. Hamor said the punishments by deaths which some said were "cruell, unusuall and barbarous" were necessary and no worse than is done in France and other countries. In 1624, 29 of the "ancient planters" signed a complaint about their sufferings during his administration of 1611-1616, including torture that made them run to the Indians to get relief. (Hamor, 1615, 27-28; Whitaker in Hamor, 60; Jl. Va. Burgesses, 31)

Even the ultimate in barbarism, cannibalism, was reported among the English in America. One such incident was included by Hakluyt in the *Principal Navigations*. Hakluyt reconstructed, through interviews, the course of the expedition of M. Hore to Newfoundland in 1536. In their extreme need, some of the crew members were alleged to have killed and "broyled" others one by one. There were also reported incidents of cannibalism in Jamestown during the worst starving time. The Virginia Assembly wrote that "Many" of the colonists had eaten human flesh and that one man had become addicted to it and "could not be restrayned, until such tyme as he was executed for it." Some of the 'poorest sort" are said to have dug up a buried Indian and eaten him. Another man was executed for killing and powdering (salting) his wife. John Smith even found this an occasion for a little joke: "Now whether shee was better roasted, boyled or carbonado'd, I know not; but of such a dish as powdered wife I never heard of." (Hakluyt, 1589f, 392; Purchas, 1614, 747; Smith, 1624, 498-499; Jl. Va. Burgesses, 21, 29)

All these marks of barbarism, from laziness up to cannibalism, are found in the civilized English as well as in the Indians, and they are reported by the same writers in both cases. There were no personal or cultural traits which fundamentally or absolutely separated English and Indians. Mankind was disorderly and the purpose of society was to restrain this disorder with as much force as was necessary. This was true for English and Indians alike.

Of all the accusations made against the Indian, the most universal and perhaps the most serious was that he was treacherous. The treacherous nature of the Indians seems to be accepted almost without reservation. Some writers even say they know the Indians to be treacherous even though they have never themselves seen any sign of treachery in them. "They are naturally given to trechery, howbeit we could not finde it in our travell up the river, but rather a most kind and loving people." (Archer, 1607a, 103-104; Cushman, 1622, A3r) Modern historians have argued that the universal belief that the Indians were treacherous stemmed from beliefs about the savage character—Indians were treacherous because savage. This belief was important because it was the expectation of treachery which the English used to justify a campaign of intimidation and expropriation against the American Indians. (Washburn in Smith, ed, 1959, 19; Nash in Dudley and Novak, eds., 1972, 65-72)

The evidence actually points to a different interpretation of the accusation that Indians are treacherous, especially if care is taken to make the crucial distinction between eyewitnesses and writers who never left England. Clearly, these accusations were not meant to be merely a literal report of Indian behavior. Instead, the charge reflected the English response to the actual situation, especially the extreme dependence and vulnerability of the colonists combined with their feelings of guilt and apprehension for their expropriation and bullying of the native Americans. The belief that the Indians would be treacherous in these circumstances was not rooted in beliefs about the nature of the "savage." Treachery was certainly not a quality especially inherent in the Indian character. Rather, the expectation of treachery was deeply rooted in the English view of human relations.

Treachery means betrayal of trust. The Indians had neither invited nor encouraged such trust. The English had rather built up a picture of the tractable Indian who would willingly jettison his own culture and religion in order to accept what the English saw as their own obviously superior religion and culture. They had needed to tell themselves that the Indians could be won over to European culture easily, just as they had told themselves that the riches of America would be there for the picking up, to make the project of colonization seem workable. If some Indians proved recalcitrant, then the other aspect of English culture, its supposed technological superiority, would come into play and the reluctant Indians would simply be overawed. In either case "these simple people" would quickly be won over to the English side. It was this belief which proved treacherous, not the Indians. Most Indians rejected assimilation and it was not all clear that European culture had the superiority it claimed in any sphere. (Lurie in Smith, ed., 1959, 47-48, 51) Most English colonists and promoters knew that this picture was false, despite the warm welcome which most early groups received from the American natives. The picture of the tractable Indian underestimated Indian culture, both in its competence and its integrity. The colonists understood this increasingly as time passed. The universal expectation of treachery from the American Indians, then, proceeded from the colonists' understanding that they would fight for their land as it became clear that nothing less than full possession was the intention of the English. Colonists assumed the Indians would be treacherous because they had placed themselves in a position of great vulnerability with respect to people whose interests they threatened, people who in fact did not want to become part of English culture. The Indians were expected to be treacherous in exactly the same way we might say an icy sidewalk is treacherous when we slip on it. The sidewalk is obviously not malevolent. Its treachery grows out of the fact that we have made ourselves vulnerable by walking on it without proper preparation and in the belief that it will be clear and negotiable.

The colonists knew they were expropriating the Indians, whatever their talk about *vacuum domicilium,* and despite the fact that the large number of Indian deaths made the Indian population so small that they seemed not to need the land. Writers from Hakluyt on, eyewitnesses and non-eyewitnesses, argued that the English must expect treachery from the Indians because the Indians would not give up their land without a fight. When John Smith asked an Indian who he thought the English were, the reply was "we were a people come from under the world, to take their world from them." Even Edward Waterhouse, who wrote the Virginia Company's official description of the massacre of 1622 filled with venomous prose, admitted that the event was caused by the Indians' fear of dispossession. (Smith, 1624, 427 and 1612b, 443; Waterhouse, 1622, 22; Va. Co., 1606, 50-52; Alexander, 1630, 28) The Indian would be treacherous, then, not because he was savage and inferior, but because he was a man and a man worthy of respect. When a soldier such as John Smith speaks of Indian treachery he is actually saying that the Indians are worthy opponents. They must be taken seriously. They are not negligible, they will fight and fight effectively.[11] That the Indian is treacherous is a cause for grudging respect, not contempt.

Early modern Englishmen expected treachery, not only from Indians, but in all areas of life. Treachery had nothing to do with savagery. It was rather simply an important fact of life. The person who does not keep his guard up should expect and may even deserve treachery. This can be seen vividly in the dealings of the colonists with

11. For a more detailed development of this argument and full documentation, see Karen Ordahl Kupperman, "English Perceptions of Treachery, 1583-1640: The Case of the American 'Savages,' " *The Historical Journal,* 29 (1977), 263-287.

one another. English people expected treachery from the "perfidious Spaniard" and the "vile Portingals." These adjectives appear so often that they almost seem part of the name. In fact a main reason for colonization of America was to obtain those products which England now imported from the Iberian peninsula and free her from dependence on these treacherous Roman Catholic countries. The early colonists hated their dependence on Portuguese pilots and on the French, Dutch, and Polish experts in such things as mineral and silk production which the promoters sent over. They pointed to many acts of treachery by these foreign experts. (Kupperman, 1977a, 278-285)

Most striking of all is the fact that English colonists expected and got treachery from their fellow English men, both colonists and those in England. And it often seems that the victim receives at least part of the blame because he, by his vulnerability, invited the treachery. The treachery of the mariners on whom the colonists depended for passage and supplies was predicted by many writers on colonization. Colonists were warned to expect it and prepare for it. We have seen the mariners' stealing and extortion from the colonists. There is ample testimony in the letters and records to show that the colonists believed they had suffered mightily from these perfidious dealings. The loss of the Roanoke colonists was blamed on the crews of the ships sent to make contact with them who diverted their voyages to privateering instead. (Smith, 1612b, 393, 417 and 1616, 219 and 1624, 525 and 1631, 930; Va. Co., 1610a, 15-17 and 1606, 53; Purchas, 1625 rpt. 1906, XIX, 117; White, 1588, 564-568; Strachey, 1953, 15; Bradford, 1953, 12)

Malcontents within the colonies were also expected to be treacherous. Every colony took elaborate steps to see to it that the discontented could not go home to England or write home about their feelings, and to censor the letters of those suspected of malice.[12] William Bradford wrote that, in his capacity as magistrate, he was justified in opening and reading and even detaining letters of people thought to be capable of treachery. (Bradford, 1953, 152-153) Virtually every book published about America during this period complained about the treacherous slander circulated by malcontents who had done poorly there and blamed the country. Almost without exception the beginnings and endings of such books explain that they were written only in order to correct such slander. Fear of their malice also goes a long way to explain

---

12. Kingsbury, ed., *Virginia Company Records*, III, 22, 28, 293; IV, 17, 116, 176, 179, 182, 225-6, 475; McIlwaine, ed., *Jls. Virginia Burgesses*, 34, and *Minutes of the Virginia Council and General Court*, 116; Shurtleff, ed., *Massachusetts Bay Records*, I, 52-3; Winthrop, *Journal*, ed. Hosmer, I, 165; Bradford, *Of Plymouth Plantation*, ed. Morison, 152-3, 156, 163, 365.

the colonists' wrath against such people as Thomas Morton, who chose to live separately.

Every colony also took steps to prevent its officers from revealing the secrets of the colony. This shows fear of a double treachery because they looked for treachery from their officers and they feared what their enemies could do with private information about the inner workings of the colony.[13] The New England towns also legislated against the free entrance of "strangers" into their communities. (Plymouth Recs., 106, 131, 142; Mass. Bay Recs., I, 196, 228) One group of officers came in for a great deal of suspicion and that was the interpreters. Many of these were the boys who had been left with the Indians, now grown up. The Virginia colonists especially regarded them as potential traitors. It is probable that part of the reason for this is the fact that these men were seen as too sympathetic to the Indians they knew so well, but it must also have proceeded from the colonists' knowledge that they were dependent on them. It seems to be the case that English people of this period believed that to be dependent or vulnerable was to invite treachery. (Fr. White, 1634, 41; Va. Co. Recs., I, 310; III, 174-175; 242-245)

Rivalries within and between colonies generated a constant stream of accusations of treachery. During Jamestown's early years, there was strife between the various members of the governing council, with factions forming around the leaders. These factions accused each other of all sorts of evil practices. Edward Maria Wingfield, who was president for a time, complained on virtually every page of the plots against him by his two chief rivals, "Captayne Gosnold, or Master Archer; for the one was strong with freinds and followers, and could if he would; and the other was troubled with an ambitious spirit, and would if he could." (Wingfield, 1608) John Smith became president later and he also believed that he was the target of constant plotting. He even believed that malcontents in Jamestown had stirred up an Indian attack against an exploring party he led. As his *Map of Virginia, Part II* says, it "would be too tedious, too strange, and almost incredible, should I particularly relate the infinite dangers, plots, and practises, hee daily escaped amongst this factious crue . . ." (Smith, 1608, 189 and 1612b, 384, 386, 403, 441, 452-454, 456) In fact, treachery is not an essentially "barbarous" or "heathen" quality for John Smith. The

---

13. Kingsbury, ed., *Virginia Company Records*, IV, 481, 560-61; McIlwaine, ed., *Minutes Virginia Council and General Court*, 14, 174; J. Hammond Trumbull, ed., *The Public Records of the Colony of Connecticut, Prior to the Union with New Haven Colony, May 1665* (Hartford, 1850), 39; Shurtleff, ed., Massachusetts Bay Records, I, 32-3, 49; Hall, ed., *Narratives of Early Maryland*, 115.

hostility of the Indians frequently pales into insignificance alongside the treachery and hostility of his fellow Europeans in Smith's story. John Rolfe wrote of his eleven years' experience in Virginia: "I never amongst so few, have seene so many falseharted, envious and malicious people (yea amongst some who march in the better ranck)." (Va. Co. Recs., III, 247)

Plymouth colony remained relatively small throughout the 17th century. It was anxious to keep its independent existence and to establish economic independence. There was a lively rivalry between Plymouth and Massachusetts Bay which led to charges of treachery. The first area of concern was the rich Connecticut River valley. Plymouth moved along the valley setting up trading posts with the consent of Massachusetts during the time this area was dominated by the Pequots. Later, when the Pequots were no longer a threat, Massachusetts men began to move into this rich area in large numbers. Plymouth felt betrayed. On his part, John Winthrop of Massachusetts was indignant over Plymouth's reluctance to join Massachusetts in the war against the Pequots which made that move into Connecticut possible. Winthrop later accused Connecticut of trying to detach some Indian allies from Massachusetts to give itself an independent power base. Connecticut abandoned this only because they were made vulnerable by the threat of the Dutch. Another dispute centered on a fur-trading post which Plymouth founded in Maine. It was attacked several times, sometimes by other Englishmen. Eventually it was taken over by the French. Bradford was indignant because, not only did Massachusetts Bay not help Plymouth to recover the post, but even traded provisions and weapons for furs with the French there. When Winthrop denied this, Bradford bluntly wrote that he was not telling the truth. (Bradford, 1953, 259, 263-268, 279-280, 304-308, 394-396; Winthrop, 1908, I, 61, 103, 213, 287-290, 301)

A similar inter-colonial rivalry between Virginia and Maryland also led to suspicion of treachery. Lord Baltimore and his colonists assumed that Virginia would undermine the Maryland colony if given the chance. Since Maryland was dependent on the older colony for information and interpreters, this is a good example of the mixture of dependence and fear which figures so heavily in the early colonial story. The colonists believed that Capt. Clayborne, who preceded them as a settler in Lord Baltimore's patent area, was attempting to stir up the Maryland Indians against the new settlers by telling them that the colonists were actually the advance party of a large number of Spaniards who were coming to destroy all the Indians. Some in Maryland thought that some of "the principall Councellors of Virginia might justly be suspected to have animated Cleyborne to his foule practises." (Lord Baltimore, 1633, 17, 20-1; Fr. White, 1634, 33, 39, 41; Yong, 1634, 56-61; Anon., 1634, 14)

The most fundamental treachery of all seems to be that of those English people with power against those English people who were vulnerable. We see this within the colonies and also on the part of those in England on whom the colonies were forced to rely. The ubiquitousness of treacherous acts, or at least of accusations of treachery, is shocking. Scarcity of manufactured goods and ordinary provisions made virtually every colonist vulnerable and the evidence abounds in the colonial records that there were many people who were willing to take advantage of this vulnerability. Many colonists accused the members of the Council of State in Virginia of using their official position to practice "rapine and extorcion" and to oppress the ordinary planters. Merchants, mariners, and colonists were all accused of extortion in the sale of the supplies which the colonists needed. Such accusations came not only from the humble or from malcontents, but even from people as exalted as Lady Wyatt, wife of the governor.[14] New colonists had their supplies taken from them and replaced by coarsely ground maize, which was seen by the Virginia Company as the cause of the "bloody flux" which killed so many of them. (Va. Co. Recs., III, 495) Officials in Virginia were also accused by many sources of having used their position to accumulate land and wealth more than they deserved, thereby cheating the Virginia Company and its backers in England. (Va.Co. Recs., II, 19, 27, 54-55, 108, 219, 402; III, 106, 125, 684; IV, 110-111, 178)

Virginia colonists were convinced that members of the Virginia Company in London had controlled the trade to and from the colony to enrich themselves at the expense of the colony, particularly the tobacco trade. As late as 1632 the Virginia House of Burgesses was complaining that the colony has long "groaned under the cruell dealings unconscionable marchaunts," and vowed no longer to "labour as slaves to other mens purses."[15] Colonists made extra efforts to control the sale of

---

14. Captain Thomas Yong, "Extract from a Letter to Captain Thomas Yong to Sir Toby Matthew, 1634," in Hall, ed., *Narratives of Early Maryland*, 60; Kingsbury, ed., *Virginia Company Records*, I, 28, 333; II, 350, 373, 375, 394, 401-2, 522-3, III, 69, 99, 119, 486-7, 495, 504, 518; IV, 11, 89, 94, 177-8, 217, 228, 231, 261, 264, 271-2, 444-5, 453, 521; McIlwaine, ed., *Minutes of the Virginia Council and General Court*, 19-20, 121, 132, 135-6, and *Jls. Virginia Burgesses*, 24.

15. Kingsbury, ed., *Virginia Company Records*, II, 52, 54-5, 375, 394, 526-7, 542; III, 219-220, 486-7, 504, 519, 520, 684; IV, 14, 23, 69, 144-5, 153-4, 212, 223; George Donne, "Virginia Reviewed," ed. Breen, *William and Mary Quarterly*, 3rd Ser., 30 (1974), 459; McIlwaine, ed., *Jls. Virginia Burgesses*, 45, 49, 55, 58-9.

wine, because its use led to high prices and disorders, and because it was alleged that merchants were dumping "base and infectious" wine in Virginia. (Va. Co. Recs., IV, 11, 453; Mins. Va. Council and Gen. Ct., 5, 106-107)

New England colonies had similar problems as can be seen in the charges of extortion made in the colonial courts and inferred from the many attempts to set prices and wages which were followed by prosecutions or by acts repealing the prices set. In 1640 Winthrop complained of oppression in the sale of commodities: "This evil was very notorious among all sorts of people."[16] What is even more striking is the fact that the Pilgrims of Plymouth colony, even though their agents were people who shared their religious convictions for the most part, felt that these men had served their own interests at the expense of the Pilgrims. Bradford's journal points to instance after instance where the colonists' trust was betrayed by treacherous dealings, even of men like Allerton, who was a member of the original Pilgrim group. (Bradford, 1953, 105, 107, 121, 124-125, 136, 141, 147-157, 211, 216, 217-218, 220, 226-229, 232-234, 238, 239-244, 245, 250, 256, 288, 298, 376, 388-389, 393)

All this requires a new reading of the denunciations of the Indian character which we find in colonists' accounts of their experiences. Historians have too often read these as attempting to create a distinction between the characteristics of civilized man and the "savage." This has led to the idea that the "savage" was perceived as being irrecoverably sunk in a mire of weaknesses and evil tendencies, of which the most serious and most significant was his treacherousness. In fact, the vices of the Indian were the vices of English people and there is no sharp dividing line, no gulf between the English and the natives. Human beings for these writers are best represented by a continuum, with the best of the English at one extreme and all other men, Indian and English, scattered along the line. There would certainly be places on this continuum where civilized and uncivilized would be mixed. Social status would be one important indicator of where a person fitted on the continuum.

Thus far we have been arguing that there was no special "savage" character which set the Indians off from civilized man as represented

---

16. Winthrop, *Journal*, ed. Hosmer, I, 112, 152, 165, 169, 200, 315-6; II, 20; Shurtleff, ed., *Massachusetts Bay Records*, I, 109-110, 111, 115, 126, 141-2, 149, 159, 160, 166, 167, 183, 192, 200, 223, 260, 278, 281, 283, 284, 286, 290, 296; Everett Emerson, ed., *Letters from New England: The Massachusetts Bay Colony, 1629-1638* (Amherst, 1976), 64-5; Bradford, *Of Plymouth Plantation*, ed. Morison, 112, 127, 175-7; Shurtleff, ed., *Plymouth Records*, I, 137; Trumbull, ed., *Connecticut Records*, 18, 19; Hoadly, ed., *New Haven Records*, 35, 36-8.

by the English. There is another way of approaching the question of whether the English saw the Indians as alien and that is by looking at the issue of treatment. In Chapter 9 we will look at English treatment of and relationship to Indians in detail. We know that English colonists exploited the Indians when they could; that is, when the weakness of the Indians made them vulnerable. The argument to be made here is that English people were fully as willing to exploit each other when opportunity arose. We have already seen the complaints of extortion and stealing in extreme conditions in all the colonies. In these cases, all the colonists were vulnerable and all suffered. What must be seen now is that there were groups or classes of people who were permanently available for exploitation, whether in England or America. The humble portion of the population was seen as a class of people who would not be useful to the state unless they were forced and therefore the state had the right to force them to work in the occupations which society thought best.

America was seen as a great sinkhole into which England's "superfluous multitude" could be sent. English parishes were encouraged to send their "swarming" poor "with whome they are pestred." The king ordered the Virginia Company to make arrangements to send over a group of "dissolute persons" he wanted to get rid of. The company said they would have to send them in small batches in order to avoid mutiny at sea. All these people were being sent regardless of their wishes in the matter. There is evidence that considerable numbers of people were sent against their will. The Jesuits in Maryland wrote that Roman Catholics were frequently sent to Virginia and sold. Grigory Dorey said he was pressed on to a ship for Virginia just because he happened to be nearby, and John Winthrop wrote that the Privy Council was especially impressed with Massachusetts because people of all sorts went there voluntarily whereas the other colonies got their people by trickery and force. (Va.Co. Recs., I, 212, 253, 259, 271, 479, 489, 555; II, 465, 526; Jesuit letters, 1634, 118 and 1638, 123; Winthrop, 1908, I, 272)

What is even more striking to the modern reader is that many of the English people sent into servitude in Virginia were children, what Hakluyt called the "frye" of wandering beggars. (Hakluyt, 1584, 319) In this use of the word fry, as in the image of the swarming poor, it scarcely seems these men are writing about human beings. The images are taken from the animal world. Yet, it is their fellow English people they are talking about. The Virginia Company made a contract with the city of London to send vagrant children to Virginia in batches of 100 per year. Three such groups were sent. The first group, which was composed of children between the ages of 8 and 16, were promised grants of land when their apprenticeships were up. Terms were changed for the second and third groups. The minimum age was changed to 12 and the company decided that they would not get land at the end of their apprenticeships. The children were to remain apprentices for seven years or until they were 21 if boys and until 21 or marriage if they were girls. After that they would become tenants on land belonging to the Virginia Company and would receive half of everything they earned. This would last for another seven years after which they could remain tenants or go off to shift for themselves. When the second group of children, kept in Bridewell while they were awaiting shipment, balked at being sent to Virginia, Sir Edwin Sandys asked for and received permission from the Privy Council to compel them to go. He promised the Privy Council that the city would thereby be "disburdened" and "in Virginia under severe Masters they may be brought to goodnes." The company hoped that parishes all over England would send their burdensome youths.[17] Peter Wilson Coldham recently marshalled evidence that a "thriving ugly trade was taking place to sell children as slave labour" in Virginia and that this trade in kidnapped London children existed from the earliest Virginia plantations. When kidnappers were prosecuted, they were punished with low fines or none at all. (Coldham, 1975, 280-287) Despite all their efforts, Sir George Yeardley wrote the Virginia Company, the colonists could not get the Indians to give them some of their children to be brought up as Christians in the colony. The reason was "their tendernes of them & feare of hard usage by the English." One wonders if it was the example of the English children in Virginia which made the Indians fear the colonists' treatment of Indian children if they were in their power. (Va. Co. Recs., I, 588)

It was not only the children who were exploited in Virginia. Evidence abounds that servants were overworked, that they were forced to work for abnormally low wages, and that they were sometimes kept working after their terms should have been up.[18] The Virginia Company tried to make the settling of contracts between servants and masters more

---

17. Kingsbury, ed., *Virginia Company Records*, I, 216, 270-1, 305-6, 310, 411-2, 424-5, 583, 626; II, 75, 90; III, 259; McIlwaine, ed., *Minutes Virginia Council and General Court*, 84, 154; Robert C. Johnson, "The Transportation of Vagrant Children from London to Virginia, 1618-1622," in Howard S. Reinmuth, Jr., ed., *Early Stuart Studies* (Minneapolis, 1970, 137-151.
18. Kingsbury, ed., *Virginia Company Records*, I, 542; II, 442; III, 489; McIlwaine, ed., *Minutes Virginia Council and General Court*, 179, and *Jls. Virginia Burgesses*, 33-4; Winthrop, *Journal*, ed. Hosmer, I, 104, 175; Emerson, ed., *Letters from New England*, 107; Shurtleff, ed., *Plymouth Records*, I, 118.

orderly because they found "ungodly people" worked to "allure and entice younge and simple" people into servitude on promises of rewards which they could not perform and which they had no intention of fulfilling. If a servant does not have every detail of their agreement in writing, the master "makes his service of the longest and hardest nature." (Va. Co. Recs., II, 113, 129-131)

The word slavery appears again and again in Virginia records. It was used in two general contexts; the treatment of servants by masters and treatment of the whole body of colonists by their government. Servants claimed to be overworked and sometimes to have been tricked into longer terms of servitude. They were also bought and sold. Maryland colonists reported that they had been able to rescue several Roman Catholic servants from Virginia by buying their time. Thomas Best wrote home that his master "hath sold me for a 150^{li} sterling like a damnd slave . . ." (Jesuit Letters, 1634, 118 and 1638, 120, 123; Va. Co. Recs. IV, 235 also I, 337; II, 465; IV, 82) Mr. Weston refused to bring servants to Virginia because "servants were sold heere upp & downe like horses, and therfore he held it not lawfull to carie any." (Mins. Va. Council and Gen. Ct., 82) The minutes of the Virginia Council and General Court record many instances of servants being transferred for money or goods. (Mins. Va. Council and Gen. Ct., 12, 71, 90, 109, 126, 134, 178) John Rolfe wrote that there had been "many complaints against the Governors, Captaines, and Officers in Virginia: for buying and selling men and boies, or to bee set over from one to another for a yeerely rent, was held in England a thing most intolerable." (Rolfe in Smith, 1624, 542)

Thomas Morton originally rose to prominence at Mount Wollaston, later Merrymount, by leading a revolt of servants against the master, Wollaston, who was selling his servants' time in Virginia. (Bradford, 1953, 205) The Plymouth colony records record many transfers of servants from one master to another, often for monetary considerations, though some of these make clear that the wishes of the servant were taken into account. In these cases, the obligations on each side were clearly set out. (Plymouth Recs., I, 12-13, 15, 37, 45, 94, 100, 107, 111-113, 141; Mass. Bay Recs., I, 311)

One other aspect of the master-servant relationship gives credence to the use of the word slavery by the complaining servants. That is the physical abuse given to servants in the name of correction or because of sexual attraction. A favorite word used to describe Indians, "barbaric," occurs with regularity in these accusations of beatings, many of which are recorded in chilling detail. Several servants died of this "correction." (Va. Co. Recs., IV, 560-1; Mins. Va. Council and Gen. Ct. 7,

22-23, 34, 42, 62, 201; Jl. Va. Burgesses, 23; Plymouth Recs., I, 49, 75, 141; Mass. Bay Recs., I, 247, 275, 282, 311; New Haven Recs., 47; Winthrop, 1908, I, 310-314, 319-320)

The word slavery, always used of Englishmen's treatment by Englishmen, appears in other contexts in official colonial records. Slavery was sometimes imposed as a punishment by colonial courts, though it seems clear that this was not the life-long, inheritable servitude which eventually came to be defined as slavery. (Va. Co. Recs., III, 93; Mass. Bay Recs., I, 246, 269, 284, 297, 300) Massachusetts recorded the freeing of two such slaves. (Mass. Bay Recs., I, 269, 300)

Those of the original Virginia colonists who survived to be ancient planters by 1625 recalled the period of martial law as a time of "more then Egyptian Slavery and Scythian Cruelty." (Jl. Va. Burgesses, 21, 25, 31) Martial law was imposed following the starving time in 1610. Its use became an issue in the fight which led to the dissolution of the Virginia Company in 1624. The group around Sir Edwin Sandys took control of the Virginia Company in 1618. From then until the dissolution when Virginia became a royal colony, the records of the company ring with charges and counter-charges of fomenting faction, manipulating company affairs and all forms of "distemper" and malice.[19] The controlling faction around Sir Edwin Sandys accused the group supporting Sir Thomas Smith, which had controlled the Virginia Company for its first 12 years, of conspiring against the colonists' liberties and rights. (Craven, 1964) The *Quo Warranto* proceeding against the Virginia Company patent in the hands of the Sandys group pointed out that the Lords Lieutenant in England had similar martial powers in certain circumstances. (Va. Co. Recs., IV, 384, 386) The Sandys faction and the planters in Virginia who remembered that time, however, felt that the circumstances had not demanded such harshness. They felt that this "Booke of the most Tyrannycall Lawes written in blood" by denying the colonists the basic rights of English law, rendered them no better than slaves. (Va. Co. Recs., I, 284, 323; II, 376, 393, 401-2, III, 605-6, IV, 83, 410, 414-5, 518, 520, 521-2) Under the martial law, punishments were alleged to have been carried out with no or improper trials, and the punishments themselves were barbaric, all contrary to the instructions of the king that the laws of Virginia should reflect the laws of England as much as possible. The Virginia Assembly answered a

---

19. Kingsbury, ed., *Virginia Company Records*, III, 424-5, IV, 169, 171, 173-4, 181, 198, 212, 418, 524; McIlwaine, ed., *Minutes Virginia Council and General Court*, 14, and *Jls. Virginia Burgesses*, 24-5, 28, 43.

favorable description of the Sir Thomas Smith administration by saying the food they were given was loathsome:

> which forced many to flee for reliefe to the Savage Enemy, who being taken againe were putt to sundry deaths as by haninge, shootinge and breakinge uppon the wheele & others were forced by famine to filch for their bellies, of whom one for steelinge 2 or 3 pints of oatmeale had a bodkinge thrust through his tongue and was tyed with a chaine to a tree untill he starved, yf a man through his sickness had not been able to worke, he had no allowance at all, and so consequently perished many through these extremities, being weery of life digged holes in the earth and hidd themselves till they famished. (Jl. Va. Burgesses, 21, 31; Va. Co. Recs., I, 363)

Following the massacre of 1622, absolute authority was restored in the particular plantations, and Governor Wyatt asked for authority to hold martial courts. (Va. Co. Recs., IV, 105, 188, 190, 209)

When colonists said they had been treated as slaves or made slaves what did they mean? Were they simply indulging in colorful rhetoric? It seems not, in that they seem to be drawing on one of the meanings of slavery to define what was happening. Their perception of this in turn reflects on the general question of exploitation of fellow human beings. There is no evidence that any English servant was held in lifetime slavery, so they cannot intend the modern meaning of the term when they use it. It also seems clear that the modern meaning, that of perpetual, inheritable servitude, was the dominant meaning at the time. (Jordan, 1969, esp. Chap. II) However, there is another meaning which we can sometimes glimpse directly and which is surely behind some of the allegations that English people have been treated as slaves. This meaning assumes that the word slave means approximately the same thing as the word base; that is, a slave is a person from the lowest rung of the social status ladder whether he is a servant or not. The most famous instance of this is Hamlet's reference to himself: "O what a rogue and peasant slave am I." The shift in definition of slavery from being only sometimes concerned with servitude to always meaning servitude would have occurred because the base person was naturally expected to serve his betters. He was generally exploited by those above him and could not be expected to raise himself from that status. This brings us back to the quotation from Michael Drayton which opened this chapter. Drayton said he did not want to know about the Indians because there were plenty of "savage slaves" in England. He clearly did not mean that they were lifetime servants, but that there were people of such low condition in England that they were savage because they did not share in English culture. Thomas Best, who we have just seen claiming that he was sold like a "damn'd slave" goes on to say of his master, "as he is for using me so baselie." Again, Best does not mean that his master has become a slave in our sense, but that he is base in his actions and is in this sense a slave. (Va. Co. Recs., IV, 235) One final quotation shows clearly the conjunction of being base with being expected to serve. When the Virginia Assembly wrote of their sufferings under the administration of Sir Thomas Smith, one of the things they felt bitter about was that people of good estate had been treated as if they were base. After telling that some of the colonists had come from ancient houses and had been born to estates of £1000 per year, they wrote: "Those who survived who had both adventured theire estates and personnes were constrayned to serve the Colony as if they had been slaves, 7 or 8 yeeres for their freedomes, who underwent as hard and servile labor as the basest fellow that was brought out of Newgate." (Jl. Va. Burgesses, 21) Though it is hard to separate the meanings absolutely here, the colonists seem to be saying that the problem was not that some colonists were made to labor as slaves, but that men of good estate were obliged to labor as if they had been base. It is the base man who is expected, because of his position in society, to labor for others. Eventually slavery came to refer to the labor and servitude only and dropped the association with social status. In the period under study here, usage is mixed.

Indians, like base or humble English people, were expected to be of service to the society. Indians of the "better sort" were not expected to be of service. The fluid situation in America made it possible to realize more fully the exploitative possibilities inherent in English practice of the time. This was true for dependent English people as well as for Indians. The Indians were exploited, not because they were seen as so alien or inferior that they did not fit into any English categories, but because they fitted only too well into the mass of people at the bottom of society whose role it was to serve others.

7

English Social Ideals and Indian Culture

Many of the early English commentators on America were profoundly unhappy about their own society. They believed that they lived in a country which was undergoing rapid change and that the change was almost all for the worse. As they wrote about Indian culture, they praised aspects of it as a way of pointing a lesson to readers in England about how English society should be improved. By looking at what they praise in the Indians we can extrapolate their picture of an ideal society. The society which they long to return to is the, possibly mythical, tightly-knit community of the medieval manor. (Thomas, 1973, 672; Quinn, 1974a, 367) What they admire about Indian society is its hierarchical nature in which rights and duties are clearly understood and each member knows what to expect from his neighbors. They like the fact that the society is characterized by sharing and mutuality rather than competition. In this writing, of course, they are romanticizing the English past as well as the Indian present. The things they say are true, though, in the sense that they are a guide to their view of the world. We can understand them better by seeing what they believed to be true.

What is most striking about this nostalgia for a more comfortable past is that these men are not old country gentlemen whom the world has passed by. They are themselves the field representatives of the new capitalism which is causing the changes they deplore in English society. They have been sent by the joint-stock companies to break new ground for profit-making. They embody the competitiveness which they believe has replaced the cooperative life of the English parish and there is virtually no diary or journal which does not record evidence of the most ruthless competition among people involved in colonization. Yet these writers show marked unanimity when they select aspects of Indian society to praise, implicitly criticizing English society.

Often these writers criticize English society directly. A vivid picture of the contentious, selfish society that has replaced the old sense of community emerges from the writings on America. The root of the breakdown of the old community, for these writers, was the search for money and profit, in fact unrestricted capitalism. Its effect has been the concentration of wealth and the severing of ties of obligation to the poor and helpless. Formerly, in their version of the past, those who had wealth and power realized that these were given to them in trust and the holders were expected to use their wealth and power for the good of those who were powerless. Now, these men use their wealth and power as weapons of oppression. English society is characterized by restlessness and greed. Alexander Whitaker of Virginia wrote of the English wealthy: "How many hungry, naked, fatherlesse, widowes, poore men and oppressed, perish for want of that which God hath lent to these rich theeves? (for no better than theeves are they . . .)" (Whitaker, 1613, 6, 11) John Donne also pointed to this rejection of responsibility. The rule in England is now "tush! thrust the beggar out of dores . . ." (Donne in Smith, 1624, 285) So serious does Daniel Price find the unrestricted search for profit that he compares the English businessman to the most barbaric "savage." To those who live by "building upon the ruines of broken poore Citizens" he says, "The bread thou eatest is the flesh of man, the wine thou drinkest is the bloud of man, thou art a Canibal . . ." (Price, 1609, F; Gray, 1609, Dv; Symonds, 1609, 20-1; Cushman in Bradford and Winslow, 1622, 72)

One way the breakdown of social cohesion manifested itself was in the immense amount of litigation which late 16th and early 17th century Englishmen indulged in, litigation that often went on for years. So much were lawsuits a part of life that time spent at the Inns of Court was considered an important part of a prospective landowner's education. In the past, it was believed, the manorial court system and religious guilds offered resolution of problems and disputes that now became entangled in the complex court system. Excessive reliance on litigation had become mixed in people's minds with the problems of the poor and "middling" citizens. (Thomas, 1973, 672; Hill, 1965, 263; Price, 1609, F, Cushman in Bradford and Winslow, 1622, 70) For John Smith part of the attractiveness of America is that "here are no hard Landlords to racke us with high rents, or extorted fines to consume us; no tedious pleas in law to consume us with their many years disputations for Justice . . ." He gives a scornful but vivid picture of the legal system: "wee not having any use of Parliaments, plaies, petitions, admirals, recorders, interpreters, chronologers, courts of plea, nor Justices of peace, sent M. Wingfield and Cap. Archer with him for England to seeke some place of better imploiment." (Smith, 1616, 195-6 and 1612b, 394)

This spirit of contention had also crept into religion. Many writers, Puritans as well as Anglicans, complained about the fact that English people were consuming themselves in wrangling about religion. Many writers ridiculed those who preferred to stay in London and argue about religion rather than go into the English "remoter parts" or to convert the American heathen. One ship to America, according to John Donne, is more vexing to Roman Catholics than twenty "Lectures in matter of Controversie." (Donne, 1626, 22; Cushman in Bradford and Winslow, 1622, 71; Whitaker in Hamor, 1615, 60; Symonds, 1609, 53-4)

The naked greed of Englishmen of this period was shown by their conversion of the legal and political system to weapons of extortion for their own benefit. The wealth so accumulated was wasted on self-indulgence, on "soft unprofitable pleasures." Crashaw compared those who chose self-indulgence over the good work of converting the American natives to "Sowes that still wallow in the mire of their profit and pleasure." The search for pleasure and gluttony in eating and drinking are symbolic of the insatiable greed of Englishmen in all aspects of life. (Hakluyt, 1599, 457; Eburne, 1624 rpt. 1962, 84; Whitaker, 1613, 6, 27-8; Crashaw, 1610, Cv-C2, D2; Peckham, 1583, 449)

Against this background, the writers' praise of Indian society is the more striking. Even acknowledging the fact that they are romanticizing their picture of Indian society and that they are more or less consciously pointing up lessons for their English audience, it is still interesting how much the writers found in Indian society "which may well become Christians to imitate." (Anon., 1635, 37) If greed was the most outstanding characteristic of English culture, satisfaction and simplicity were the most outstanding characteristics of Indian culture. It is praised for its moderation, justice, the loyalty and concern of its people for each other. Those in authority are respected by the people below them: "no people in the worlde carry more respect to their King, Nobilitie, and Governours, then these doe." (Barlowe, 1584, 103) This respect proceeds not from the external trappings of office, but from the dignity of the king and the loyalty and orderliness of the subject: "For though hee hath no Kingly Robes, to make him glorious in the view of his Subjects, nor dayly Guardes to secure his person, or Courtlike attendance, nor sumptuous Pallaces; yet doe they yeeld all submissive subjection to him, accounting him their Soveraigne; going at his command, and comming at his becke, not so much as expostulating the cause . . ." (Wood, 1634, 79-80; Smith, 1612a, 369; Rosier, 1605, E3; Whitaker, 1613, 26)

There is an implicit contrast to the sumptuousness of the Stuart monarchs' lives and the disorderliness of their subjects. Many writers remark on the simplicity and dignity of the sachem's life, as when *Mourt's Relation* described Iyanough: "a man not exceeding twentie-six yeeres of age, but very personable, gentle, courteous, and fayre conditioned . . ." (Bradford and Winslow, 1622, 50) Honor and reputation are greatly valued among Indians. They listen only to those who speak with gravity and condemn garrulousness. The *Relation of Maryland* reported Indian disgust with the Jamestown assembly because everyone talked at once. The Indian reporter said "wee doe not so in our Match-comaco." (Anon., 1635, 38-9; Morton, 1637, 28-9; Wood, 1634, 73)

Not only does the king receive obedience and reverence, but so do all who deserve it. Children respect their parents. Wives respect husbands. The young respect the old. Thomas Morton considers this so important that he devotes an entire short chapter to it, saying in part: "It is a thing to be admired, and indeede made a president, that a Nation yet uncivilized, should more respect age then some nations civilized; since there are so many precepts both of divine and humane writers extant." It is his hope that his writing will reach "our irregular young people of civilized Nations," and that they will be "ashamed of their former error in this kinde." (Morton, 1637, 24-5; Whitaker, 1613, 26; Anon., 1635, 33; Winslow, 1624, 58; Wood, 1634, 97)

In return for the obedience of his subjects, the king carries out his obligations faithfully. In contrast to the England of "thrust the beggar out of dores," the Indian king personally takes care of those members of society who are unable to care for themselves, just as the Bible enjoins Christians to do. The king assumes responsibility for orphans, widows, the aged and such as are "any way maimed." He personally entertains travelers. Many writers stress that hospitality and neighborliness are the rule for all Indians. Wood describes almost unlimited hospitality for English travelers in Indian houses. Morton says the young provide for the old. Friends go to stay with and comfort the sick. The *Relation of Maryland* characterized the "friendly Offices" of the Indians toward the English as being "as any neighbour or friend uses to doe in the most Civill parts of Christendome." (Whitaker, 1613, 6, 15-6, 20; Morrell, 1625, 18-9; Winslow, 1624, 56-8; Bradford and Winslow, 1622, 50; Morton, 1637, 24-5; Anon., 1635, 32; Wood, 1634, 70)

Though several of the writers say the sachem receives tribute from his subjects, it is also clear that he does not live off the labor of his people. This is one reason why the Indians were amazed that King James, who was a widower, could live without a wife to help him. (Levett, 1624, 21; Bradford and Winslow, 1622, 45) John Smith offered a detailed list of the work Powhatan did for himself: "For the King himselfe will make his owne robes, shooes, bowes, arrowes, pots; plant, hunt, or doe anything so well as the rest." (Smith, 1624, 400 and 1612a, 355; Anon., 1635, 33)

One of the king's most important roles was as the fount of justice. Justice in Indian society is swift and fair, the decisions are accepted without complaint. Much of this is due to the simplicity of the system. Wood shows the king and his wisest men personally deciding all cases and says, "as their evill courses come short of many other Nations, so they have not so many Lawes." (Wood, 1634, 80) Many writers agree with Wood that the Indian legal system is simple because the Indians need less regulation than the English. They have no need of "bonds nor bills," but only their vow, because they "keepe just promise and love equitie." (Morrell, 1625, 22; Anon., 1635, 38; Bradford and Winslow, 1622, 62) When punishments are necessary, the sachem personally administers the sentence and the person punished never complains. (Smith, 1612a 371-372; Winslow, 1624, 59-60)

Indians were also praised in their roles as parents. Parent-child relationships were interesting to English writers and they praised the affectionate bond between Indian parents and their children. Lawrence Stone asserts that the characteristic child-parent relationship of the 16th and 17th centuries in Europe was so bad as to create a "psychic numbing" and "emotionally stunted" adults. Before the 18th century, he says, the typical response to children was indifference. (Stone, 1974, 25-6, 28-9) Indifference is not indicated by these writers' picture of the good society. Many writers report the tender love of Indian parents for their children. (Rosier, 1605, C2; Smith, 1612a, 356; Spelman, 1613, cviii, Strachey, 1953, 113; Va.Co. Recs., I, 311) They describe how the boys are trained in the use of the bow and arrow, and how children are hardened by drinking bitter herbs, bathing the skin in special ointments, and exposure to cold to make them impervious to hardships and foul weather. Such descriptions do not portray Indian parents as sadistic. All this training is seen as an expression of benevolent concern. (Levett, 1624, 21; Morrell, 1625, 19-20; Winslow, 1624, 56; Smith, 1612a, 356) The Indian mother's care is so tender that the children "generally are as quiet as if they had neither spleene or lungs." (Wood, 1634, 96) Henry Spelman indicated that one important reason why the

Indian king with whom he lived valued him was that no one could quiet the king's young child as well as Spelman could. (Spelman, 1613, cviii)

English parents in the 17th century usually sent their children to live and work away from home when they reached early adolescence, or even earlier. (Macfarlane, 1970a, 92-93; Illick, 1974, 321) The *Relation of Maryland* reports, by contrast, that Indian parents keep their children at home until they are ready for adult life. (Anon., 1635, 34) Many of the writers report the grief of Indian parents at separation from their children. Ralph Lane and John Smith made use of this affectionate relationship by kidnapping children to ensure the cooperation of Indian villages. (Lane, 1586. 262; Smith, 1612b, 404) Ralph Hamor and Samuel Argall report the extreme grief of Powhatan when he learned that Pocahontas had been kidnapped. His concern for his daughter continued after he had accepted her marriage. (Hamor, 1615, 6, 40; Argall, 1610, 93) When Powhatan was asked to send another daughter to Jamestown, he replied: "that he loved his daughter as deere as his owne life, and though he had many Children, he delighted in none so much as in her, whom if he should not often beholde, he could not possibly live . . ." Hamor also reported that Powhatan forged a similar bond of affection for Thomas Savage, the boy whom Capt. Newport had left with him. (Hamor, 1615, 38, 42) The King of Rappahannock refused to give his son as a pledge of peace as demanded because, "having no more but him he could not live without him." (Smith, 1624, 429) If a child dies, the father will "put his own most special jewels and ornaments in the earth with it; also will cut his hair, and disfigure himself very much, in token of sorrow." (Winslow, 1624, 58) Early plans for conversion of the Indians to Christianity involved taking young Indians and placing them in English society in the colonies where they could learn the ways of European civilization along with the rudiments of Christianity. These plans inevitably led to failure because of the reluctance of all but a few Indian parents to part with their children.[1]

The most important characteristic of Indian life was its contentedness and freedom from envy. English writers thought this accounted for their long and healthy lives, "content with heir state, and livinge frendlye together . . ." (Hariot, 1590, 423, 435) Indians are not covetous because they want only useful things and no more of those than are necessary to them. Not only are they content with little, but they also share all that they have with their fellows: "so much the more perspicuous is their love, in that they are as willing to part with their

---

1. Exceptions occur in Anon., *Relation of Maryland*, ed. Hawks, 40; Morton, *New English Canaan*, in Force, comp., *Tracts*, II, 35.

Mite in poverty, as treasure in plenty." (Wood, 1634, 69; Rosier, 1605, E3) Though all this has a rhetorical ring, many writers authenticate their claims by telling of specific instances when an Indian, given something by an explorer or colonist, carefully cuts it up so that all his companions have an equal share. English writers, concerned about the decay they see in their own society, are quick to point out that sharing and contentedness are key Christian virtues. It is ironic for them that the heathen should practice these virtues more systematically and sincerely than the nominal Christians. Writers like Thomas Morton also point out that the simplicity and mutuality of Indian life echo the greatest philosophers of classical antiquity. (Wood, 1634, 63; Anon., 1635, 44; Morton, 1637, 39)

Praise of Indian life reached a crescendo with descriptions of their temperance in eating and drinking. Gluttony was the most serious sin in the catalogue of English habits. The Indians, by contrast, eat and drink no more "than seemed to content nature." (Rosier, 1605, Cv) Their simple diet keeps them healthy. The English are not only gluttonous, but their restless greediness causes them to search constantly for new food sensations. Symbolic of all that was wrong with English society for these writers was the devising of "variety of Sauces to procure appetite." (Morton, 1637, 39; Anon., 1635, 37-8; Hariot, 1590, 430; Smith, 1631, 939; Cushman in Bradford and Winslow, 1622, 72) Thomas Hariot cries out most strongly against English gluttony. Even when they "make good cheere together," the Indians are "moderate in their eatinge wher by they avoide sicknes. I would to god wee would followe their example. For wee should bee free from many kynes of diseasyes which wee fall into by sumptwous and unseasonable banketts, continuallye devisinge new sawces, and provocation of gluttonye to satisfie our unsatiable appetite." (Hariot, 1590, 430, 438)

Shot through these discussions of Indian culture as an example to the English is the fear that England may be an old and declining culture. John Smith uses historical examples to warn England that the ruin of empires comes when they fall into covetousness and negligence. Rapid social change in England generated uneasiness and descriptions of Indian society demonstrate the extent of change, of how far the English have strayed from their own professed ideals. Many writers hope that Englishmen will be moved by the example of the "naturally most curteous" Indians. (Smith, 1616, 210-211; Vaughan, 1626, I, 8; Lane, 1585, 209; Barlowe, 1584, 110; Cushman, 1622, A3)

No writer seriously considered the possibility that England might copy Indian society in any fundamental way. All the desirable aspects of Indian life were qualities which English society had recently shared. England could resume these without making fundamental changes in her culture. In fact English people of this period feared change. There was widespread fear that the colonization effort as well as life in America might cause changes in English society against the will and intention of colonial sponsors. The good society was hierarchical with fixed categories. That colonization was causing change, especially change in the hierarchical nature of society, was vehemently denied by a large number of writers, but these same writers at other times affirmed that different relationships might be demanded by the drive to colonize America.

John Smith is the best example of this ambivalence. He often complained about the high proportion of gentlemen in Virginia, saying that the determiners of high status in England are meaningless in America. "For in Virginia, a plaine Souldier that can use a Pick-axe and spade, is better than five Knights, although they were Knights that could breake a Lance." He told the Virginia Company that 100 "good labourers and mechanicall men" would have "done more then a thousand of those that went." The ignorant gentlemen can scarcely do what is necessary to save themselves on an exploring trip. He ridicules the rebellious "Tuftaffety humorists" in the colony, men more accustomed to silks than hard work. (Smith, 1612a, 342 and 1612b, 387, 452 and 1624, 537, 616) Smith, however, sometimes argues as vehemently that it was the gentlemen alone who saved Jamestown from utter ruin. The gentlemen, under the force of necessity, became proficient at basic skills, showing that there was an underlying quality that made one a gentleman as well as the accident of birth. (Smith, 1612a, 342 and 1631, 930)

Other writers report that gentlemen are working in Jamestown, especially in times of necessity. William Strachey wrote of the inspiring example of gentlemen working: "how contentedly doe such as labour with us, goe forth, when men of ranke and quality, assist, and set on their labours?" (Strachey, 1610, 9, 11, 28, 48-9; Va. Co., 1610a, 20; Purchas, 1617, 947) Smith and the Virginia Company propagandists are quick to add that the fact that the gentlemen are making themselves useful should not be construed as proof that frontier life is causing them to be degraded. Rather, they elevate work to the level of recreation by their voluntary cheerfulness. John Smith says the colonists of rank did work at felling trees and became masters at it though "the axes so oft blistered there tender fingers" that a penalty for oaths had to be administered:

By this, let no man think that the President, or these gentlemen spent their times as common wood-hackers at felling of trees, or such like other labours, or that they were pressed to any thing as hirelings or common slaves, for what they did (being but once a little inured) it seemed, and they conceited it only as a pleasure and a recreation. Yet 30 or 40 of such voluntary Gentlemen would doe more in a day then 100 of the rest that must been prest to it by compulsion. (Smith, 1612b, 416; Va. Co., 1610a, 20)

It is of very great importance to many writers to argue that those involved in colonization are not just from the lower ranks of society. Lists of colonists or explorers often give detailed information about the status and even the incomes of those involved. (Hakluyt, 1589f, 390; Barlowe, 1584, 115; Rich, 1610, B2v) The Virginia Company felt it was very important that a great peer like Baron de la Warr would be willing to adventure his own person in Virginia, but his death made some writers think the country was still too rough for "such a personage" and that gentlemen grow discontented when they cannot live the life they are accustomed to. William Crashaw ridiculed this fear of hardships: "it discovers the pusillanimitie, the basenesse, the tendernesse and effeminateness of our English people; into which our nation is now degenerate . . ." (Crashaw, 1610, F4-F4v; Va. Co., 1610a, 20-1; Smith, 1624, 536-7)

People antagonistic to colonization apparently went on making allegations about the low standing of those who went to America, because pro-America writers kept insisting that such charges were not true. The sorts of allegations which were made against the colonists can be inferred from William Crashaw's description of Alexander Whitaker. Whitaker, he says, is "a Scholler, a Graduate, a Preacher, well borne, and friended in England, not in debt nor disgrace, but competently provided for, and liked, and beloved where he lived, not in want, but (for a scholler, and as these dayes be) rich in possession . . ." (Crashaw in Whitaker, 1613, A4) Whitaker went to Jamestown as a preacher and, as a Cambridge University graduate, he was well prepared for his profession. Crashaw's description, though, demonstrates concern over another type of change being forced by the drive to explore and colonize America. This was in the educational establishment. On one level, we have plain John Smith's disdain for book learning. He points to his experience in the field "which indeed is the very ground of reason," and ridicules the "tender educats" who complain about the hardships of the country. The school of hard knocks is the only university that makes sense for this life. On the other hand, Thomas Morton accused the Plymouth colonists of taking up a know-nothing attitude and despising learning. They have driven out men of learning and high social status because "the Seperatists love not those good parts when they proceede from a carnall man (as they call every good Protestant.)" They vilify the two universities because they are incapable of appreciating that "learninge does inable mens mindes to converse with climents of a higher nature then is to be found within the habitation of the Mole." Colonization is allowing them to set up a version of English society in which the test of religious conformity is the only important test. (Smith, 1612a, 373 and 1631, 952, 956-7; Morton, 1637, 92, 101-2, 121-2) In both these cases, colonization has produced a situation in which kinds of experience other than education is the key to status.

The educational establishment was challenged in a much more fundamental way by writers on colonization. As early as 1582 Richard Hakluyt began a campaign of criticism of the two English universities on the grounds that they were retaining the medieval curriculum and ignoring the entire subject of exploration, navigation, and the practical mathematics and geography which were their basis. Hakluyt pointed to the lectures on mathematics and navigation offered in Spain and Portugal and the high status of the lecturers. He praised Sir Thomas Gresham for the practical lecture series he endowed in London, and Sir Walter Raleigh for realizing the connection between practical science and exploration:

Ever since you perceived that skill in the navigator's art, the chief ornament of an island kingdom, might attain its splendour amongst us if the aid of the mathematical sciences were enlisted, you have maintained in your household Thomas Hariot, a man pre-eminent in those studies, at a most liberal salary in order that by his aid you might acquire those noble sciences in your leisure hours, and that your own sea-captains, of whom there are not a few, might link theory with practice, not without almost incredible results. (Hakluyt, 1587a, 365-7; 1582a, 14-16 and 1598a, 429-432 and 1600, 473)

Sir Humphrey Gilbert, leader of one of the earliest expeditions, was the author of a scheme for a third university which would have stressed practical, particularly scientific, training and would have put less emphasis on abstract knowledge. The plan reflects the needs of a changing society and the groups which needed practical training to participate in its control. (Quinn, ed., 1940, I, 27-28) University men were responding to the challenge with hostility. Sir George Peckham, who wrote about Gilbert's voyage, said that he was not adequate to the task of writing a book and had long hoped that "some of those rype, and perfect witts" would step forward to write about America, but instead the critics of colonization are "such as doo take uppon them to be more then meanely learned." (Peckham, 1583, 436, 458)

Not only did the colonization effort raise questions about the relevance of traditional skills, particularly those of the "better sort," it also appeared to offer a chance for new individuals and groups within English society to rise. It was a situation in which traditional restraints of all sorts were off, allowing both beneficial and harmful behavior. People bettering themselves was one response. The oppressive actions of those in control of the Virginia colony was another. The colonization effort was a catalyst in this; that is, it speeded up and made clear a process which was already taking place. The fundamental question was what kind of society England was to be. What was the relevance of the traditional social classes and their role as England moved to a commercial economy? What will be the status of the merchants as their economic role becomes crucial? There was very great ambivalence among writers on America when they touch on these questions. Many vehemently deny that colonization will produce social change either in America or England and then just as warmly praise the opportunities which the whole enterprise offers to those who want to change their status.

The Virginia Company was an uneasy alliance between powerful merchants and members of the gentry. The merchants needed the aristocratic cachet and influence at court just as much as the aristocrats needed the merchants' economic power and knowledge. John Donne gloried in the fact that Virginia Company backing came from all levels of society. He emphasized that there are no social distinctions in Christ. More significantly, he said that the distinctions between aristocrats and merchants are so unstable that there should be no incompatibility between the two groups: "merchants growe up into worshipfull Families, and worshipfull Families let fall branches amongst Merchants againe . . ." (Donne, 1626, 32, 34-5; Crashaw, 1610, G3v) The alliance between merchants and gentry forced consideration of a question which was symbolic of the changes occurring in English society in general. Should the merchants or the gentry and aristocrats dominate? Francis Bacon warned against allowing merchants to control the company. Government by the gentry would be better because the merchants look too much for gain. This line of reasoning sees the gentry as embodying concern for the public good and rising above personal self-interest. On the other hand, everyone involved in the Virginia venture wanted to make money from it and some writers faced directly the fact that the merchants were more skilled in organizing and directing commercial ventures. King James himself was reported to favor merchant control for this reason. Some reasoned that merchants' concern for their self-interest would serve the interests of all by making the colony a greater success. In the event the cries of oppression and extortion by merchants and gentlemen alike in the Virginia enterprise raised doubts about whether the traditional virtues of the gentry still inhered in that class. (Bacon, 1625, 202; Va.Co. Recs., II, 35, 233-5)

John Smith pointed to the basic facts of colonization: "For, I am not so simple to thinke, that ever any other motive then wealth, will ever erect there a Commonweale." (Smith, 1616, 212) This did not necessarily mean merchant domination, because the gentry were as interested in wealth as anyone. But there was an even more fundamental question about the future shape of English society which grew out of the sources of wealth expected from colonization. The Spanish, in stumbling upon a country where gold was readily available almost for the taking, had been able to sustain the swashbuckling aristocratic image of overseas expansion. That was not to be the case with England. Again it was Smith who pointed out that England's wealth would come from humbler, but steadier sources. The privateers and the Spanish with all their "mynes of golde and Silver" do not have a source of income to equal what the "Hollanders" have accomplished by the "contemptible trade of fish." Holland is now a wealthy country and "the benefit of fishing is that *Primum mobile* that turnes all their *Spheres* to this height of plentie, strength, honour and admiration." If England is to become wealthy, she will do it by copying Holland's example and concentrating on mercantile sources of wealth. (Smith, 1616, 194-5)

Christopher Hill has pointed to the "anti-aristocratic overtones of the patriotic motif in Elizabethan literature. Not only was the balance between classes changing in England partly under the pressure of colonization, but many writers proclaim that the colonies are the place for individuals of "great spirits and smal meanes" who wish to raise their station. Writers point out with historical examples that God often chooses humble men to do his work and rewards them. Exploits as a soldier has been one way for the humble to rise. Colonization offers another theater in which "hidden vertue" can be revealed. (Hill, 1965, 193; Smith, 1616, 208-9, 213; Symonds, 1609, 32, 54; Strachey, ed., 1612, 56-7; Peckham, 1583, 448, 457)

People who looked for social change also feared it. They feared that the fluid colonial situation would allow sweeping changes in transplanted English society there. Jamestown's early years seemed to confirm their worst fears. The original government was to be by a council which would elect its own president. The "aristocratic government" in which all were "Keisars" led to a tumultuous scene of disorders. The Virginia Company moved to the opposite extreme, imposing martial law to curb the impression that "wee lived there lawlesse."[2] Extraordinary measures were called for because the bulk of the colonists were from the meanest level of English society, the "very scumme of the Land." (Copland, 1622, 24) Though colonists came to feel that the martial law had been as much a distortion of English society as the previous disorder, the fear continued that freed indentured servants would have no reason to observe the laws laid down by those in command and would attempt to live as libertines. (Va.Co. Recs., III, 177) The Puritans of Plymouth and Massachusetts Bay also struggled with settlers who chose to live outside their organized society. John Winthrop recorded that he had defended the idea that "in the infancy of plantation, justice should be administered with more lenity than in a settled state, because people were then more apt to transgress, partly of ignorance of new laws and orders, partly through oppression of business and other straits." The ministers disagreed and convinced him that stricter discipline was required in the unsettled conditions of plantations. (Winthrop, 1908, I, 171)

Who should administer this control in the colonies? Life in America brought up the issues which colonization posed for England, but in a new form. Promoters had to face the issue of what kind of background prepared a man to be a governor in America. Colonial leaders felt strongly that experience of the country and command there were more important than any other single factor. (Va.Co. Recs., II, 487; IV, 16, 103) On the other hand, in such a status-conscious society, rank was also important, "Sithence itt is nott easye to swaye a vulgar and servile Nature, by vulgar & servile Spiritts." The Virginia Company attempted to bridge this gap by arranging for the knighting of one governor, George Yeardley. This satisfied no one. (Va. Co. Recs., III, 217, 231-2) George Sandys wrote home his estimations of the members of the Virginia Council in 1623. His description of Lt. Pierce, the governor of Jamestown, shows the confusion in his mind between the benefits of experience and the inherent virtues of men of rank. He says Pierce is not "inferiour to anie, expert in the Countrie, who refuses no labour, nor stickes at anie expences, that may advantage the publique, and of a Capacitie that is not to bee expected in a man of his breedinge . . ."

---

2. William Strachey, ed., *For the Colony in Virginea Britannia. Lawes Divine, Morall and Martiall, &c.* in Force, comp., *Tracts*, III, 5; Virginia Company, *True and Sincere Declaration*, 6, 12; Kingsbury, ed., *Virginia Company Records*, II, 350; III, 92; George Donne, "Virginia Reviewed," ed. Breen, *William and Mary Quarterly*, 3rd Ser., 30 (1973), 460; Rolfe, *True Relation of Virginia*, 34-5.

(Va.Co. Recs., IV, 111) All the colonies punished people who spoke against the government, sometimes with great savagery, and people of mean estate who spoke out against their betters were also punished. Accusations against people of high birth were often voided by the colonial courts, and different punishments were ordained for persons of quality.[3]

Despite claims of colonial promoters that talented people of humble estate could rise in America, colonists were eager to refute the allegation that levelling was taking place there. One accusation that Thomas Morton made against the separatists at Plymouth was that they degraded gentlemen and raised unworthy people to that dignity. He also charges that the pastor has "preheminence above the Civile Magistrate," and that ordinary people are allowed to preach. (Morton, 1637, 110-111, 115-8) John Underhill felt it necessary to explain the apparently large ratio of captains to men in the English army of the Pequot War. The fact that the Indians split into small groups to fight required the English to do the same. He explained that the word captain simply referred to anyone responsible for a group of men, so the colonists were not devaluing distinctions between people. (Underhill, 1638, 3-4)

All the colonies passed sumptuary laws, attempting to maintain distinctions between people by regulating the lavishness of dress. Virginia and Massachusetts Bay attempted to prescribe in very great detail just what materials and cut of clothing were allowed. Lack of success is indicated by repetitions of such orders. John Winthrop confided to his journal that it was difficult for the elders to control "the great disorder general through the country in costliness of apparel" since the elders' wives participated in it. (Winthrop, 1908, I, 279; Mass. Bay Recs., I, 126, 183, 274-5; Va. Co. Recs., III, 469) John Pory wrote from Virginia in 1619 indicating that all standards had broken down: "our Cowe-keeper here of James city on Sundayes goes acowterd all in freshe flaming silkes and a wife of one that in England had professed the black arte not of a scholler but of a collier of Croydon, weares her rough bever hatt with a faire perle hattband, and a silken suite therto correspondent." In the same year the first General Assembly acknowledged the breakdown by shifting the ground of sumptuary legislation from the moral plane to that of expediency and self-interest. They

---

3. Kingsbury, ed., *Virginia Company Records*, IV, 584; McIlwaine, ed., *Minutes Virginia Council and General Court*, 12, 14, 15-6, 18-20, 57, 59, 85-6, 93, 132-6, 148; Shurtleff, ed., *Plymouth Records*, 87, 97, and *Massachusetts Bay Records*, I, 84, 86, 88, 91, 94, 100, 108, 132-3, 135, 136, 152, 156-7, 161, 189, 200, 207ff, 212-3, 217, 224, 237, 265, 269, 286, 296; Trumbull, ed., *Connecticut Records*, 33, 51; Winthrop, *Journal*, ed. Hosmer, I, 67, 147.

legislated that a man's church tax rate would be set according to the apparel of himself and his wife. Frontier conditions meant wealth for some who would not have had it in England and unexpected poverty as well. In these circumstances, the old relationships and their badges did not last. (Va. Co. Recs., III, 165, 221)

Just as the writers were concerned for fear distinctions between classes might be affected by frontier life, they were also anxious to assert that relationships between the sexes would be maintained as in England. Many writers vehemently denied that rough colonial conditions would necessitate hard work for English women, or that English men, freed from the constraints of English society, would "usurpe over their Wives, and keepe them in servile subjection." (Morrell, 1625, 21, Underhill, 1638, 5-6; Wood, 1634, 97-8). Less clearly stated but certainly just as important is the other side of the problem: would more fluid and demanding colonial conditions mean that women would become more central to the economy of the community and therefore more powerful and important as Indian women were? Women clearly were very important in early colonial ventures. Colonies were not successful until after they were transformed from military outposts to recreations of English society. The crucial factor in this transformation was the presence of women. The Virginia Company repeatedly sent cargoes of women to be wives for colonists and they frequently repeated their conviction that men would not be committed to the country until they had families there. This recognition is demonstrated also by the fact that many colonies gave shares of land for every child and woman brought over as well as for men. The Virginia House of Burgesses, in a petition sent from their first meeting to the Virginia Company said, "in a newe plantation it is not knowen whether man or woman be more necessary." (Va. Co. Recs., III, 160 and I, 256-7, 268-9, 391, 566; III, 493, 505, 526, 640; Smith, 1624, 543)

It also seems clear that, despite denials, English colonists, male and female, did work harder than they expected to and the less well-established social structure of the colonies allowed scope for activities not normally allowed. Women who did not conform to the sexual standards of English society seem to have shocked colonists by their openness. Women were also the victims of oppression, sexual and other, by their masters. Women were expected to do extraordinary duty in protecting the colonies in case of attack and in extending settlements. One of the most grievous of all the ways in which women went beyond traditional bounds was in their religious activities. Anne Hutchinson was one of many women in early New England who kept a conventicle. Colonial authorities worked constantly to maintain women's roles in the familiar English patterns. They could tolerate neither an enlargement of women's sphere nor a diminution of the protection which they believed traditional forms offered to women. (Levett, 1624, 36-7; Wyatt, 1624, 121; Winthrop, 1908, I, 234, 259; Morton, 1637, 115; Va. Co. Recs., IV, 82, 231-2, 473; Mins. Va. Council and Gen. Ct., 27, 61-2, 91, 101, 117, 155; Mass. Bay Recs., I, 193, 224)

Because English colonists were so concerned about maintaining distinctions within their own society they were adamant about forbidding English people to blur these distinctions by attempting to live in the Indian style. However much Indian society possessed qualities the writers felt were lost in English society and however critical they were of their own culture, none was prepared to countenance the step of forsaking the company of fellow Europeans and going to live with Indians. John Smith reported that French explorers lived with the Tarrentines "as one nation or family." (Smith, 1616, 203) This was no precedent for the English. English writers, at least theoretically, looked forward to a time when the Indians would grow out of their own culture and adopt European Christianity and civilization. For Europeans to regress to Indian ways would be ludicrous in their view.

This was not the way the question appeared to many colonists. There were people in every colony for whom Indian life was enormously attractive. During the early period of colonization more Englishmen chose to live with Indians than natives adopted English civilization. As with some of the runaways from Jamestown, English people who were "delivered" from Indian captivity often chose to run away to the Indians again. (Smith, 1624, 542; Winslow, 1624, 39; Axtell, 1975, 56, 61-2) Virginia and Massachusetts Bay both legislated against being absent from the plantation without permission. People who did run away to the Indians might expect very extreme punishments, even up to the death penalty. (Va. Co. Recs., III, 74; Jl. Va. Burgesses, 21, 31; Mins. Va. Council and Gen. Ct., 105, 148; Mass. Bay Recs., I, 88; Vaughan, 1965, 208)

The boys who had been left with the Indians during Jamestown's early years grew into men who appear to have lived in the fringes between Indians and English. They were so useful to the colonies as translators that they could not be rejected outright. They and other people who lived between the two cultures not only interpreted for the colonies but also advised them on where to settle and where to find the commodities they were looking for. Despite their usefulness they were regarded with great suspicion for fear they might be identifying their interests with the Indians rather than their fellow Englishmen, or playing one set of colonists off against another. The work that Henry

Spelman and Thomas Savage did for Virginia as guides and translators is frequently mentioned, often coupled with the fact that the colony never properly recompensed either for the work they did. The colonists' dilemma is aptly illustrated by the story of Henry Spelman. Another interpreter, Robert Poole, told the Virginia authorities that Spelman had ridiculed the present governor before Opechancanough, telling him that a much greater man was coming in his place, thereby making the chief contemptuous of the entire colony. Such treachery corresponded with their fears, but they decided not to execute Spelman, but to degrade him from his rank of captain "and made him a servant to the Collony for Seaven years in quallytie of an Interpriter." Clearly if Spelman was treacherous, then using him as an interpreter greatly increased the vulnerability of the colony, but the colony needed him and must use him regardless. The governor later pardoned Spelman and then the colonial authorities found that the treachery had been rather on Poole's part. He, they now found out, was "very dishonest" and in fact had "even turned heathen." They found he had been distorting both the governor's messages to Opechancanough and the Indian chief's messages to the colony. The basic problem remained: the colonial government was forced to rely for its most basic safety on people whom it did not trust. (Smith, 1624, 528, 569, 606; Purchas, 1625 rpt. 1906, XIX, 119; Anon., 1635, 6-7; Va. Co. Recs., I, 310; III, 174-5, 242-5; Fr. White, 1634, 41; Leonard Calvert, 1638, 150-7; Yong, 1634, 56; Lurie in Smith, ed., 1959, 49)

Part of the reason why the example of defectors from English culture was so disliked lies in the fact that those men who did leave were attempting to escape the constraints of society, to live in "prophane course of life." William Wood pointed to the bad habits many Indians had acquired from such English people, especially one who lived with his family on Richmonds Island, "living as he list amongst them, making his covetous corrupt will his law." Eventually he and his family were murdered by Indians, "so that these that lived beside the Law of God, and their King, and the light of Nature, dyed by their hands that car'd neither for God, King, nor Nature." This is certainly part of the reason for the great animus against Thomas Morton in New England. It seems clear that the major objection to living away from colonial control was that it allowed one to live lawlessly rather than that Englishmen might in some direct way be influenced by the Indian example. That is, frontier conditions allowed a kind of disrespect for the rules of English society which would not occur at home. Small plantations, such as those of Wessagusset in New England and Capt. Martin's Hundred in Virginia, were seen as sources of disorder and lawlessness. In both cases, colonial authorities moved to end these colonies' separate existences, alleging in the case of Martin's plantation that he had made it a "receptacle of disordered persons." When the first Virginia Assembly met, they petitioned London to allow them to enforce the laws they passed immediately without waiting for them to be endorsed by the Virginia Company, "for otherwise this people (who nowe at length have gotten the raines of former servitude into their owne swindge) would in shorte time growe so insolent, as they would shake off all government, and there would be no living among them."[4] Ironically it was Thomas Morton who objected to Englishmen living with Indians on equal terms on the purely practical grounds that this was impossible. He claimed that English culture and its representatives always dominated in his plantation. (Morton, 1637, 77)

The idea that those who leave English society for Indian might be unusually unruly individuals cannot be the whole explanation for the uneasiness with which men who lived on the fringes of civilization were regarded. The boys who grew into interpreters had been left with Indians by those in authority, and there is no indication that they were living immoral lives. In these cases, especially since the men were fulfilling an absolutely necessary function, the dislike must have emanated from the uncomfortable feeling that they were anomalous, not Indian but not really English either. It was not that the colonists saw an awful warning that the veneer of civilization could slip and they could descend to a savage state. None of the anomalous men did that. What they did do was generate the profound uneasiness felt in the presence of men who do not conform fully to the category of persons to which they belong.[5]

---

4. Wood, *New Englands Prospect*, 61; Kingsbury, ed., *Virginia Company Records*, I, 611; II, 42-3; III, 163, 177; IV, 70, 515, 517-8, 565; McIlwaine, ed., *Minutes Virginia Council and General Court*, 61-3; Bradford, *Of Plymouth Plantation*, ed. Morison, 113, 116, 141, 205, 219; Vaughan, *New England Frontier*, 208.

5. This concept is drawn from Mary Douglas, *Purity and Danger: An Analysis of Concepts of Pollution and Taboo* (New York, 1966), Chap. III, esp. pp. 53-4.

8

England's Special Relationship with North America

God revealed the existence of America as a part of the unfolding of his universal plan, in which the English nation was invited to take a major role. This sense of being God's agents in a great mission, of serving an "Apostolicall function," as John Donne put it, is all-pervasive in English writings on colonization during the first 60 years of experience. (Donne, 1626, 43) The belief that the colonization of America represented the working out of God's plan and that the English had been specially selected to bring his work to fruition was strongly urged by all segments of that community, by Anglicans and Roman Catholics as well as Puritans.[1] This belief sprang from the common theological framework of the age, not from the disputes within that framework. Virginians saw their colony as a "Sanctum Sanctorum, an holy house" just as New Englanders did. (Hamor, 1615, A3v-A4; Dale in Hamor, 51) This belief forced action: the carrying of the Gospel to the natives of America.

The sense of urgency found in many of the writings was a product of the widespread belief that they were not merely fulfilling a part of God's universal plan, but that they were participating in its last act, the events which would bring the millenium, the 1000 year reign of Christ after his victory over Antichrist. Tremendous energies were generated by the widespread belief that the millenium was near and that the English were involved in a "cosmic struggle." (Webster, 1975, 1-31, 44-47; Sanford, 1961, 78, 91) As William Symonds put it, after listing

1. The argument that this belief was limited to the Puritans of New England can be found in Richard S. Dunn, "Seventeenth-Century English Historians of America," in Smith, ed., *Seventeenth-Century America,* 196, and Vaughan, "Evolution of Virginia History," in Vaughan and Billias, eds., *Perspectives on Early American History,* 36.

the great events of the Old Testament, "These things were done in a corner, in comparison of that which is in hand . . ." (Symonds, 1609, A2v) America was crucial in this last act, because the end could not come until all the world's people had heard the Gospel. In fact, the sense of divine mission shared by colonists and promoters placed the Indians and their conversion squarely in the center of their concerns. Confidence in the imminence of the millenium and the importance to it of English efforts in America was shared by representatives of all religious groups. Again and again, Roman Catholic, Anglican, and Puritan writers stressed the need to preach the Gospel to all before the end.[2] John Donne urged the Virginia Company to "Further and hasten you this blessed, this joyfull, this glorious consummation of all . . ." (Donne, 1622, 43) To the objection that the apostles had been commanded to preach to all the world and that therefore this necessary step had already been accomplished, several ministers answered that the apostles preached to the then known world and that the task was handed on to their successors.

Not only did the writers affirm that this spreading of the Gospel must occur before the millenium, but many of them, again of all persuasions, said plainly that the moment was near, that the "world is olde and now in her dotage." (Benson, 1609, 41) English people of this period searched the Book of Revelations for indications of how to predict the end of the world. Writers of different religious professions united in seeing in their own time "infallible arguments of the worlds end approching." (Hayes, 1583, 388) Gordon of Lochinvar sums up the tradition. After asserting that the Gospel must be preached to all, he asks rhetorically, "And is it not as certaine a Conclusion amongst all the Divines, that these are the latter Dayes, wherein we live, well knowne by the signes that were to come before, sette downe by God himselfe in his sacred Worde, and for the most part alreadie manifested?" (Gordon of Lochinvar, 1625, B3)

England had a special role to play in this spreading of the Gospel.

---

2. This set of beliefs about the millenium and England's role in it can be found generally in Hayes, *Report of the voyage by Gilbert*, in Quinn, ed., *Gilbert Voyages*, II, 388; George Peckham, *A True Reporte of the Newfound Landes*, ibid., 476; Virginia Company, *True and Sincere declaration*, 3 and *True Declaration of Estate*, in Force, comp., *Tracts*, III, 5; Johnson, *Nova Britannia*, ibid., I, 14, 27; White, *The Planters Plea*, ibid., II, 7-9; Robert Cushman, "Preface" to *A Sermon Preached at Plimmoth in New-England* (London, 1622), A3; George Benson, *A Sermon Preached at Paules Crosse* (London, 1609), 41, 60, 92; John Donne, *A Sermon Preached to the Honourable Company of the Virginia Plantation*, 1622 (London, 1626), 15-6, 42-3; Eburne, Plain Pathway, ed. Wright, 28-9; Symonds, *Virginia. A Sermon*, 47-8.

God had kept America hidden until the Reformation and he had saved North America for the leader of the protestant forces. The outpouring from English ministers and laymen of all shades of religious opinion on England's role in the divine mission forms a striking contrast to the experience of Holland, the other protestant power deeply involved in colonization. (Boxer, 1973a, 127) English writers argued voluminously that God had reserved North America for the English and that this could be proven from history, geography, climate and reason. Writers of all circumstances and experience in the period before 1640 would have agreed with William Crashaw and Alexander Whitaker writing of Virginia that "God himselfe is the founder, and favourer of this Plantation." (Crashaw in Whitaker, 1613, A4v, C4; Whitaker, 1613, 21, 33) Many would have gone as far as Robert Gray did when he wrote that to oppose Virginia was to be in "opposition against God, the King, the Church, and the Commonwealth." (Gray, 1609, D2; Price, 1609, F2)

Failures of other European countries to establish permanent bases in North America were often pointed to as evidence that God had intended that continent for England. The Roman Catholic Sir George Peckham found such evidence in Mercator's new map where North America can be seen to "stretche out it selfe towardes England onelie." (Peckham, 1583, 448, 476) John Donne argued from geography, seeing England as lying between Europe and North America. The Virginia Company will make "this Iland, which is but as the Suburbs of the old world, a Bridge, a Gallery to the new." (Donne, 1626, 44) James Rosier, a Roman Catholic, argued that God had directed the expedition he traveled with. (Rosier, 1605, E) Puritans and Anglicans, ministers and laymen, all knew God had reserved North America for England. (White, 1630, 12; Vaughan, 1626, III, 5; Hayes, 1583, 387-8; Winslow, 1624, 52; Smith, 1631, 933; Morrell, 1625, 13)

Promoters of colonization were disturbed by the charge that their efforts would produce change or novel situations. This spreading out of populations, they argued, was not unprecedented. Sir William Alexander argued that the colonization of America approached "the puritie . . . of the infancie of the first age" when people spread out to populate the world. (Alexander, 1630, 37; Gray, 1609, Bv) A favorite answer was to compare colonization to the habits of the "Painefull Bee" who, when the hive becomes overfull, takes a portion of its population to found a new hive. The analogy comparing colonization to the swarming of bees appears in virtually every writer. Just as the new hive is an exact reproduction of the old one, so will the colonists found "a new Brittaine in another world." (Crakanthorpe, 1609, D2v; Morrell, 1625, 24; Purchas, 1625 rpt. 1906, XX, 132; Parkhurst in Peckham, 1583, 441; Cushman, 1622, A2)

Some of these writers argue that the English are not so delicate that they cannot face new situations. Englishness is an inner quality that the colonists will carry with them wherever they go. Sir William Pelham in a commendatory poem to Peckham's *True Reporte* puts it, "To valiaunt mindes each land is a native soile." (Pelham in Peckham, 1583, 437) Richard Eburne argues that Englishmen are adaptable and can learn to live even in inhospitable climates. England itself is an expandable concept: "And if you will needs live in England, imagine all that to be England where Englishmen, where English people, you with them, and they with you, do dwell. (And it be the people that makes the land English, not the land the people.)" (Eburne, 1625 rpt. 1962, 12, 47-8) Finally, William Symonds reminds his hearers that to leave one's country at the commandment of God is to receive God's blessing. "The trueth is; that none doe so shine in pietie as those that feare God & are out of their Countrie." (Symonds, 1609, 30)

Another way such writers reinforced their contention that God had intended North America to be England's special province was by demonstrating how well-suited Englishmen were to live there, incidentally offering an interesting picture of the English character. All the arguments of English-American compatibility are based on the assumption that the English always choose the mean, that they can thrive only in moderate circumstances. The North American coast, they argued, was perfectly suited to English habitation because it was neither too hot nor too cold, too flat nor too mountainous, too far north nor too far south. The passage to English America was not, like other voyages, subject to "the untemperate heate of the Sunne on the one side, or the danger of the Ice on the other side." It was "as though God himselfe had built a bridge for men to passe from England to Virginia."[3] John Smith argued that New England lies at the "very meane betwixt the North Pole and the Line," by which he meant the

---

3. Crashaw, *A Sermon Preached in London*, Ev; Richard Hakluyt (Elder), *Inducements to the Liking of the Voyage intended towards Virginia written 1585*, in E. G. R. Taylor, ed., *The Original Writings and Correspondence of the Two Richard Hakluyts* (London, 1935), II, 328; John Brereton, *A Briefe and true Relation of the Discoverie of the North part of Virginia*, 2nd ed. (London, 1602), 20; Edward Hayes, *A Treatise, conteining important inducements for the planting in these parts, and finding a passage that way to the South Sea and China*, in Brereton, *ibid.*, 15; T. C., *A Short Discourse of the New-Found-Land* (Dublin, 1623), B3v; Samuel Purchas, *Purchas his Pilgrimage*, 3rd ed. (London, 1617), 946; Peckham, *True Reporte of the Newfound Landes*, in Quinn, ed., *Gilbert Voyages*, II, 447; Whitaker, *Good Newes from Virginia*, 39.

equator. (Smith, 1620, 253) Thomas Morton also pointed to New England's middle location which makes it "participate of heate and cold indifferently." This land between 40 and 45 degrees of latitude "may be truly sayd to be within the compasse of that golden meane, most apt and fit for habitation and generation, being placed by Allmighty God the great Creator, under that Zone, called *Zona Temperata,* and therefore most fitt for the generation and habitation of our English nation, of all other . . ." (Morton, 1637, 14) Even the lay of the land in New England was suited to the moderation of Englishmen: it was "neither too flat in plaines, nor too high in hils." (Smith, 1631, 949) Similar arguments were made for Newfoundland. (Eburne, 1625 rpt. 1962, 136; Vaughan, 1626, III, 5; Whitbourne, 1620 rpt. 1622, 47)

God had reserved this part of the world for which the English were so well-suited in order that they might plant there and fulfill his plan. This fulfillment, the preaching of the Gospel to the Indians, could not take place without the prior establishment of colonies. Many of the writers were aware that the Spanish had done more to convert the natives to what John Smith called "their adulterated faith." (Smith, 1616, 217; Eburne, 1626 rpt. 1962, 25-6) But the Spaniards, as Las Casas had pointed out, were willing to perform mass baptisms without thorough instruction in the faith the convert was accepting. (Hanke, 1959, 19-20) There was general agreement among the protestant English that conversion could not be accepted until the convert clearly understood the principles of the faith and, for some of the writers, not until he or she could read the Bible. English colonial promoters were obviously thinking of a long-range program of work with the Indians. Plantation in America was required because such conversion required extensive education: "there is no other, moderate, and mixt course, to bring them to conversion, but by dailie conversion, where they may see the life, and learne the language each of other." (Va. Co., 1610a, 6; Gordon of Lochinvar, 1625, B3v) John White, in 1630, said the Indians and English already understand enough of each other's language to trade and to teach the "morall precepts" of Christianity as well as the forms of worship. "But how shall a man express unto them things meerely spirituall, which have no affinity with sense, unlesse wee were thoroughly acquainted with their language, and they with ours?" (White, 1630, 29) These writers agreed with the Roman Catholic Sir George Peckham that since the Indians could not come in large numbers to England, Christians, of whom England had a superfluity, must plant in America. (Peckham, 1583, 450-1)

Christianity was a part of the European culture which the English wrote of carrying to the Indians, and they clearly saw this culture as unified. One could not be a Christian without first becoming civilized as the English understood civilization. Thomas Hariot early pointed to a sequence which began with attracting the Indians by superior English "knowledges and craftes," proceeding through friendship to "civilitie, and the imbracing of true religion." (Hariot, 1588, 372) This sequence was seen as standard and necessary by the writers who discussed the process of conversion. Through planting colonies the English can first attract the Indians with their technological superiority and then go on to civilization and Christianity. (White, 1630, 29; Carleill, 1583, 357; Whitbourne, 1620 rpt. 1622, 14-5; Eburne, 1625 rpt. 1962, 25) When the high Anglican Nicholas Ferrar and his family and friends wanted to contribute to the conversion of Indian children, they gave their money to found a "Christian college" in Virginia. (Waterhouse, 1622, 52; Maycock, 1963, 24-5) The program had to be, as William Crashaw said, to bring the Indians "to civility, and so to religion." He says the object of the Virginia Company is conversion of the "Savages . . . (after they first be made civill men.)" (Crashaw, 1610, C3v, Kv) Historians criticize as arrogant this assumption that conversion could not occur without prior acceptance of European civilization, but the colonists' argument points to the unified nature of both Indian and English culture, especially to the fact that the religious leadership and the political authority proceeded from the same set of beliefs. Francis Jennings points out that, in abandoning his powwow, an Indian was also abandoning his physician. (Jennings, 1975, 232, 248; Washburn, 1975, 111-112; Jacobs, 1975, 601) Modern writers are simply repeating the perception of the 16th and 17th century English writers in a different way. Both Indian and English culture were unified in this way. Both sides were aware that if the Indian were to accept Christianity, he would have to abandon his own culture and accept the entire European culture. The blind spot of the English writers exists in the fact that, despite their admiration for some aspects of Indian life, they never questioned their assumption that English culture, including English religion, was superior. They saw themselves as having willingly given up their pagan religion and customs when offered that opportunity and they expected a similar response from the Indians. It seemed obvious to people of this period that those who are set over others in order to guide their development ought to have virtually unlimited power. William Strachey ridicules people who claim that colonization might injure the Indians by quoting William Symonds' statement of this idea: " 'It is as much' (saith he) 'as if a father, should be said to offer violence to his child, when he beats him, to bringe him to goodnes':" A beating given for your own good is not violence. (Strachey, 1953, 24)

In his last work John Smith bitterly accused the Virginia Company of having made "Religion their colour, when all their aime was nothing but present profit." (Smith, 1631, 928) The Jesuit John Floyd ridiculed the ministers who "preached Virginia" but did not go themselves, so the company sent "away the riffraff, and rascality of the Land to be the Converters of Nations." (Floyd, 1612, 321-323) The charge of insincerity has stuck ever since and is often applied to the entire colonial effort, the avowal of interest in converting the Indians being seen as "a pious hope to sweeten a more worldly and selfish ambition." (Foss, 1974, 59; Cawley, 1938, 299) Several historians take the other side, expressing their conviction that the emphasis on religious motives found in the writers before 1640 is sincere. (Washburn, 1975, 111-113; Jordan, 1969, 21-22; Craven, 1944; 67) Those who question the sincerity of the religious avowals argue from the fact that more effort was put into producing food and commodities than to converting Indians. The money which was given to establish an Indian college was actually used as part of the financing of the iron works set up in 1620 near Richmond on the James River. This can be seen either as a cynical diversion of piously given funds or as an attempt to make an investment which would grow and produce income for the college as an endowment. It all came to nothing, as the iron works were completely destroyed in the massacre of 1622. (Purchas, 1625 rpt. 1906, XIX, 145, 152, 237, 247; Hatch and Gregory, 1962, 267-8, 274) Lack of missionary work in the early years is partially explained by Alden Vaughan and Larzer Ziff who point to the fact that, under Protestantism, each minister was tied to his own congregation. There was no separate group to be sent to evangelize as the Roman Catholic friars had been in the south. (Ziff, 1973, 169; Vaughan, 1965, 237-9)

If we look at the question as contemporaries did, the issue of sincerity can be seen to be a false one. The process of conversion was expected to be a long one which would require extensive and prolonged contact between the two cultures. Therefore, contemporaries argued, the first task was to establish the colonies on a firm footing. Then, when the colonies were assured of survival, they could turn their attention to missionary work. This would be made all the easier by the fact that the Indians would have had ample time to see the superiority of the English way of life and each side would have some facility in the language of the other.

Many writers warn that an unrestricted search for profits will be fatal to the colonial effort. They argue strongly, however, that profit is not bad in itself. In fact, profit is absolutely necessary to the colonial effort. Since that effort is essential to the fulfillment of the divine plan, it is

God himself who offers the planters their reasonable profit. Colonization was an expensive proposition. This became more clear after the early failures demonstrated that infant plantations would need sustenance for several years before they could even hope to be self-sufficient. Since this was so, God, as a realist, offered sure hope of reward in return for Englishmen undertaking this task. As John Smith said, "For I am not so simple to thinke, that ever any other motive then wealth, will ever erect there a Commonweale." (Smith, 1616, 212; Lane, 1586, 273)

What is important is that profit and virtue were not incompatible in their eyes. John Smith goes on to write of the "unparalleled vertues" of the Spanish and Portuguese and "their mountaines of wealth (sprong from the plants of their generous indevours)." (Smith, 1616, 215) Good flows naturally to men who do good. William Haller has pointed to the moral and practical significance of the parable of the talents for the Puritans. (Haller, 1957, 124) Robert Johnson, an Anglican, cautions against making gain the chief aim, but "God that hath said by Solomon: Cast thy bread upon the waters, and after many daies thou shalt find it: he will give the blessing." (Johnson, 1609, 13) The Roman Catholic Sir George Peckham points to other biblical justification: "But heerunto it may be objected, that the Gospel must be freely preached . . . Yet for further aunswer, we may say with Saint Paule. If we have sowen unto you heavenlie thinges, doo you thinke it much that we should reape your carnall things? And withall, The workman is worthy of his hier." (Peckham, 1583, 468; Hawkins in Peckham, 442) The Anglican ministers who spoke for Virginia during the dark days of 1609 and 1610 urged strongly the connection between virtue and profit. As William Crashaw put it, "he that is zealous of Gods glorie, God will be mindfull of his profit." Crashaw demonstrates that God has directed the English to a land that has the commodities which England lacks. (Crashaw, 1610, G3; Price, 1609, F3; Tynley, 1609, 68) As Edward Winslow of Plymouth believes, the plantation of America is one of those cases "where religion and profit jump together." (Winslow, 1624, 52, 64)

The most obvious and most powerful biblical precedent for colonization resulting in profit was that of the Israelites entering the land of Canaan. Because the colonizers in that case were allowed to violate the rights of and even to kill the inhabitants of Canaan, it is interesting to see how the late 16th and early 17th century colonial promoters handled this precedent. Writers of all religious opinions used the Canaan simile and they used it with care. Some confusion arises from the fact that the Canaan precedent involved two aspects. One of these was that the Israelites were given a land flowing with milk and honey, with its implications of a better and, possibly, an easier life. The other aspect was the assignment of the Canaanites to the ranks of people without rights, open to extermination. If this could be seen as a precedent for the colonization of America, the effect would be momentous. Though they stressed that men cannot live without labor, many writers spoke of America as a land flowing with milk and honey, obviously linking it to Canaan. (Price, 1609, F3v; Johnson, 1612, 8) Moreover, many of the writers said that America exceeded Canaan: "that land flowed with milke and honie, our abounds with as good or better." (Crashaw, 1610, F3v; Purchas, 1625 rpt. 1906, XIX, 233) Thomas Morton says New England is in a more temperate climate than Canaan. (Morton, 1637, 63) Canaan was also slandered just as America is. Robert Johnson and Robert Gray both point out that 10 of the 12 men sent to reconnoiter in Canaan returned to the Israelites "with tydings of impossibilitie to enter and prevaile." The Israelites did not retire from the field and Johnson and Gray, who wrote in Virginia's worst hour of 1609-1610, urged their readers similarly not to be discouraged. (Johnson, 1609, 15; Gray, 1609, C3-C3v)

Great care was used in attempting to apply the second aspect of the Canaan precedent, that of "Worthy Josuah . . . who hanged up so many shields in the house of God." (Symonds, 1609, 12) In the many deliverances surrounding the tempest which destroyed the great Virginia fleet but cast up the survivors in a land of abundance from which they saved Jamestown, the Virginia Company's *True Declaration of the Estate of the Colonie in Virginia* saw "the arme of the Lord of Hosts, who would have his people to passe the redde Sea and Wildernesse, and then to possesse the land of Canaan." (Va.Co., 1610a, 19) Two writers discuss the position of the Canaanites in comparison to that of the natives of America. Both specifically reject the idea that the behavior of the Israelites in Canaan could be a precedent for the English in America. William Crashaw, an Anglican preacher known for his learning put it this way: "the Israelites had a *commandement* from God to dwell in *Canaan,* we have *leave* to dwell in *Virginea:* they were *commanded to kill* the heathen, we are *forbidden to kill* them, but are commanded to *convert* them." (Crashaw, 1610, F3-F3v) Robert Cushman, a leader of the separatist Puritans at Plymouth colony said similarly: "Neither is there any land or possession now, like unto the possession which the Jewes had in Canaan, being legally holy and appropriated unto a holy people the seed of Abraham." (Cushman in Bradford and Winslow, 1622, 66)

The English believed they had been selected by God to play a special role in the last act of the divine drama. They liked to think that this quality of being chosen made them in some ways like the Jews in the Old Testament, but they never deluded themselves into thinking that they had the same role as the Jews. God favored them only because he could, through them, bring salvation to all people. He did not favor the English exclusively or at the expense of others and they knew it. In the final chapter, we will see how and why the English colonists came to be destroyers rather than saviors.

9

The Nature of the Relationship

Thomas Morton is a unique figure in the early history of English colonization of America because he presided over a plantation in which English men and Indians, men and women, lived together. Morton's writing is characterized by an openness, a willingness to appreciate the strengths of Indian culture and to see it as attractive. His plantation horrified the Puritans among whom he lived in Massachusetts and historians have continued the Puritan practice of seeing Morton as diametrically opposed to everything the Puritans stood for. One thing has changed. Recent treatments see Morton as a more attractive figure in these contests than the Puritans did.[1] Morton can be asked to bear too great a load as the harbinger of modern attitudes. In most respects, his attitudes were more like those of contemporary English people, Puritans or not, than we allow for. This comes through especially clearly when he describes his relationship to the Indians among whom he lived. First he plays up his rejection of Puritanism and his admiration for the Indians: "but I have found the Massachussets Indian more full of humanity, then the Christians, & have had much better quarter with them..." But he then goes on to state quite clearly that he expected the relationship to be one in which he dominated the Indians: "yet I observed not their humors, but they mine, although my great number that I landed were dissolved, and my Company as few as might be: for I know that this falls out infallibly where two Nations meete, one must rule, and the other be ruled, before a peace can be hoped for: and

---

1. See for example Slotkin, *Regeneration Through Violence;* Michael Zuckerman, "Pilgrims in the Wilderness: Community, Modernity, and the Maypole of Merry Mount," *New England Quarterly,* 50 (1977), 255-277.

for a Christian to submit to the rule of a Salvage you will say, is both shame and dishonor: (at least) it is my opinion, and my practise was accordingly, and I have the better quarter by the meanes thereof." (Morton, 1637, 77-8) Morton assumed that the English person would rule even when he was greatly outnumbered.

English people saw their role in America as tutelary. The Indians were not simply "our brethren," they were "our younger brethren." This is important because younger brothers, like women, were dependents in English society of this period. After the death of their father, younger brothers in gentry families owed obedience to the inheriting older brother similar to the obedience they had shown their father. If younger brothers did not show the proper respect and obedience to the oldest brother he could effectively cut them off from marriage and career opportunities. The superiority of the oldest brother worked in two ways, then: not only did he receive the largest share of the family's resources, but his siblings were subordinate to his wishes. In return the older brother took responsibility for shaping and instructing his younger brothers. His authority was similar to the authority of husband over wife in Renaissance England. In the husband-wife relationship, the wife was seen as requiring constant guidance on how to act, what to read, when to read, whom to see, and so on. The superior member knew what was best for the dependent. (Slater, 1976; Macfarlane, 1970a, 48-51; Kelso, 1956, 83)

The ideal version of the English-Indian relationship involved a tutelary relationship similar to that of older brother to younger and husband to wife. Reports to and from America constantly refer to the Indians as "our kinsmen and younger brethren." (Johnson, 1612, 8; Vaughan, 1626, III, 31) The colonists, as the older brothers, would instruct and shape the Indians and their culture. Indian tuition could mean nothing short of the destruction of their culture and religion and their replacement by European civilization and Christianity. People in superior positions naturally assumed the right and necessity to shape and instruct in England as well as America. That such instruction involved the priceless gift of Christianity enhanced the obligation to assume the tutelary role.

English theorists willfully deluded themselves when they translated this tutelary image into policy. They assumed that the process of getting the natives to accommodate themselves to English settlement would be much easier than in fact it was. The English were let down by their own preconceptions and wishful thinking. English writers commonly foresaw a two-step approach: gentleness to be followed, if necessary, by severity. The elder Richard Hakluyt is the first of a long series of advisers who urge the importance of maintaining peaceful relations with the Indians by using "humanitie and curtesie and much forbearing of revenge." (elder Hakluyt, 1578, 118 and 1585, 334; Peckham, 1583, 451; Winslow in Bradford and Winslow, 1622, 61; Whitbourne, 1620 rpt. 1622, 2, 5; Anon., 1635, 31-2; Mass. Bay Co., 1629a, 159)

In fact it was clear from the beginning that the second step, the use of severity, would dominate. Early colonial leaders were chosen for their experience in chastising recalcitrant populations. The younger Hakluyt first enunciated the idea that the English could draw on experience gained in the cruel European and Irish wars in handling the American natives. In his preface to de Soto's *Virginia Richly Valued* he advocated treating the Indians with gentleness, but "if gentle polishing will not serve, then we shall not want hammerours and rough masons enow, I meane our old soldiours trained up in the Netherlands, to square and prepare them to our Preachers hands." (Hakluyt, 1609, 503 and 1587b, 377) The policy of treating the Indians as a conquered population originated with Ralph Lane, the governor of the first large-scale colony at Roanoke. Lane, with military experience in Ireland, like John Smith and the long line of Virginia governors whose prior experience was military, saw the problem of organizing both settlers and Indians as essentially martial. (Lane, 1586, 274, 262-3fn; Smith, 1631, 925) All the early governors in Virginia followed a policy of intimidation, certainly insofar as it meant requisitioning food for the colonists and using whatever methods were necessary to ensure this food supply. Small excuses were sought to justify actions calculated to impress the Indians. Ralph Lane and John Smith found it useful to kidnap children to use as hostages when they entered Indian Villages. Smith endorsed this policy in a marginal note: "How to deale with the Salvages." (Smith, 1612b, 404 and 1624, 419) Colonists and theorists in England alike understood that the Indians must be overawed if the colonies were to be safe. People in England believed that English weapons and technology were so obviously superior that overawing the Indians would be natural, and that the Indians could be dominated through fear.

In fact the early colonists were extremely vulnerable. Despite the frequently friendly first meetings between new colonists and natives, English writers assumed that Indians would be fundamentally hostile to the settlements. This was not because the Indians were seen as savage and treacherous, but because they were human beings. All men have dignity and pride in their identification with their own land. Hakluyt believed so strongly that the Indians would necessarily fight for their birthright that he warned the first Jamestown settlers that war would be inevitable. Therefore he urged the colonists to trade for corn and supplies before the Indians realized a permanent settlement was planned. (Va. Co., 1606, 50-52) The Virginia Company's instructions to its governors and Matthew Cradock's letter of instructions to Massachusetts Bay draw on the same assumptions about Indian behavior toward the colonies. The colonists are always warned to treat Indians justly but to expect hostility even from those natives who appear friendly. In 1609 the Virginia Company wrote "it is Clere even to reason" that the Indians would not like "our neighbourhood," and that they would be helpful to the colonists either out of fear or because they thought the English could be helpful to them in their intertribal wars. The Ancient Planters of Virginia later attested that fear had been the only source of loyalty in the Indians. (Va. Co. Recs., III, 17-21; Jl. Va. Burgesses, 22, 33, 35) John Smith recorded the Indian belief that "we were a people come from under the world to take their world from them." (Smith, 1624, 427)

Official colonial policy throughout was friendliness and fairness combined with swift and decisive punishment of any "insolency." Because they knew the Indians could do them great harm and because they knew the Indians had every reason to want to see them out of America except as traders of European tools for furs, the colonial officials assumed that the Indians would be constantly prodding and testing for signs of weakness. (Va. Co. Recs., III, 164, 469, 487; Mass. Bay Recs., I, 385; Winthrop, 1908, I, 63, 79, 90-92) Writers from every colony as well as advisors in England all stressed keeping together, keeping strong, fortifying themselves, and keeping up military discipline.[2] Their military vulnerability was clearly on their minds.

Even more important was the superiority of the Indians in coping with the American environment, particularly in food production. Early colonists were vividly aware of the fact that they were dependent on the Indians for food, that in fact Indian technology made a living for both English and Indians from land which English technology and efforts, in the short run, could not make fruitful. Ralph Lane of Roanoke admitted the extreme dependence of his party on Indian help. His expedition to the northwest almost starved when the Indians withdrew. His colony could not grow or gather food for themselves: "For at that

---

2. Hariot, *Briefe and true Report*, in Quinn, ed., *Roanoke Voyages*, I, 381-2; Anon., *Relation of Maryland*, ed. Hawks, 31-2, 45; Bradford and Winslow, *Mourt's Relation*, 61-2; Eburne, Plain Pathway, ed. Wright, 134; Donne, *Sermon Preached to the Virginia Company*, 43; Massachusetts Bay Company, "The Company's First General Letter of Instructions to Endicott and his Council. April, 1629," in Alexander Young, ed., *Chronicles of the First Planters of Massachusetts Bay, 1623-1636* (1836; rpt. New York, 1970), 157; Vincent, *True Relation of the Late Battell*, 15; Wood, *New Englands Prospect*, 53.

time wee had no weares for fishe, neither could our men skill of the making of them, neither had wee one grayne of corne for seede to put into the ground." His colonists could not even repair the weirs when they were broken. (Lane, 1586, 266-7, 270, 276, 282-3) When the Indians around Jamestown withdrew from contact with the settlers, the Virginia Company saw it as a form of aggression. (Va. Co., 1610b, 11) John Smith repeatedly demonstrated the utter dependence of the Jamestown colony in its early years on food from the natives. When things were at their worst under his governorship, he sent out colonists to live with the "Salvages" in order to learn how they utilized the natural products of the area. (Smith, 1612b, 448) Gabriel Archer gives a glimpse of their relative positions when he says the colonists were "dispersed in the Savages townes, living upon their almes for an ounce of Copper a day . . ." (Archer, 1609, 3) John Smith also makes it clear that the Indians understood how dependent the colonists were. He recorded a "discourse of peace and warre" that Powhatan made to him. In it Powhatan warns Smith that war will be beneficial to neither Indians nor colonists. If pressed too hard, the Indians will flee the area and be forced to live in fear in the woods eating "acorns roots, and such trash." If this should happen, "you must famish by wronging us your friends." The Indians will have a less comfortable life, but the colonists will "famish." (Smith, 1612b, 426, 443-4)

Throughout the period the colonists in Virginia continued to be dependent on Indian neighbors for food, and they continued to attempt to cope in their writings with the meaning of this dependence. (Va. Co. Recs., III, 16, 74, 300; IV, 5) In 1618 Governor Argall prohibited trade with "ye perfidious Savages nor familiarity lest they discover our weakness." (Va. Co. Recs., III, 93) Three years later the Virginia Company criticized the colonists because they were still trading in corn extensively: "for we conceive it would be much better for the Plantation and more honor for you and our nation, that the naturalles should come for theire provision to you; then you to begg your bread of them . . ." (Va. Co. Recs., III, 495-96) Earlier that same year, the colonists wrote to London that if their tobacco was not received in England, "the heathen" would triumph over the colony and "saye Where is now their God?" (Va. Co. Recs., III, 425) Planters who had been longest in Virginia described their sufferings during the first 12 years of the colony as their contribution to the fight in London over control of the Virginia Company. Their story returned again and again to the loathsome things they were forced to eat when they could not get corn from the Indians, and to the fact that many colonists ran to the Indians for relief. (Jl. Va. Burgesses, 21, 28-31, 35) The tribute of one bushel of corn for every bowman which the Chickahominies were said to have paid the English annually by agreement with Sir Thomas Dale, and which the company later made much of, was actually paid for: "we were to give to each man one peece of copper and one iron tomahawke, and to the eight chiefe men each a suit of redd cloth, which clothes and truckinge stuffe we esteemed of more worth then their corne." (Jl. Va. Burgesses, 33; Va. Co. Recs., IV, 93, 134-5, 217-8)

In New England Weston's colonists at Wessagusset were described as being reduced to doing menial labor for the Indians in order to get corn. Colonial records show the same ambiguous situation in New England as in Virginia. Prohibitions on trade for corn or attempts to regulate that trade are repeatedly followed by reports of unlawful trading or by new proclamations authorizing trading expeditions. There were also attempts to regulate the prices at which wampum circulated. (Winslow, 1624, 34; Bradford, 1953, 116; Mass. Bay Recs., I, 208, 302; Plymouth Recs., I, 50-1, 54, 130; Conn. Recs., 11, 17, 19; New Haven Recs., 44; Emerson, ed., 1976, 65, 74, 125)

The colonists' awareness of their own vulnerability combined with their feelings of guilt at the mistreatment of those Indians they could dominate to produce the rage and hostility which is characteristic of many of their actions. Colonists acknowledged a sense of guilt from the beginning of colonization. Thomas Hariot ascribed the change in relations with the Indians at Roanoke to English mistreatment of the Indians. The English had "shewed themselves too fierce . . . upon causes that on our part, might easily enough have bene borne withall." Richard Hakluyt in England made a dramatic assessment of the same evidence. He described the storm and the resultant haste with which the colony packed and left Roanoke, "as if they had bene chased from thence by a mightie armie, and no doubt so they were, for the hande of God came upon them for the crueltie, and outrages committed by some of them against the native inhabitantes of that Countrie." (Hariot, 1588, 381; Hakluyt, 1589d, 478) John Smith said he would need soldiers to lead an expedition to New England "because of the abuses which have been offered the poore Salvages." Many writers acknowledged that the spreading of the Virginia colony and the false dealings of the colonists were the root cause of bad relations with Indians in the Chesapeake area: "Wee our selves have taught them to bee trecherous by our false dealinge . . ." (Va. Co. Recs., IV, 89; Smith, 1616, 200) The Virginia Company acknowledged that fear of dispossession inspired the Indian attack on the Virginia plantations in 1622. (Va. Co. Recs., II, 351; Waterhouse, 1622, 22) John Penreis testified that perfidious dealing with friendly Indians continued after 1622 and continued to trouble the consciences of some colonists. Penreis said killing and seizing corn under pretence of friendship was "contrarie to ye equity of God & natures lawes, whereby ye name of God, our King & Cuntry are all dishonored, we being formerly for our Justice and vertuous Government Called Gods, but now through treacherous & inhumaine Cruelty esteemed worse then Divels for which (I feare me) Gods punishment is & wilbe uppon us." (Va. Co. Recs., IV, 277, 515)

Philip Vincent and John Underhill of Massachusetts Bay admitted, when writing of their burning an Indian fort with its 400 inhabitants of both sexes and all ages, that conditions in America have caused them to do things which are outside their own code. They both say they would have been moved to pity but for the bad actions of the Pequots. Vincent says "severe justice" was substituted for pity. Underhill's *Newes from America* refers those who think they were too cruel to the story of David's war: "but we will not dispute it now. We had sufficient light from the word of God for our proceedings." (Vincent, 1637, B4v; Underhill, 1638, 40)

Guilt and vulnerability reinforced each other in the American colonies. Colonists' fear caused them to overreact to small provocations or to make pre-emptive strikes as in the Pequot War. Their dependence on Indians for food led to bullying when they could get by with it. Their feelings of guilt and vulnerability generated rage and hostility against those who caused them to have these feelings. The psychological mechanism is similar to that in the witchcraft trials of the 17th century in England as studied by Alan Macfarlane and Keith Thomas. People against whom accusations were made were usually people who had been rejected by the community, despite the community's acknowledgment that the rejected person was entitled to help and support. Those who have turned away someone whom they ought to have helped then feel guilty because they have made a breach in their own social code. This "conflict between ideals and behaviour" produces an uncomfortable feeling of guilt which combines with a fear of retribution. Though the person turned away is usually a powerless person, an old widow for instance, the person rejecting her comes to believe that she may have other forms of power. If some misfortune befalls him, he can believe that the rejected person has attacked him with supernatural powers. He can then assuage his own feelings of guilt and vulnerability by accusing her of a much more serious crime, that of being a witch. (Macfarlane, 1970b, 174, 195-6, 206; Thomas, 1973, 663, 673)

In the case of the colonists, their guilt and conviction that the Indians must fight for their land combined with their very real appreciation of their vulnerability to produce the truism that Indians are treacherous. This could then justify retribution in advance of any real evidence of such treachery. In fact this psychological mechanism is clearly at work when we find so many of the writers saying they know Indians are treacherous even though they have never seen any evidence of it, even though they find the Indians trustworthy and praiseworthy in every other respect. More importantly guilt reinforced the reaction of rage when open Indian attacks made the colonists too aware of just how vulnerable they were.

The massacre of 1622 signalled the failure of Virginian attempts to conciliate and dominate their Indian neighbors. It was certainly the most important event in Indian-English relations during the first period of colonization, especially in its psychological effects. Gary B. Nash has argued that after the massacre all obligations to respect the humanity of the Indians were removed for Englishmen in general, that the Indians were now seen as "vicious, cultureless, unreconstructable savages rather than merely as hostile and primitive men, though men with an integral culture and way of life worthy of notice." (Nash, 1972, 218-220) Examination of the documentary record shows that this was not the case for Virginians. Nash's judgment involves an anachronistic picture of the relative strength of colonists and Indians in the post-massacre period.

Immediately following the massacre, the Virginia Company moved to explain it to the English public. Edward Waterhouse wrote the authorized version of the events and their cause in 1622. His account was reprinted by Samuel Purchas in his compilation *Hakluytus Posthumus or Purchas his Pilgrimes* and by John Smith in his *Generall Historie*. Waterhouse denounced the Virginia Indians as resembling beasts more than men. He stressed the barbarity of their attack in the massacre, which was successful not because of their strength, but because of their perfidy. Purchas, in a separate essay, "Virginia's Verger," went further, saying the Indians were "more brutish then the beasts they hunt." Waterhouse and Purchas agreed that the Virginia natives were now unworthy of consideration and could therefore be enslaved, thus making the massacre a blessing in disguise for Virginia. Even in the midst of these denunciations, however, Waterhouse demonstrated the organized political life of the Indians. Not only do they live by planting corn, but the massacre was done "at one instant of time, though our severall Plantations were an hundred and forty miles up one River on both sides." Clearly it was not the work of people who range over the land like beasts. (Waterhouse, 1622, A3v, 15-6, 19, 22-4, 26; Purchas, 1625 rpt. 1906, XIX, 157-164, 222-3, 231-246, 266)

Neither Waterhouse nor Purchas was an eyewitness of America, and certainly not of the events and people they described. John Smith had left Virginia many years before the massacre, but it is interesting to see what changes he made in Waterhouse's narrative as a result of his understanding of the true situation between natives and English settlers in Virginia. While Waterhouse had stressed that the massacre had occurred in the midst of a universally beneficial peace, Smith clearly shows relations between English and Indians in Virginia as a continuing struggle for mastery and control between two formidable opponents, despite rhetorical references to the "poore, weake Salvages." As Smith tells the story, the English had succeeded in tipping the balance in their favor. The peace which Waterhouse saw as proceeding from the mutual benefits it conferred on English and Indians, Smith converted into military domination by the English. Smith offered his analysis of why the massacre occurred. He preceded his rendition of Waterhouse's account by telling of the murder of the Indian leader Nemattanow, "otherwise called Jack of the Feather," and described Opechancanough's grief, which led him to plan the massacre. Smith also analyzed the underlying causes of the massacre, the fact that the English had ceased to be as vigilant as they had formerly been, reinforcing his perception that the Virginia situation was and continued to be a struggle for control. He added a long section in support of his contention that "they hurt not any that did either fight or stand upon their guard." Smith argued against Waterhouse's attempt to trivialize the Indians. He reprinted the description of Opechancanough's delight over the house with a locking door which George Thorpe built for him, but he omitted Waterhouse's allegation that Opechancanough's former cottage had resembled "a denne or hogstye." More importantly, Smith commented parenthetically on Waterhouse's assertion, which he reprinted, that the Indians were "naked and cowardly:" "(But I must tell those Authors, though some might be thus cowardly, there were many of them had better spirits.)" He further argued that the English would not win final mastery over the Indians until they abandoned their palisades and European techniques and paid a "running army" to pursue them continually. In fact, Smith returned again and again to his theme that the massacre involved nothing new in Indian-English relations and that his policy of fortified places combined with a running army was the only key to success. The reiteration is necessary because so many people have come to think the Indians "are grown invincible." Smith, unemcumbered by moral indignation on either side of the issue, is clear about what the purpose of the running army will be: "to inforce the Salvages to leave their Country." It is their country, and if the English want it, they will have to win it by military invasion. They cannot do it by underestimating the Indians or by deceiving themselves about their own intentions. (Smith, 1624, 572-588, 594, 600, 619; Waterhouse, 1622, 12, 16; Purchas, 1625 rpt. 1906, XIX, 160, 168-9)

 Documents from the colony reveal, as is to be expected, enormous hostility after 1622, but this is hostility toward a formidable enemy, not denunciation of cultureless animals. Published works about Virginia fall off rapidly following the massacre largely because the Virginia Company was involved in its final struggle, which culminated in Virginia's being made a royal colony in 1625. Between 1625 and 1640 published works about Virginia stop altogether. Therefore, the documentary evidence offers the only source about the plans and attitudes of the colonists following the massacre. All the plans for dealing with the Indians demonstrate the competence of the Indians and the fear of the settlers. One animal comparison occurs, but it is obviously meant as a figure of speech. William Capps, angry that a decisive blow had not been struck against the Indians, wrote of them as "the Heathen kennell of dogges," but in the same passage he said the English were "weatherbeaten Crowes" and compared English cultivation of tobacco to the rooting of hogs. (Va. Co. Recs., IV, 38-9) Plans for revenge were not written, except perhaps in the safety of London, in a spirit of exhilaration that the inhibitions were now off, and even those plans which came from London reminded the colonists of the duty of converting the young Indians. (Va. Co. Recs., III, 672-3) Rather those plans that proceeded from the colonists were tinged with desperation and real fear. When they were warned by the Virginia Company to drive away their enemies fairly and in accordance with justice and truth, the colonists answered that they could not win unless they adopted treacherous tactics. The colonists planned to lull the Indians into a false sense of security by "A perfidious treatye" and then strike when they least expected it, "that wee may followe their Example in destroying them." (Va. Co. Recs., IV 71, 75, 221, 269-70, 451) This willingness to adopt unworthy tactics proceeded not from contempt for the enemy, but respect for his ability. George Wyatt, advising his son Sir Francis, who was governor in Virginia, offered the most realistic assessment of the colonists' situation from England. His main message was against underestimating the enemy. "Yet I doe not with contempt reccon of them as cowards, as our common opinions esteemes. Neither did this their enterprise or execution, either want politie or corage." He went on to say that their striking and running away was an intelligent strategy and that they had an efficient intelligence system. His best advice was to follow the example of the Indians in understanding all about the enemy and being always prepared for war. He sent his son several stratagems to use, the art of which is "a politie of war by wils of wit rather then force to make benefit of an Enimise Error." The Indians also make use of stratagems "as you have felt." (Wyatt, 1624, 116-121, 127)

The most striking thing about the letters from Virginia to England in the years following the massacre is the number and variety of expressions of the fear that the colonists lived in. As late as 1626 and 1627 orders were going out to strengthen the watch and the palisades, along with expressions of fears of a new assault. (Va. Co. Recs., IV, 58-61, 147, 159; Mins. Va. Council and Gen. Ct., 106, 120) For one thing the colonists said they did not have the men to fight such an enemy. The 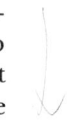 Indians, rather than fighting formal battles, preferred to make lightning raids or to hide in woods and cornfields and pick off colonists who were caught unawares. (Jl. Va. Burgesses, 38) To field an army against this enemy would have left the plantations unprotected even if the army had been strong enough. As George Sandys wrote: "or how would their weakness have indured the want of their ablest men to have gonne upon the Indians, when out of the whole Collonie wee Could but raise 180 (whereof 80 were fit onelie to Carrie burthens) to incounter 1000?" (Va. Co. Recs., IV, 67, 12) The governor, Sir Francis Wyatt, presented his arithmetic to demonstrate the "Antipathy" between "theyr [the Virginia Company's] vast Commands and our grumbling Obedience: They talke of an Army of 500 to issue out upon th' Indians in all parts and after a running Armye of 150 to vex them in all places: This joyned with the 5th man for the Fort would leave some xx men to guard 40 Plantacions, halfe a man to each counting any that were tolerable shott for a man I know what I say and to whom I speake it." (Va. Co. Recs., IV 159, 237, 572)

The first problem faced by the colony was the extreme food shortage. In the disarray following the massacre, while people were being brought to safer concentration points from the far-flung plantations, the 1622 planting time was lost. Letters sent home in the spring of 1623 all talk of the sufferings of the colonists from famine. (Va. Co. Recs., IV 231, 233, 234, 235, 238, 239; Powell, 1958, 44-75) The food shortage continued and this was directly attributable to the threat of the Indians. The colonists said they could not plant corn in large enough quantities because Indians would lurk in the fields and kill the workers. Therefore, they had to go out in large parties and set some of their number to act as sentinels. The colonists said they could not leave the immediate area of the plantation except in large and armed parties, so they had little meat from hunting and fishing. One faction in the Virginia Company summed up the letters: "it seemes doubtfull to us by the letters which we have seene whether the poore people that there remayne are in more danger of starving at home, or of having their throates cutt abroad." This is amply confirmed by the letters of early summer 1623, even in a letter of the newly-arrived Lady Wyatt. The colonists were commanded by their government not to venture forth except when fully protected. (Va. Co. Recs., IV, 41, 167-8, 186, 216-7, 228-230, 234-5, 476, 583; Mins. Va. Council and Gen. Ct., 44, 106; Jl. Va. Burgesses, 38.)

All this explains why the colonists said they had to drive the Indians from the land. It seemed clear to them that only that could offer them survival. It was their very inability to do any such thing that made them talk in such extravagant terms, not gladness that at last they could give free rein to their genocidal tendencies. The colonists believed that their perception of the situation was the same as the Indians': "without doubt either wee must drive them, or they us out of the countrey . . ." (Va. Co. Recs., II, 351; III, 683; IV, 105; Jl. Va. Burgesses, 37) The fact that the Indians remained a problem for the settlers shows through the record in the plans for marches against the natives which continued through the years. In 1637 the colonists were still writing about "the tyranny of the Natives." (Jl. Va. Burgesses, 52, 59, 62-3; Va. Co. Recs., IV, 292, 584; Mins. Va. Council and Gen. Ct., 151, 155, 184-5)

Virginian plans for conquering the Indians not only reveal them as formidable opponents, but also emphasize the civil and organized nature of Indian life. When Waterhouse was arguing that the massacre would ultimately be beneficial to Virginia, one reason he gave was that it would enable colonists to seize Indian cornfields "(which are situate in the fruitfullest places of the land.)" (Waterhouse, 1622, 23) Virtually every serious plan involved striking at the Indians through their cornfields. It was agreed that the Indians must be starved out rather than vanquished in a direct attack. (Va. Co. Recs., IV, 10, 98) Even that was more difficult than it seemed, because the Indians could plant in secret and hidden places. Thus, what was required, according to the Council of State in Virginia, was a false peace, so when the Indians "grow secure uppon the treatie, we shall have the better Advantage both to surprise them, & cutt downe theire Corne, by knowinge where they plant, which otherwise they will plant in such Corners, as it will nott be possible for us to finnde owte." (Va. Co. Recs., IV, 99) That Indian life was sedentary and based on agriculture is revealed by the colonists' conviction that, if their attack were delayed until late summer, the Indians would be unable to leave the area of their cornfields and, once their fields were burned, it would be impossible for them to find food for the winter. (Va. Co. Recs., II, 482; III, 704; IV, 102, 222, 250-1, 568-9) There is no attempt to hide the fact that the perfidious treaty, a device to which the English had been driven by desperation, was essential to these plans. Though the revenge tactics were not notably successful, the colonists continued to believe in them. In 1626, 1627, and 1628 similar plans were announced for expeditions against the enemy. In progress reports, the colonists reveal the large-scale planting of the Indians. In January 1623/4, the Council reported that they had "Cut downe theire Corne in all places which was planted in great abundance, uppon hope of a fraudulent peace..." and in one expedition the governor carried away "a marvelous quantitie of Corne." In December of the same year a report of a victory over the Pamunkeys includes the statement that they cut down corn "Sufficyent to have Sustayned fower Thousand men for a Twellv mounthe." The colonists were particularly pleased by this victory because they hoped it would diminish the reputation of the Pamunkeys with Indians to the north, one tribe of whom had sent an observer. (Va. Co. Recs., IV, 71, 74-5, 450, 507-8, 568-9; Mins. Va. Council and Gen. Ct., 151, 155, 172)

One point made by many historians is that when the Indians were helpful or loving in their relationships with the English, they were not given the credit for it, rather the credit for their actions was given to God for moving their hearts. (Washburn in Smith, ed., 1959, 19) This is certainly true in all the records as well as the published reports. (Va. Co. Recs., IV, 473; Waterhouse, 1622, 13, 18, 20-1; Smith, 1624, 578) What is also true is that the harm the Indians did to the colonists was also attributed to God. Virtually every reference to the massacre of 1622 in the Virginia records spoke of the Indian attack and the subsequent scarcity and mortality from famine and disease as God's punishment on them for their sins. The Indians were frequently referred to specifically as God's instruments. (Va. Co. Recs., III, 612, 646, 666, 678, 698; IV, 11, 22, 162, 234, 235, 237, 263, 493; Jl. Va. Burgesses, 23, 36) While this looks like simple rhetoric, a few of the writers offered an explanation of the connection between their sins and the massacre which made it a convincing explanation. Chief among their sins was greed, which manifested itself in cultivating tobacco to the exclusion of all else. This in turn made the settlers dependent on the Indians for their food supply. Tobacco cultivation required large amounts of land, so the colonists were forced to live dispersed and this made them more vulnerable. Further, those lands which were best for tobacco cultivation were said to be the most unhealthy for men. Greed was not the only sin being punished. George Sandys said the desire to live dispersed was fed by the colonists' wanting to "lyve like Libertines out of the eye of the Magistrate." He said that even if they had had ample warning of the Indians' plans, they were too dispersed to help each other. (Va. Co. Recs., IV, 70, 73, 172, 179)

Finally, the relative positions of the English and the Indians following the massacre are clearly shown by the fact that the colonists continued to be dependent on native suppliers for corn, and therefore continued to be vulnerable. In the months following the massacre, different types of expeditions were sent out for corn. Some were sent to territories defined as enemy and they were authorized to simply seize whatever they could. Others were sent to trade, but authorized to fight if "occasion shall be given by the Indians." Ralph Hamor in May, 1622, was authorized to take corn from the Indians if they would not trade, but his commission added parenthetically "(if he be able)." (Va. Co. Recs., III, 622, 678-9; 696-700; IV, 7) By 1623 the necessity to become self-sufficient in corn was clearly understood. Here begins a pattern of commanding the settlers to plant corn, and forbidding trading in corn. As often as these proclamations are made, exemptions are granted in the form of special licenses. In 1623 trading was forbidden partly because the governor believed Indians ostensibly trading actually came "to spy and observe the weaknes of our plantationes." (Va. Co. Recs., IV, 167) In May Governor Wyatt commanded the colonists to plant corn because it was dishonourable and dangerous to rely on "these base Salvages" for "our most necessarie food." Three days later he gave Gilbert Peppet a commission to trade for corn. (Va. Co. Recs., IV, 172, 189) In September, 1623 trading for corn was absolutely forbidden because it had devalued the English trading goods and kept people from planting corn. In November of the same year, Wyatt himself led an expedition to settle trade in the bay area. By January, 1624, the Council was saying that the food shortages were temporary and to be expected after such a massacre, and they pointed to a basic problem. The colonists could not make war on the Indians according to their basic strategy and be home tending their own corn. What they wanted was to be left free to cultivate their own fields, not to burn those of the Indians. (Va. Co. Recs., IV, 275-6, 399, 451-2; Jl. Va. Burgesses, 23-4) Also in January Ralph Hamor was given a license to carry on trade for the public benefit of the country. He was cautioned not to compel the Indians to trade, unless he suspected treachery on their part. On March 5, 1624, the Council and Assembly in Virginia ordered that all trading in corn with the "Savages" would be ended after June, 1624, and everyone was ordered to plant sufficient corn for his own family, with the price of corn being allowed to float. On March 16 Rawleigh Croshawe was given a commission to trade similar to Hamor's. In December of 1624 Robert Poole reported on his trading voyage, saying that they stayed at "Pocotanck" for "23 or 24 days in hope the Indyans would have furnisht them with Corne." (Va. Co. Recs., IV, 447-8, 470, 582-3; Mins. Va. Council and Gen. Ct., 30) The pattern of forbidding trading and punishing people who traded illegally and commanding planting of corn while making constant exceptions and sending out trading parties continued for many years. (Mins. Va. Council and Gen. Ct., 48, 50, 73, 86, 104, 136, 147, 167, 184-5, 193, 198) In 1638 George Donne felt he could sum up the cause of Virginia's troubles best by quoting Samuel Purchas's judgment after the massacre, which included: "Injuries to and from the savaldges and yet A necessity of their use and helpe." (Geo. Donne, 1638, 455)

New England's policy of vengeance paralleled that of Virginia. In addition to urging good treatment as the most intelligent approach to Indian relations, the New England colonists also attempted to win native support by manipulation of rivalries between tribes. But every provocation, they felt, must be met with a show of force. The settlers felt they had almost constant reinforcement for their idea that overawing the natives was the only proper approach to them. Again and again, the journal-keepers speak of the many tribes who came to them and sued for peace or alliance after a punitive expedition. Confirmation also came from the example of the improvident Wessagusset colonists who, according to the Plymouth historians, became utterly dependent on the Indians and were treated with extreme contempt by them. Thomas Dudley said the Indians "oppressed these weak English." So important was this policy of overawing the natives that the colonists considered revenge even when they clearly acknowledged that the Indians' acts against individual Englishmen were justified by extreme provocation on the Englishmen's parts. (Bradford, 1953, 88-9, 115-6, 259; Winthrop, 1908, I, 69, 139, 237-8, 269, 271, 299; Dudley in Emerson, ed., 1976, 69)

It was not the policy but the degree of vengeance exacted that troubled some writers. The Plymouth colony's move against the Indians at Wessagusset was criticized by their Leyden pastor, John Robinson, in one of the most famous letters of this literature:

Oh, how happy a thing had it been, if you had converted some before you had killed any! Besides, where blood is once begun to be shed, it is seldom staunched of a long time after. You will say they deserved it. I grant it; but upon what provocations and invitements by those heathenish Christians? Besides, you being no magistrates over them were to consider not what they deserved but what you were by necessity constrained to inflict.

Robinson goes on to say that at most they should have killed one or two principals as an example, "according to that approved rule, The punishment to a few, and the fear to many." (Bradford, 1953, 374-5)

In the Pequot War the justification was the conviction of the colonists that the Pequots were too dangerous to ignore. Massachusetts Bay took the lead in a policy which aimed at nothing less than the elimination of the Pequots as a tribal entity. Large numbers of Pequots were either killed or taken prisoner. Women and children were sometimes among those killed, as in the burning of the Pequot fort, and in one case, Winthrop admits, a captive was tortured to death by the Saybrook men in retaliation for torture deaths of some of their men. Those who were taken prisoner were dispersed among the towns of Massachusetts Bay and Connecticut and their status can only be guessed. Two women and 15 boys who were sent to Old Providence in the West Indies were almost certainly made slaves. (Bradford, 1953, 397-8; Winthrop, 1908, I, 218-9, 225-8) Plymouth was a reluctant ally in the Pequot War. Bradford wrote to Winthrop his conviction that it was Massachusetts which had occasioned the war. Winthrop's complex answer revolved around his conviction that if even 100 were left alive, they could do as much harm as the entire tribe was ever likely to do. Thus, as in Virginia after the massacre, a policy of vengeance was based on or justified by the right of self-preservation. (Winthrop, 1908, I, 194) In 1640 the plantations in Connecticut wrote jointly to Massachusetts "wherein they declared their dislike of such as would have the Indians rooted out, as being of the cursed race of Ham, and their desire of our mutual accord in seeking to gain them by justice and kindness . . ." Winthrop wrote back "our consent" but Massachusetts refused to join in any pact with Aquiday, a dissident plantation. (Winthrop, 1908, II, 18-19)

John Winthrop and the leaders of Massachusetts felt they were acting on a recognized principle in exacting extreme vengeance for wrongs done. This was not lawless justice justified by the fact that the enemy was racially or culturally inferior. There is one clear statement of the principle of vengeance in this literature and in it John Winthrop is justifying Indian vengeance against Englishmen. Winthrop records that Connecticut wrote to him asking for advice on a legal problem. They had found out that Sequin and his "Indians of the river" had "procured" the Pequots to make an onslaught on Wethersfield the previous year. Sequin had given the land to the settlers on the condition that he could settle by them and be protected by them. "When he came to Weathersfield, and had set down his wigwam, they drave him away by force." Since he was relatively weak, he secretly got the Pequots to do his vengeance. The answer of the elders and magistrates assembled by Winthrop is surprising and interesting enough to justify extensive quotation:

That, if the cause were thus, Sequin might, upon this injury first offered by them, right himself either by force or fraud, and that by the law of nations; and though the damage he had done them had been one hundred times more than what he sustained from them, that is not considerable in point of a just war; neither was he bound (upon such an open act of hostility publicly maintained) to seek satisfaction first in a peaceable way; it was enough, that he had complained of it as an injury and breach of covenant.

Winthrop further recorded that Connecticut took their advice and made a new treaty with Sequin. (Winthrop, 1908, I, 265-6; Conn. Recs., 16, 19-20)

Puritan writers were convinced that their victories represented the will of God, that God delivered their enemies into their hands. (Winthrop, 1908, I, 221, 227-8) The most extreme statement of this belief occurs in Bradford's description of the burning of the Pequot fort with its inhabitants:

It was a fearful sight to see them thus frying in the fire and the streams of blood quenching the same, and horrible was the stink and scent thereof; but the victory seemed a sweet sacrifice, and they gave the praise thereof to God, who had wrought so wonderfully for them, thus to enclose their enemies in their hands and give them so speedy a victory over so proud and insulting an enemy. (Bradford, 1953, 296)

This formulation, though not in such extreme form, appears again and again with fellow Englishmen, not Indians, being the subjects of divine vengeance. It was dangerous to be the enemy of these Puritans. Winthrop reported that two wicked servants drowned, the "evident judgment of God upon them." God prevented the escape of several who had broken the law. (Winthrop, 1908, I, 103-4, 322) Sir Ferdinando Gorges, who held a rival claim to New England, and his agents were prevented by God from prospering. (Winthrop, 1908, I, 152-3; II, 11) Finally several critics of Massachusetts Bay who tried to divert prospective colonists from coming to New England suffered devastating losses, all demonstrations of the judgement of God against them. One family ended up as slaves in Algiers. Mariners who had scoffed at the divine worship of the Puritans, were blown up with their ship, "wherein the judgment of God appeared." (Winthrop, 1908, II, 9-12) Sometimes, William Bradford is more cautious than Winthrop. Twice he reports that some people think the losses of Plymouth's enemies are God's judgment, "but God's judgments are unsearchable." But elsewhere he drops this caution. A sailor on the Mayflower who ridiculed the Pilgrims died and was buried at sea, which his fellows noted was "the just hand of God upon him." As in Winthrop's story, those who scoff at or attempt to cheat the Pilgrims too often find, as John Pierce did, that "the Lord marvelously crossed him." (Bradford, 1953, 58, 118-9, 124, 177, 233, 290) It was the quality of being an enemy which set all these people apart with the Pequots burning in their fort.

Each colony learned for itself that the Indians could not and would not accept the role of the younger brethren of the English. European culture was not the powerful magnet for Indians which colonization promoters assumed it would be, so Indians were not willing to submerge or forsake their own culture in favor of the "civilization" offered by the English. Nor was English technology at first the powerful instrument for forcing Indian cooperation which promoters assumed. The technology and culture of Indians on America's east coast were genuine rivals to those of the English and the eventual outcome of the rivalry was not at first clear. In these circumstances, whatever those comfortable people who remained in England wrote, colonists were faced with the necessity of coping with a formidable people on whom they were encroaching and on whom they, intermittently at least, were dependent. Much of what is taken for contempt in their writings is really the voice of vulnerability speaking. One can only speculate what the outcome of the rivalry would have been if the impact of European diseases on the American population had not been so devastating. If colonists had not been able to occupy lands already cleared by Indian farmers who had vanished, colonization would have proceeded much more slowly. If Indian culture had not been devastated by the physical and psychological assaults it had suffered, colonization might not have proceeded at all in the 16th and 17th centuries. European diseases did more than European technology to vanquish the American Indian in the early years of colonization.

We began by documenting the enormous interest on the part of English people, colonists and those who stayed home, in the culture and life of the American Indians as the colonies were being founded. One of the conclusions which English people derived from the wealth of information sent home was that the Indians had an interesting culture and one that clearly fulfilled the requirements of civil life. This realization was reinforced by the conclusion that American Indians were in no fundamental way different from Europeans, that they were racially similar and that they would soon be indistinguishable from Europeans. Despite the military clashes and exploitation, this line of reasoning about the Indians continues in some writers throughout the period. Some of the most enthusiastic descriptions of Indian culture come from the end of the period.

Just at the end of the period, though, those people who admire Indian culture begin to diverge from the earlier themes in one way; that is, they begin to see Indian culture as something which Europeans might respect and leave alone at least in some of its aspects. No writer could assume that Christianity should not be imposed on Indians, but observers such as Thomas Morton and William Wood begin in a very tentative way to suggest that the Indians need not become indistinguishable from Europeans. Though this seems to underly much of what they write, it is stated clearly only when they discuss Indian clothes. Clothes, as we have seen, were of primary importance as a badge of identity. To accept that the Indians should continue to dress in their traditional way was to accept a continuation of their separate identity. Yet, this is just what Morton and Wood proposed. (Morton, 1637, 23; Wood, 1634, 65)

Unfortunately, this new idea that the Indians should be viewed as permanently separate from the English contained the seeds of racism. As long as the English believed that the Indians were their "younger brothers," that the Americans were different in no fundamental way, they could not be viewed as inherently inferior to Europeans. Once the differences between the two groups came to be seen as important and continuing, it would be a short step to seeing the different life of the Indians as less valuable than the European way of life, and to attributing their different patterns of development to qualities inherent in each group. Both of these traditions developed through the remainder of the 17th century, though the attitude of respect grows much rarer. When English colonists later in the century began to rely massively on African slaves as a labor supply and to categorize servants purely on the basis of race, this could meld with the idea that Indians were permanently different from Europeans to make them co-victims of racism. The criteria by which people were classified shifted from manipulable cultural traits to theoretically inherent racially bound traits.

The belief that expropriation and enslavement of the Indians was legitimate grew as a result of experiences in America. The fact that the precedent of the Israelites' war against the Canaanites was used so sparingly and so carefully points to the assumption that there was no intention in the beginning to sweep away the Indians in America. The American experience allowed, in the absence of the normal constraints of English society, unrestricted power over other human beings. It was the ultimate powerlessness of the Indians, not their racial inferiority, which made it possible to see them as people without rights.

Europeans of the late 16th and early 17th centuries were capable of acting with barbarity toward those who were powerless, whether these were Indians, Africans, or fellow Europeans. The civilization of which they were so proud and so confident was not fully internalized. When they were outside their normal society and its constraints, their deviations from the standards of civilization could be enormous. This was especially true if, as in the case of colonization, the condition of being separated meant personal risk and the possibility of great power over other human beings. It was the effect of unrestricted power, not preconceived racism, which caused the English to treat the American Indians as they did. If, in the period after 1640, the American Indians were the subjects of racism by English people, the conclusion must be that this racism was a product of, not the cause of, the treatment of Indians by colonists.

Appendix
Profiles of the Writers[1]

These profiles give the writers' social status first. Gentry status is assigned on the basis of a writer's identification of himself, or of his having been to a university or the Inns of Court,[2] having served in Parliament or city government, or on the board of directors of one of the great trading companies. Governors of colonies have been assumed, in most cases, to have been gentlemen.

After status, the profiles give education, occupation, travel experience and religious affiliation where these are known. Where religion is unknown, adherence to the Church of England is assumed.

The names of eyewitness writers are set in bold type.

Sir William Alexander (Scot.). Gent., created Earl of Stirling, 1633. Glasgow and Leyden Universities. Courtier, poet, royal tutor. Continental travel. Anglican, supporter of Laud. (Calder, 1966, 87)

Capt. Gabriel **Archer.** Gent. Cambridge University; Gray's Inn. Military career. Anglican (assumed). (Barbour, 1964, 122-123)

Capt. Samuel **Argall.** Gent., knighted 1622. Military career, acting Governor of Virginia. Served in continental wars. Anglican (assumed). (Barbour, 1969, 67-70)

Arthur **Barlowe.** Origins unknown. Naval career. Continental travel. Anglican (assumed). (Quinn, 1955, 15)

Thomas **Best.** Servant in Virginia.

William **Bradford.** Yeoman family. Governor of Plymouth colony. Lived on continent. Separatist Puritan.

John **Brereton.** Gent. Caius College, Cambridge, M.A. Cleric. Anglican (assumed).

---

1. Information for these profiles is taken from biographies in the *Dictionary of National Biography;* the *Dictionary of American Biography;* the *Dictionary of Canadian Biography;* Brown, *Genesis of the United States,* II; and Theodore K. Rabb, *Enterprise and Empire: Merchant and Gentry Investment in the Expansion of England, 1575-1630* (Cambridge, Mass., 1967). Where information from other sources is used, these sources are noted.

2. Kelso, *Doctrine of the English Gentleman,* p. 27.

Capt. Nathaniel **Butler.** Gent. Naval career, Governor of Bermuda. Anglican (assumed). (Davis, 1955, 178-179)

T.C. Identity unknown.

Cecilius Calvert, Lord Baltimore. Gent. Founder of Maryland. Roman Catholic.

Leonard **Calvert.** Gent. Brother of Lord Baltimore. First Governor of Maryland. Roman Catholic.

Thomas **Canner.** Gent. Barnard's Inn. Anglican (assumed).

William **Capps.** Origins unknown. Ancient planter in Virginia.

Christopher Carleill. Gent., son-in-law of Sir Francis Walsingham. Cambridge University. Military career. Served in continental wars and in Ireland. Anglican (assumed).

Richard **Clarke.** Origins unknown. Navigator and privateer. Continental travel. Anglican (assumed).

Patrick Copland. Origins unknown. Cleric. African travel. Anglican, became radical Puritan in later life. (Levy, 1960, 94, 128)

John Cotton. Not an eyewitness when he wrote *The Planter's Plea*. Gent. Trinity College, Cambridge; fellow and Head Lecturer of Emmanuel College. Cleric. Puritan.

Matthew Cradock. Gent. First Governor of Massachusetts Bay Company, Member of Parliament. Puritan.

Richard Crakanthorpe. Gent. Queen's College, Oxford, fellow. Cleric, Chaplain to James I and the Bishop of London. (Wright, 1943, 96)

William Crashaw. Gent. St. John's College, Cambridge, fellow. Cleric, active in Virginia Company. Anglican or moderate Puritan.[3]

Robert **Cushman.** Origins unknown. Worked as wool-comber in Leyden, but was a man of means. Lived on continent. Separatist Puritan.

Sir Thomas **Dale.** Gent., knighted 1606. Military career, Governor of Virginia. Served in continental wars. Anglican (assumed).

Thomas **Dermer.** Origins unknown. Explorer, commander of expedition. Anglican (assumed).

George **Donne.** Gent. Second son of John Donne. Military career. Service and prison on continent. Anglican (assumed). (Donne, 1638, 449-451)

John Donne. Gent. Oxford University; Lincoln's Inn. Cleric. Continental travel. Anglican.

Grigorey **Dorey.** Servant in Virginia.

---

3. L. B. Wright says Crashaw condemned "Catholics and nonconformists with equal severity," *Religion and Empire*, p. 100. Babette Levy and Alexander Brown classify Crashaw as a moderate Puritan: Levy, "Early Puritanism," p. 101; Brown, *Genesis of the United States*, II, 867.

Michael Drayton. Gent. Page in household of Sir Henry Goodere. Poet. Anglican (assumed).

Thomas **Dudley.** Gent. Latin School, page in household of Earl of Northampton. Steward of Earl of Lincoln, Governor of Massachusetts Bay. Service on continent. Puritan.

Richard Eburne. Origins unknown. Cleric. Anglican (assumed).

John **Eliot.** Gent. Jesus College, Cambridge. Cleric, missionary to the Indians. Puritan.

Capt. John **Endecott.** Gent. Leader of advance party sent by Massachusetts Bay Company to Salem, 1628. Puritan (assumed).

Sir Robert Gordon of Lochinvar (Scot.). Gent. Anglican (assumed).

Sir Ferdinando Gorges. Gent., knighted 1591. Oxford University. Military career, Member of Parliament, Governor of Plymouth Fort. Served in the continental wars. Anglican. (Preston, 1953)

Bartholomew **Gosnold.** Gent. Cambridge University; Middle Temple. Naval career. Anglican (assumed). (Gookin and Barbour, 1963)

Thomas **Graves.** Origins unknown. Engineer. Puritan (assumed).

Robert Gray. Gent. St. John's College, Cambridge. Cleric. Anglican (assumed). (Wright, 1943, 92)

John **Guy.** Gent. Governor in Newfoundland, Alderman of Bristol, Member of Parliament. Anglican (assumed).

Richard Hakluyt, elder. Gent. Middle Temple. Lawyer. Anglican (assumed).

Richard Hakluyt. Gent. Christ Church, Oxford. Cleric, editor. Continental service. Anglican.

Ralph **Hamor.** Gent. Brasenose College, Oxford. Important figure in Virginia. Anglican (assumed).

Thomas **Hariot.** Gent. St. Mary's Hall, Oxford. Scientist, mathematician. Anglican, accused of skepticism.

Edward **Hayes.** Gent. King's College, Cambridge. Projector. Possible continental travel. Anglican, possible Puritan outlook. (Quinn, 1974a, Chap. 8)

Robert **Hayman.** Gent. Exeter College, Oxford; Lincoln's Inn. Governor in Newfoundland. Anglican (assumed).

Francis **Higginson.** Gent. Jesus College, Cambridge, M.A. Cleric. Puritan.

Nicholas **Hoskins.** Gent. Roman Catholic (assumed).

David **Ingram.** Origins unknown. Sailor. Possible African travel. Anglican (assumed).

Robert Johnson. Gent. Grocer, Director of several companies for overseas exploitation, Sheriff and Alderman of London. Anglican.

Ralph **Lane.** Gent. Military career, Governor at Roanoke. Service in Ireland. Anglican (assumed).
Christopher **Levett.** Gent. Woodward of Somersetshire, commanded ship against Spain, 1625. Continental travel. Anglican, with Puritan leanings. (Baxter, 1893)
Francis Magnel (Irish). Sailor. Interrogated in Spain about Virginia.
Capt. John **Martin.** Gent. Son of Lord Mayor of London. Inns of Court. Military career, Member of Council in Virginia.
John **Mason.** Gent. Magdalen College, Oxford. Cartographer, Governor in Newfoundland. Anglican.
William **Morrell.** Gent. Carried Church of England commission to oversee New England churches, but never used it. Cleric. Anglican.
Thomas **Morton.** Gent. Clifford's Inn. Lawyer. Anglican.
George Mourt, born Morton. Gent. Merchant. Lived on continent. Puritan.
Anthony **Parkhurst.** Gent. Merchant and adventurer. African and Caribbean travel. Anglican (assumed).
Sir George Peckham. Gent., knighted 1570. Promoter. Roman Catholic, imprisoned for harboring priests. (Quinn, 1974a, 371)
John **Penreis.** Gent. Vice Admiral in Virginia. Anglican (assumed).
George **Percy.** Gent. Son of Earl of Northumberland. Military career, acting Governor in Virginia. Served in continental wars. Anglican (assumed).
John **Pond.** Servant in Massachusetts Bay.
Robert **Poole.** Origins unknown. Interpreter in Virginia, agent for George Sandys. (Davis, 1955, 166)
John **Pory.** Gent. Gonville and Caius College, Cambridge, M.A. Writer, Member of Parliament, Secretary of State in Virginia, First Speaker of Virginia House of Burgesses. Travel on continent and in Near East. Anglican.
Dr. John **Pott.** Gent. Cambridge University. Physician, acting Governor in Virginia, 1628. Anglican (assumed). (Morgan, 1975, 122; Davis, 1955, 190)
Capt. Daniel **Powell.** Origins unknown. Roman Catholic (assumed).
Daniel Price. Gent. Exeter College, Oxford; Middle Temple. Cleric, Chaplain to James I and Charles I. Anglican.
Martin **Pringe.** Origins unknown. Ship Captain. World travel. Anglican (assumed).
Samuel Purchas. Gent. St. John's College, Cambridge, M.A. Cleric, Chaplain to Archbishop Abbot, editor. Anglican.
R. **Rich.** Identity unknown. Gent. Military career. Anglican (assumed). (Rich, 1610, vii-viii)

John Robinson. Gent. Cambridge University, probably fellow of Corpus Christi College. Cleric. Lived on continent. Puritan.
John **Rolfe.** Gent. Member of Council in Virginia. Anglican.
James **Rosier.** Gent. Roman Catholic. (Quinn, 1974a, 389)
Sir Edwin Sandys. Gent. Son of Archbishop of York, knighted 1603. Corpus Christi College, Oxford; Middle Temple. Member of Parliament, Treasurer of Virginia Company in London, 1619 to 1624. Traveled on continent. Anglican.
George **Sandys.** Gent. Brother of Sir Edwin. St. Mary's Hall, Oxford; Middle Temple. Poet, Treasurer in Virginia. Travel on continent and Near East. Anglican. (Davis, 1955)
John **Smith.** Yeoman family, grant of arms from Sigismundus Bathori was registered by the Garter King at Arms. Grammar school. Military career, Governor in Virginia. Anglican. (Arber and Bradley, 1910, I, vi-vii)
Henry **Spelman.** Gent. Nephew or son of Sir Henry Spelman, the antiquary. Interpreter, Captain in Virginia. Anglican (assumed).[4]
Master **Stockam.** Gent. Cleric. Anglican (assumed).
John **Stoneman.** Origins unknown. Pilot. Anglican (assumed).
William **Strachey.** Gent. Emmanuel College, Cambridge; Gray's Inn. Writer, Secretary of Virginia Colony. Continental travel. Anglican.
William Symonds. Gent. Magdalen College, Oxford. Cleric. Anglican.[5]
Capt. George **Thorpe.** Gent. Member of Parliament, Gentleman of the Privy Chamber, Deputy in charge of the Indian College in Virginia, Member of Council in Virginia. Anglican (assumed).
William **Tucker.** Gent. Ship Captain, merchant's factor in Virginia, Member of Council in Virginia. Anglican (assumed).
Capt. John **Underhill.** Origins unknown. Military career. Continental service. Puritan, became extreme sectarian.
Sir William **Vaughan** (Welsh). Gent., knighted 1628. Jesus College, Oxford, M.A.; Vienna, L.L.D Writer, Sheriff of Carmarthenshire. Studied on continent. Anglican (assumed).
Philip **Vincent.** Gent. Peterhouse College, Cambridge. Cleric. Travel on continent and in Guiana. Puritan.
Edward Waterhouse. Origins unknown. Secretary of the Virginia Company. Anglican (assumed).

4. Brown, *Genesis of the United States,* II, 1020-1021, and Arber and Bradley, eds., *Travels and Works of John Smith,* ci, say Spelman was the antiquarian's third son. The *Dictionary of National Biography* follows them in this. Barbour, Jamestown Voyages, I, 5 says he was a nephew.

5. L. B. Wright contends that Symonds later went to Virginia, *Religion and Empire,* p. 90.

Thomas **West,** Lord De La Warr. Noble. Oxford, M.A. Military career, Governor in Virginia, implicated in the Essex rebellion. Served in the continental wars. Anglican.

Alexander **Whitaker.** Gent. Father of Master of St. John's College, Cambridge, Regius Professor Divinity. Eton; Trinity College, Cambridge, M.A. Cleric. Moderate Puritan. (Levy, 1960, 99-100)

Richard **Whitbourne.** Origins unknown. Sea Captain, Governor in Newfoundland. Traveled from age 15. Anglican (assumed).

Fr. Andrew **White.** Gent. S. Albans College, Valladolid; St. Hermenegild's College, Seville; Douai. Member of the Society of Jesus. University teacher, missionary to the Indians. Roman Catholic. May be author of *A Relation of Maryland*.

John **White.** Gent. Painter, Governor in Roanoke. Anglican (assumed).

John White. Gent. New College, Oxford, M.A., elected Warden. Cleric. Puritan.

William **White.** Origins unknown. Listed as laborer in Smith's *Map of Virginia, Part II*.

Roger **Williams.** Gent. Son of a shopkeeper. Patronage of Sir Edward Coke enabled him to attend Charterhouse and Pembroke Hall, Cambridge. Cleric, Chaplain to Sir William Masham. Puritan, became extreme sectarian.

Capt. Edward Maria **Wingfield.** Gent. Military career, First President of Council in Virginia. Service on continent. Of Roman Catholic family.

Edward **Winslow.** Gent. Colonial agent, agent for Cromwell government. Travel on continent. Separatist Puritan.

John **Winthrop.** Gent. Trinity College, Cambridge; Gray's Inn; Inner Temple. Lawyer, first Governor of Massachusetts Bay. Puritan.

William **Wood.** Gent. Probably at Cambridge. Puritan (assumed).

Samuel Wrote. Gent. Member of Royal Council for Virginia in London. Anglican (assumed).

Sir Francis **Wyatt.** Gent., knighted 1603. Oxford University; Gray's Inn. Military career, Governor of Virginia, 1621-1626, 1639-1641. Anglican (assumed). (Davis, 1955, 190)

Lady **Wyatt.** Gent. Daughter of Sir Samuel Sandys, eldest son of Archbishop of York. Married 1618, joined husband in Virginia in 1623. Anglican (assumed).

George Wyatt. Gent. Father of Sir Francis, Grandson of poet Sir Thomas Wyatt and son of rebel of same name. Writer on historical and military subjects. Military service on continent. Anglican. (Wyatt, 1624, 104-111)

Capt. Edward **Wynne.** Gent. Governor in Newfoundland. Roman Catholic (assumed).

Sir George **Yeardley.** Gent., knighted 1617. Military career, Governor of Virginia, 1619-1621, 1626-1627. Service on continent. Anglican (assumed).

Capt. Thomas Yong. Gent. Commander of fleet of ships. Roman Catholic (assumed). (Hall, 1910)

Bibliography

I. Works written before 1640.

Anon. 1584-5. "For Master Rauleys Viage." In *Roanoke Voyages*. Ed. D. B. Quinn. I, 130-139.

Anon. 1585. *The voyage made by Sir Richard Greenvile*. In *Roanoke Voyages*, Ed. D. B. Quinn, I, 178-193.

Anon. 1602. *A briefe Note of the sending another barke by Sir Walte Ralegh*. In *Briefe and true Relation*. J. Brereton, p. 14.

Anon. 1619. "Letter. From Captaine Martyn his Plantation." In *Purchas His Pilgrimes*. XIX, 134-135.

Anon. 1625. *The description of the Countrey of Mawooshen*. In *Purchas His Pilgrimes*. XIX, 400-405.

Anon. 1635. *A Relation of Maryland*. Ed. Francis L. Hawks. J. Sabin, New York, 1865.

Alexander, William, Earl of Stirling. 1630. *The Mapp and Description of New-England*. London. Known as *An Encouragement to Colonies*.

Archer, Gabriel. 1602. *The Relation of Captaine Gosnols Voyage to the North part of Virginia*. In *Purchas His Pilgrimes*. XVIII, 302-313.

———. 1607a. *A breif discription of the People*. In *Jamestown Voyages*. Ed. P. L. Barbour. I, 102-104.

———. 1607b. *The Discription of the now discovered River and Country of Virginia*. In *Jamestown Voyages*. Ed. P. L. Barbour. I, 98-102.

———. 1607c. *A relatyon of the Discovery of our River*. In *Jamestown Voyages*, Ed. P. L. Barbour. I, 80-98.

Argall, Samuel. 1610. *The Voyage of Captaine Samuel Argal*. In *Purchas His Pilgrimes*. XIX, 73-84.

Argall, Samuel. 1613. "A Letter of Sir Samuell Argoll touching his Voyage to Virginia." In *Purchas His Pilgrimes*. XIX, 90-95.

Bacon, Francis. 1625. "Of Plantations." In *The Essayes or Counsels, Civill and Morall*. London.

Baltimore, Lord. 1633. *A Coppy of Instructions to the Governor and Commissioners of his province of Maryland*. In *Narratives of Early Maryland*. Ed. C. C. Hall. Pp. 16-23.

Barlowe, Arthur. 1584. *The first voyage made to the coastes of America.* In *Roanoke Voyages.* Ed. D. B. Quinn. I, 91-116.

Benson, George. 1609. *A Sermon preached at Paules Crosse.* London.

Best, George. 1578. *Experiences and reasons of the Sphere, to proove all partes of the worlde habitable.* In *Principal Navigations.* Ed. R. Hakluyt. VII, 252-283.

Best, George. 1938. *The Three Voyages of Martin Frobisher In search of a passage to Cathay and India by the North-West, A.D. 1576-8.* Ed. Vilhjalmur Stefansson. Argonaut Press, London.

Bradford, William and Winslow, Edward. 1622. *A Relation or Journall of the English Plantation setled at Plimoth in New England.* London. Known as *Mourt's Relation.*

Bradford, William. 1953. *Of Plymouth Plantation, 1620-1647.* Ed. Samuel Eliot Morison. Knopf, New York.

Brereton, John. 1602. *A Briefe and true Relation of the Discoverie of the North part of Virginia.* 2nd ed. London.

Brerewood, Edward. 1614. *Enquiries Touching the diversity of Languages, and Religions through the cheife parts of the world.* London.

C., T. 1623. *A Short Discourse of the New-Found-Land.* Dublin.

Calvert, Leonard. 1638. "Letter of Governor Leonard Calvert to Lord Baltimore." In *Narratives of Early Maryland.* Ed. C. C. Hall, Pp. 150-159.

Calvin, John. 1957. *John Calvin On the Christian Faith: Selections from the Institutes, Commentaries, and Tracts.* Ed. John T. McNeill. Liberal Arts Press, New York.

Canner, Thomas. 1603. *A Relation of the Voyage made to Virginia.* In *Purchas His Pilgrimes.* XVIII, 329-335.

Carleill, Christopher. 1583. *A briefe and summary discourse upon the intended voyage to the hithermost parts of America.* In *Gilbert Voyages.* Ed. D. B. Quinn. II, 351-364.

Clarke, Richard. 1583. *A relation of Richard Clarke of Weymouth.* In *Gilbert Voyages.* Ed. D. B. Quinn. II, 423-426.

Copland, Patrick. 1622a. *Virginia's God be Thanked.* London.

———. 1622b. *A Declaration how the monies were disposed.* London.

Cotton, John. 1630. *God's Promise to His Plantation.* London.

Crakanthorpe, Richard. 1609. *A Sermon at the Inauguration of King James.* London.

Crashaw, William. 1610. *A Sermon Preached in London before the right honourable the Lord Lawarre.* London.

Cushman, Robert. 1622a. *A Sermon Preached in Plimmoth in New-England.* London.

———. 1622b. *Reasons and Considerations touching the lawfulnesse of removing out of England into the parts of America.* In Bradford and Winslow, *Relation.* Pp. 65-72.

Dale, Sir Thomas. 1615. "Letter." In Hamor, *True Discourse.* Pp. 51-59.

Dermer, Thomas. 1619. "Letter." In *Purchas His Pilgrimes.* XIX, 129-134.

Donne, George. 1638. *Virginia Reviewed.* Ed. T. H. Breen. *William and Mary Quarterly.* 3rd Ser., 30 (1973), 449-466.

Donne, John. 1624. "Verse. To his friend Captaine John Smith, and his Worke." In Smith, *Generall Historie.* Pp. 284-285.

Donne, John. 1626. *A Sermon Preached to the Honourable Company of the Virginian Plantation.* In *Five Sermons upon Special Occasions.* London.

Drayton, Michael. 1619. "To the Virginian Voyage." In *The Works of Michael Drayton.* Ed. W. J. Hebel. Basil Blackwell for the Shakespeare Head Press. Oxford, 1961, II, 363-364.

Drayton, Michael. 1622. "To Master George Sandys, Treasurer for the English Colony in Virginia." In *Works.* Ed. W. J. Hebel, III, 206-208.

Dudley, Thomas. 1631. "Letter to the Countess of Lincoln." In *Letters From New England.* Ed. Everett Emerson. Pp. 66-83.

Eburne, Richard. 1624. *A Plain Pathway to Plantations.* Ed. Louis B. Wright. Cornell University Press for the Folger Shakespeare Library, Ithaca, New York, 1962.

Floyd, John. 1612. *The Overthrow of the Protestants Pulpit-Babels.* n.p.

Gordon of Lochinvar, Robert. 1625. *Encouragements to Under-takers.* Edinburgh.

Gorges, Ferdinando (?) 1622. *A Briefe Relation of the Discovery and Plantation of New England.* London.

Gosnold, Bartholomew. 1602. "Master Bartholomew Gosnolds Letter to his Father." In *Purchas His Pilgrimes.* XVIII, 300-302.

Graves, Thomas. 1630. "A Letter sent from New-England by Master Graves, Engineer, now there resident." First published in Higginson, *New England's Plantation,* 3rd ed. Rpt. in *Chronicles of First Planters of Massachusetts Bay.* Ed. A. Young, Pp. 264-266.

Gray, Robert. 1609. *A Good Speed to Virginia.* London.

Guy, John. 1611. "Master John Guy his Letter to the Counsell of the New-foundland Plantation." In *Purchas His Pilgrimes.* XIX, 410-416.

Guy, John. 1612. "Letter to the Councell, and Company of the New-foundland Plantation." In *Purchas His Pilgrimes.* XIX, 417-424.

Hakewill, George. 1635. *An Apologie or Declaration of the Power and Providence of God in the Government of the World.* Oxford.

Hakluyt, Richard (lawyer). 1578. *Notes framed by a Gentleman.* In *Gilbert Voyages.* Ed. D. B. Quinn. I, 181-186.

Hakluyt, Richard (lawyer). 1585. *Inducements to the Liking of the Voyage intended towards Virginia.* In *Writings.* Ed. E. G. R. Taylor. II, 327-338.

Hakluyt, Richard. n.d. *A briefe extract concerning the discoverie of New-found-land, taken out of the booke of M. Robert Thorne.* In *Principal Navigations.* VII, 155.

———. 1582a. *Divers Voyages Touching the Discovery of America.* Ed. John Winter Jones. Hakluyt Society, London, 1850.

———. 1582b. *A Note of Sebastian Gabotes Voyage of Discoverie.* In *Divers Voyages.* Pp. 23-24.

———. 1584. *A Particuler discourse concerninge the Westerne discoveries.* Known as the *Discourse of Western Planting.* In *Writings.* Ed. E. G. R. Taylor. II, 211-326.

———. 1587a. "Epistle Dedicatory" to *De Orbe novo Petri Martyris.* In *Writings.* Ed. E. G. R. Taylor. II, 362-369.

———. 1587b. "Epistle Dedicatory" to R. Laudonnière, *A Notable Historie containing foure voyages unto Florida.* In *Writings.* Ed. E. G. R. Taylor. II, 372-378.

———. 1589a. "Epistle Dedicatory" in *Principall Navigations.* In *Writings.* Ed. E. G. R. Taylor. II, 396-401.

———. 1589b. "Preface to the reader" in *Principall Navigations.* In *Writings.* Ed. E. G. R. Taylor. II, 401-409.

———. 1589c. *The Principall Navigations, Voiages, and Discoveries of the English Nation.* Ed. David B. Quinn and Raleigh A. Skelton. 2 vols. Cambridge, Cambridge University Press for the Hakluyt Society and the Peabody Museum of Salem, 1965.

———. 1589d. *The third voyage to the reliefe of the Colonie planted in Virginia.* In *Roanoke Voyages.* Ed. D. B. Quinn. I, 477-480.

———. 1589e. *The voyage of Madoc in the yeere 1170.* In *Principall Navigations.* II, 506-507.

———. 1589f. *The voyage of M. Hore and divers other gentlemen, to Newfoundland, and Cape Briton, in the yere 1536.* In *Writings.* Ed. E. G. R. Taylor. II, 390-394.

———. 1598a. "Epistle Dedicatorie" to *Principal Navigations.* In *Writings.* Ed. E. G. R. Taylor. II, 426-432.

———. 1598b. "Preface to the Reader" in *Principal Navigations.* In *Writings.* Ed. E. G. R. Taylor. II, 433-451.

———. 1598-1600. *The Principal Navigations, Voyages, Traffiques and Discoveries of the English Nation.* 12 vols. James MacLehose and Sons, Glasgow, 1904.

———. 1599. "Epistle Dedicatory" to *Principal Navigations.* In *Writings.* Ed. E. G. R. Taylor. II, 469-475.

———. 1609. "Epistle Dedicatory" to de Soto, *Virginia Richly Valued.* In *Writings.* Ed. E. G. R. Taylor. II, 499-503.

Hamor, Ralph. 1615. *A True Discourse of the Present Estate of Virginia.* London.

Hariot, Thomas. 1588. *A briefe and true report of the new found land of Virginia.* In *Roanoke Voyages.* Ed. D. B. Quinn. I, 317-387.

Hariot, Thomas, 1590. *Notes* to the paintings of John White. In *Roanoke Voyages.* Ed. D.B. Quinn. I, 398-444.

Hayes, Edward, 1583. *A report of the voyage by sir Humfrey Gilbert knight*. In *Gilbert Voyages*. Ed. D.B. Quinn. II, 385-423.

Hayes, Edward. 1602. *A Treatise, conteining important inducements for the planting in these parts, and finding a passage that way to the South Sea and China*. In Brereton, *Briefe and true Relation*. Pp. 15-24.

Hayman, Robert. 1628. *Quodlibets, lately come over from New Britaniola, Old New found-land*. London.

Higginson, Francis. 1630. *New Englands Plantation*. In *Tracts*. Comp. P. Force. I, no. 12.

Hoskins, Nicholas, 1622. "Letter." In *Discourse and Discovery*. R. Whitbourne.

Ingram, David. 1582. *The Relation of David Ingram of Barking*. In *Gilbert Voyages*. Ed. D.B. Quinn. II, 283-296.

James I. 1606. *Part of the first Patent for Virginia*. In *Purchas His Pilgrimes*. XVIII, 399-403.

James I. 1610. *The beginning of the Patent for New-found-land*. In *Purchas His Pilgrimes*. XIX, 406-409.

Johnson, Robert. 1609. *Nova Brittania*. In *Tracts*. Comp. P. Force. I, No. 6.

Johnson, Robert. 1612. *The New Life of Virginea*. In *Tracts*. Comp. P. Force. I, no. 7.

Lane, Ralph. 1585. "An extract of Master Lanes letter from Virginia." In *Roanoke Voyages*. Ed. D.B. Quinn. I, 207-210.

Lane, Ralph. 1586. *An account of the particularities of the imployments of the English men left in Virginia by sir Richard Greenevill*. In *Roanoke Voyages*. Ed. D.B. Quinn. I, 255-294.

Levett, Christopher. 1624. *A Voyage into New England*. London.

Magnel, Francis. 1610. *Relation of what Francis Magnel, an Irishman, learned in the land of Virginia during the eight months he was there*. In *Jamestown Voyages*. Ed. P.L. Barbour. I, 151-157.

Mason, John. 1620. *A Briefe Discourse of the New-found land*. Edinburgh.

Massachusetts Bay Company. 1629 a. "The Company's First General Letter of Instructions to Endicott and his Council." In *Chronicles of First Planters of Massachusetts Bay*. Ed. A. Young. Pp. 141-171.

Massachusetts Bay Company. 1629b. "The company's Second General Letter of Instructions to Endicott and his Council." In *Chronicles of First Planters of Massachusetts Bay*. Ed. A. Young. Pp. 172-191.

Morrell, William. 1625. *New-England*. London.

Morton, Thomas. 1637. *New English Canaan*. In *Tracts*. Comp. P. Force. II, No. 5. (Internal evidence points to the 1637 date rather than the 1632 date Force assigns.)

New England, Adventurers. 1630. *Proportion of Provisions needfull for such as intend to plant themselves in New England, for one whole yeare*. London.

Parkhurst, Anthony. 1578. "A letter conteining a report of the true state and commodities of Newfoundland." In *Hakluyt Writings*. Ed. E.G.R. Taylor. I, 127-134.

Peckham, George. 1583. *A True Reporte of the Newfound Landes*. In *Gilbert Voyages*. Ed. D.B. Quinn. II, 435-482.

Percy, George. 1607. *Observations gathered out of a Discourse*. In *Purchas His Pilgrimes*. XVIII, 403-419.

Powell, Daniel. 1622. "Another Letter to Master Secretary Calvert." In *Discourse and Discovery*. R. Whitbourne.

Price, Daniel. 1609. *Sauls Prohibition Staide*. London.

Pringe, Martin. 1603. *A Voyage set out from the Citie of Bristoll*. In *Purchas His Pilgrimes*. XVIII, 322-329.

Purchas, Samuel. 1614. *Purchas his Pilgrimage*. 2nd ed. London.

Purchas, Samuel. 1617. *Purchas his Pilgrimage*. 3rd ed. London.

Purchas, Samuel. 1625. *Hakluytus Posthumus or Purchas His Pilgrimes*. 20 vols. Rpt. James MacLehose and Sons, Glasgow, 1906.

Rich, R. 1610. *Newes from Virginia*. London.

Rolfe, John. 1615. "The coppie of the Gentle-mans letters to Sir Thomas Dale, that after maried Powhatans daughter, containing the reasons moving him thereunto." In *True Discourse*. R. Hamor. Pp. 61-68.

Rolfe, John. 1616. *A True Relation of the state of Virginia*. Rpt. Yale University Press, New Haven, 1951.

Rosier, James. 1605. *A True Relation of the most prosperous voyage made by Captaine George Waymouth*. London.

Smith, John. 1608. *A True Relation of such occurrences and accidents of noate as hath hapned in Virginia*. In *Jamestown Voyages*. Ed. P.L. Barbour. I, 165-208.

Smith, John. 1612a. *A Map of Virginia*. In *Jamestown Voyages*. Ed. P.L. Barbour. II, 327-374.

Smith, John. 1612b. *The Proceedings of The English Colonie in Virginia*. Ed. William Symonds. Known as *Map of Virginia, Part II*. In *Jamestown Voyages*. Ed. P.L. Barbour. II, 375-464.

Smith, John. 1616. *A Description of New England*. In *Travels and Works*. Ed. Arber and Bradley. I, 175-231.

Smith, John. 1620. *New Englands Trials*. In *Travels and Works*. Ed. Arber and Bradley. I, 233-272.

Smith, John. 1624. *The Generall Historie of Virginia, New-England, and the Summer Isles*. In *Travels and Works*. Ed. Arber and Bradley. I, 272-382 and II, 383-622, 689-784.

Smith, John. 1631. *Advertisements For the unexperienced Planters of New-England, or any where*. In *Travels and Works*. Ed. Arber and Bradley. II, 917-966.

Society of Jesus. 1634, 1638, 1639, 1640. "Extracts from the Annual Letters of the English Province of the Society of Jesus.: In *Narratives of Early Maryland*. Ed. C.C. Hall. Pp. 118-134.

Spelman, Henry. 1613. *Relation of Virginea*. In *Travels and Works of John Smith*. Ed. E. Arber and A.G. Bradley. I, ci-cxiv.

Stoneman, John. 1606. *The Voyage of M. Henry Challons*. In *Purchas His Pilgrimes*. XIX, 284-297.

Strachey, William. 1610. *A true reportory of the wracke, and redemption of Sir Thomas Gates Knight*. In *Purchas His Pilgrimes*. XIX, 5-72.

Strachey, William, ed. 1612. *For the Colony in Virginea Britannia. Lawes Divine, Morall and Martiall, &c.* In *Tracts*. Comp. P. Force. III, No. 2.

Strachey, William. 1953. *The Historie of Travell into Virginia Britania*. Ed. Louis B. Wright and Virginia Freund. The Hakluyt Society, London.

Symonds, William. 1609. *Virginia. A Sermon Preached at White-Chappel*. London.

Tynley, Robert. 1609. *Two Learned Sermons*. London.

Underhill, John. 1638. *Newes From America*. London.

Vaughan, William. 1626. *The Golden Fleece*. London.

Vincent, Philip. 1637. *A True Relation of the Late Battel fought in New England, between the English, and the Salvages*. London.

Virginia Company. 1606. *Instructions given by way of advice*. In *Jamestown Voyages*. Ed. P. L. Barbour. I, 49-54.

Virginia Company. 1610a. *A True Declaration of the estate of the Colonie in Virginia*. In *Tracts*. Comp. P. Force. III, No. 1.

Virginia Company. 1610b. *A True and Sincere declaration of the purpose and end of the Plantation begun in Virginia*. London.

Virginia Company. 1616. *A Briefe Declaration of the Present State of Things in Virginia*. In *Genesis of the United States*. Ed. A. Brown. II, 775-779.

Virginia Company. 1620. *A Declaration of the state of the Colonie and Affaires in Virginia*. In *Tracts*. Comp. P. Force. III, No. 5.

Waterhouse, Edward. 1622. *A Declaration of the State of the Colony and Affaires in Virginia*. London.

West, Thomas, Baron de la Warr. 1611. *The Relation of the Right Honourable the Lord De-La-Warre*. In *Genesis of the United States*. Ed. A. Brown. I, 478-483.

Whitaker, Alexander. 1613. *Good Newes from Virginia*. London.

Whitaker, Alexander. 1615. "Letter, To my verie deere and loving Cosen." In *True Discourse*. R. Hamor. Pp. 59-61.

Whitbourne, Richard. 1620 rpt. 1622. *A Discourse and Discovery of New-foundland*. London.

Whitbourne, Richard. 1622. *A Discourse Containing a loving Invitation*. London.

White, Fr. Andrew. 1633. *An Account of the Colony of the Lord Baron of Baltamore, in Maryland, near Virginia.* In *Narratives of Early Maryland.* Ed. C.C. Hall. Pp. 5-10.

White, Fr. Andrew. 1634. *A Briefe Relation of the Voyage unto Maryland.* In *Narratives of Early Maryland.* Ed. C.C. Hall. Pp. 29-45.

White, John. 1587. *The fourth voyage made to Virginia.* In *Roanoke Voyages.* Ed. D.B. Quinn. II, 515-538.

White, John. 1588. *The first voyage intended for the supply of the Colonie planted in Virginia.* In *Roanoke Voyages.* Ed. D.B. Quinn. II, 562-569.

White, John. 1950. *The fift voyage of Master John White into the West Indies and parts of America called Virginia.* In *Roanoke Voyages.* Ed. D.B. Quinn. II, 598-622.

White, John, of Dorchester. 1630. *The Planters Plea.* In *Tracts.* Comp. P. Force. II, No. 3.

Wingfield, Edward Maria. 1608. *Discourse.* In *Jamestown Voyages.* Ed. P.L. Barbour. I, 213-234.

Winslow, Edward. 1624. *Good Newes from New-England.* London.

Winthrop, John. 1908. *Winthrop's Journal: History of New England, 1630-1649.* Ed. James Kendall Hosmer. 2 vols. Scribner's, New York.

Wood, William. 1634. *New Englands Prospect.* London.

Wyatt, George. 1624. "A Letter of Advice to the Governor of Virginia." Ed. J. Frederick Fausz and Jon Kukla. *William and Mary Quarterly.* 3rd Ser. 34 (1977), 104-129.

Wynne, Edward. 1622a. "A Letter from Captaine Edward Wynne, Governor of the Colony at Ferryland." In *Discourse and Discovery.* R. Whitbourne.

Wynne, Edward. 1622b. "Another letter to Master Secretary Calvert" In *Discourse and Discovery.* R. Whitbourne.

Yong, Captain Thomas. 1634. "Extract from a Letter of Captain Thomas Yong to Sir Toby Matthew." In *Narratives of Early Maryland.* Ed. C.C. Hall. Pp. 53-61.

II. Tract Collections first published after 1800.

Arber, Edward and Bradley, A.G., eds. 1910. *Travels and Works of Captain John Smith.* 2 vols. John Grant, Edinburgh.

Barbour, Philip L., ed. 1969. *The Jamestown Voyages Under the First Charter, 1606-1609.* 2 vols. Cambridge University Press for the Hakluyt Society, Cambridge.

Brown, Alexander, 1898. *The First Republic in America.* Houghton, Mifflin, Boston.

Brown, Alexander. 1964. *The Genesis of the United States.* 2 vols. First published 1890. Russell and Russell, New York.

Emerson, Everett, ed. 1976. *Letters from New England: The Massachusetts Bay Colony, 1629-1638.* University of Massachusetts Press, Amherst.

Force, Peter, comp. 1963. *Tracts and Other Papers, Relating Principally to the Origin, Settlement, and Progress of the Colonies in North America.* 4 vols. First published 1836. Peter Smith, Gloucester, Mass.

Hall, Clayton Colman, ed. 1910. *Narratives of Early Maryland, 1633-1684.* Scribner's, New York.

Quinn, David B., ed. 1940. *The Voyages and Colonising Enterprises of Sir Humphrey Gilbert.* 2 vols. The Hakluyt Society, London.

Quinn, David B., ed. 1955. *The Roanoke Voyages, 1584-1590.* 2 vols. The Hakluyt Society, London.

Taylor, E. G. R., ed. 1935. *The Original Writings and Correspondence of the Two Richard Hakluyts.* 2 vols. The Hakluyt Society, London.

Young, Alexander, ed. 1970. *Chronicles of the First Planters of Massachusetts Bay, 1623-1636.* First published 1846. Da Capo, New York.

Young, Alexander, ed. 1971. *Chronicles of the Pilgrim Fathers of the Colony of Plymouth, 1602-1625.* First published 1841. Da Capo, New York.

III. Official Colonial Records
Connecticut
Trumbull, J. Hammond, ed. 1850. *The Public Records of the Colony of Connecticut, Prior to the Union with New Haven Colony, May 1665.* Brown and Parsons, Hartford.

Massachusetts
Noble, John, supervisor. 1904. *Records of the Court of Assistants of the Colony of the Massachusetts Bay, 1630-1692.* Vol. II. County of Suffolk, Boston.

Shurtleff, Nathaniel B., ed. 1853. *Records of the Governor and Company of the Massachusetts Bay in New England.* Vol. I, 1628-1641. William White, Boston.

New Haven
Hoadly, Charles J., ed. 1857. *Records of the Colony and Plantation of New Haven, From 1638 to 1649.* Case, Tiffany, Hartford.

Plymouth
Shurtleff, Nathaniel B., ed. 1855. *Records of the Colony of New Plymouth in New England.* Vol. I, 1633-1640. William White, Boston.

Virginia
Kingsbury, Susan Myra, ed. 1906-1935. *The Records of the Virginia Company of London.* 4 vols. U.S. Government Printing Office, Washington, D.C.

McIlwaine, H. R., ed. 1915. *Journals of the House of Burgesses of Virginia, 1619-1658/59.* Virginia State Library, Richmond.

McIlwaine, H. R., ed. 1924. *Minutes of the Council and General Court of Colonial Virginia, 1622-1632, 1670-1676.* Virginia State Library, Richmond.

IV. Secondary Sources
Allen, D. C. 1936. "Symbolic Color in the Literature of the English Renaissance," *Philological Quarterly,* 15, 81-92.

Allen, D. C. 1949. *The Legend of Noah: Renaissance Rationalism in Art, Science, and Letters,* University of Illinois Press, Urbana.

Alston, W. P. 1967. "Religion," In *The Encyclopedia of Philosophy,* MacMillan, New York, 4, 140-147.

Andrews, K. R. 1964. *Elizabethan Privateering: English Privateering During the Spanish War, 1585-1603,* Cambridge University Press, Cambridge.

Axtell, J. 1972. "The Scholastic Philosophy of the Wilderness," *William and Mary Quarterly,* 3rd Ser., 29, 335-366.

Axtell, J. 1975. "The White Indians of Colonial America," *William and Mary Quarterly,* 3rd Ser., 32, 55-88.

Bailey, A. G. 1969. *The Conflict of European and Eastern Algonkian Cultures, 1504-1700: A Study in Canadian Civilization,* 2nd ed. University of Toronto Press, Toronto.

Barbour, P. L. 1964. *The Three Worlds of Captain John Smith,* Houghton Mifflin, Boston.

Barbour, P. L. 1969. *Pocahontas and Her World: A Chronicle of America's First Settlement in Which is Related the Story of the Indians and the Englishmen— Particularly Captain John Smith, Captain Samuel Argall, and Master John Rolfe,* Robert Hale, London

Barbour, P. L. 1972. "A Possible Clue to Samuel Argall's Pre-Jamestown Activities," *William and Mary Quarterly,* 3rd Ser., 29, 300-306.

Barbour, P. L. 1975. "Captain John Smith and the London Theatre," *Virginia Magazine of History and Biography,* 83, 277-279.

Battis, E. 1962. *Saints and Sectaries: Anne Hutchinson and the Antinomian Controversy in the Massachusetts Bay Colony,* University of North Carolina Press for the Institute of Early American History and Culture, Chapel Hill.

Baxter, J. P. 1893. *Christopher Levett of York, The Pioneer Colonist in Casco Bay,* Gorges Society, Portland, Maine.

Beeching, J. 1972. "Introduction" to Richard Hakluyt, *Voyages and Discoveries: The Principal Navigations, Voyages, Traffiques and Discoveries of the English Nation,* Penguin Books, Harmondsworth.

Bernheimer, R. 1952. *Wild Men in the Middle Ages: A Study in Art, Sentiment, and Demonology,* Harvard University Press, Cambridge, Mass.

Bidney, David. 1964. "The Idea of the Savage in North American Ethnohistory," *Journal of the History of Ideas,* 15, 322-327.

Bissell, B. 1925. *The American Indian in English Literature of the Eighteenth Century,* Yale University Press, New Haven.

Blanton, W. B. 1957. "Epidemics, Real and Imaginary, and Other Factors Influencing Seventeenth Century Virginia's Population," *Bulletin of the History of Medicine,* 31, 454-462.

Boorstin, D. J. 1975a. "The Birth of Exploration," *The Listener,* 13 Nov., 633-636.

Boorstin, D. J. 1975b. "Pilgrim Fathers to Founding Fathers," *The Listener*, 20 Nov., 667-670.

Boxer, C. R. 1973a. *The Dutch Seaborne Empire, 1600-1800*, Penguin Books, Harmondsworth.

Boxer, C. R. 1973b. *The Portuguese Seaborne Empire, 1415-1825*, Penguin Books, Harmondsworth.

Brandon, W. 1961. *The American Heritage Book of Indians*, American Heritage Publishing Company, New York.

Brasser, T. J. C. 1971. "The Coastal Algonkians: People of the First Frontiers," In *North American Indians in Historical Perspective*, ed. E. B. Leacock and N. O. Lurie. Random House, New York.

Breen, T. H. 1970. *The Character of the Good Ruler: A Study of Puritan Political Ideas in New England, 1630-1730*, Yale University Press, New Haven.

Breen, T. H. and Foster, S. 1973a. "The Puritans' Greatest Achievement: A Study of Social Cohesion in Seventeenth-Century Massachusetts," *The Journal of American History*, 60, 5-22.

Breen, T. H. and Foster, S. 1973b. "Moving to the New World: The Character of Early Massachusetts Immigration," *William and Mary Quarterly*, 3rd. Ser., 30, 189-222.

Bridenbaugh, C. 1976. *Vexed and Troubled Englishmen, 1590-1642*, Oxford University Press, London.

Broude, R. 1975. "Revenge and Revenge Tragedy in Renaissance England," *Renaissance Quarterly*, 28, 38-58.

Bushnell, D. 1953. "The Treatment of the Indians in Plymouth Colony," *New England Quarterly*, 26, 193-218.

Calder, I. M. 1966. "The Earl of Stirling and the Colonization of Long Island," In *Essays in Colonial History Presented to Charles McLean Andrews by his Students*, Books for Libraries Press, Inc., New York.

Canny, N. P. 1973. "The Ideology of English Colonization: From Ireland to America," *William and Mary Quarterly*, 3rd Ser., 30, 575-598.

Canny, N. P. 1976. *The Elizabethan Conquest of Ireland: A Pattern Established, 1565-76*, Barnes & Noble, New York.

Carroll, P. N. 1969. *Puritanism and the Wilderness: The Intellectual Significance of the New England Frontier, 1629-1700*, Columbia University Press, New York.

Cawley, R. R. 1938. *The Voyagers and Elizabethan Drama*, D. C. Heath, Boston.

Cawley, R. R. 1940. *Unpathed Waters: Studies in the Influence of the Voyagers on Elizabethan Literature*, Princeton University Press, Princeton.

Ceci, L. 1975. "Fish Fertilizer: A Native North American Practice?," *Science*, 188, 26-30.

Chiappelli, F., ed. 1976. *First Images of America: The Impact of the New World on the Old*, 2 vols., University of California Press, Berkeley.

Clarkson, L. A. 1971. *The Pre-Industrial Economy in England, 1500-1750*, Batsford, London.

Coldham, P. W. 1975. "The 'Spiriting' of London Children to Virginia, 1648-1685," *Virginia Magazine of History and Biography*, 83, 280-287.

Collier, G. A. "Aboriginal Sin and the Garden of Eden: Humanist Views of the Amerindian," Unpub. Manuscript.

Conceptual Frameworks in Women's History. 1976. Sarah Lawrence College, Bronxville, New York.

Connors, D. F. 1969. *Thomas Morton*, Twayne Publishers, New York.

Cook, S. F. 1973. "The Significance of Diseases in the Extinction of the New England Indians," *Human Biology*, 45, 485-508.

Craven, W. F. 1944. "Indian Policy in Early Virginia," *William and Mary Quarterly*, 3rd Ser., 1, 65-82.

Craven, W. F. 1964. *Dissolution of the Virginia Company: The Failure of a Colonial Experiment*, Peter Smith, Gloucester, Mass.

Craven, W. F. 1971. *White, Red, and Black: The Seventeenth-Century Virginian*, University Press of Virginia, Charlottesville.

Crosby, A. W., Jr. 1972. *The Columbian Exchange: Biological and Cultural Consequences of 1492*, Greenwood Publishing Co., Westport, Connecticut.

Crosby, A. W., Jr. 1976. "Virgin Soil Epidemics as a Factor in the Aboriginal Depopulation in America," *William and Mary Quarterly*, 3rd Ser., 33, 289-299.

Culliford, S. G. 1965. *William Strachey, 1572-1621*, University Press of Virginia, Charlottesville.

Curtis, M. H. 1962. "The Alienated Intellectuals of Early Stuart England," *Past and Present*, No. 23, 25-43.

Davies, K. G. 1974. *The North Atlantic World in the Seventeenth Century*, University of Minnesota Press, Minneapolis.

Davis, R. B. 1947. "America in Sandys' *Ovid*," *William and Mary Quarterly*, 3rd Ser., 4, 297-304.

Davis, R. B. 1955. *George Sandys, Poet-Adventurer: A Study in Anglo-American Culture in the Seventeenth Century*, The Bodley Head, London.

Day, G. M. 1953. "The Indian as an Ecological Factor in the Northeastern Forest," *Ecology*, 34, 329-343.

Detweiler, R. 1971. "Was Richard Hakluyt a Negative Influence in the Colonization of Virginia?," *North Carolina Historical Review*, 158, 359-369.

Diamond, S. 1958. "From Organization to Society: Virginia in the Seventeenth Century," *American Journal of Sociology*, 63, 457-475.

Dictionary of American Biography. 1928-1937. Scribner's, New York.

Dictionary of Canadian Biography. 1966. University of Toronto Press, Toronto.

Dictionary of National Biography. 1917. Oxford University Press, London.

Dobyns, H. F. 1966. "Estimating Aboriginal American Population: An Appraisal of Techniques with a New Hemispheric Estimate," *Current Anthropology,* 7, 395-416.

Douglas, M. 1966. *Purity and Danger: An Analysis of Concepts of Pollution and Taboo,* Praeger, New York.

Driver, H. E. 1969. *Indians of North America,* 2nd ed., revised, University of Chicago Press, Chicago.

Dudley, E. and Novak, M. E. 1972. *The Wild Man Within: An Image in Western Thought from the Renaissance to Romanticism,* University of Pittsburgh Press, Pittsburgh.

Duncan, J. E. 1972. *Milton's Earthly Paradise: A Historical Study of Eden.* University of Minnesota Press, Minneapolis.

Dunn, R. 1959. "Seventeenth-Century English Historians of America," In *Seventeenth-Century America,* ed. J. M. Smith, 195-225.

Elliott, J.H. 1970. *The Old World and the New, 1492-1650,* Cambridge University Press, Cambridge.

Elliott, J.H. 1972. *The Discovery of America and the Discovery of Man,* Oxford University Press, London.

Emerson, E.H. 1971. *Captain John Smith,* Twayne, New York.

Flannery, R. 1939. *An Analysis of Coastal Algonquian Culture,* Catholic University of America Press, Washington, D.C.

Foreman, C. T. 1943. *Indians Abroad, 1493-1938,* University of Oklahoma Press, Norman.

Foss, M. 1974. *Undreamed Shores: England's Wasted Empire in America,* Harrap, London.

Galenson, D. W. 1978. " 'Middling People' or 'Common Sort'?: The Social Origins of Some Early Americans Reexamined," *William and Mary Quarterly,* 3rd ser., 34, 3, 499-524.

Gay, P. 1966. *A Loss of Mastery: Puritan Historians in Colonial America,* University of California Press, Berkeley.

Geller, L. D. 1974. *Pilgrims in Eden: Conservation Policies at New Plymouth,* Pride Publications, Wakefield, Mass.

Gookin, W. F. and Barbour, P. L. 1963. *Bartholomew Gosnold, Discoverer and Planter,* Archon Books, Hamden, Conn.

Greenblatt, S. J. 1973. *Sir Walter Ralegh: The Renaissance Man and His Roles,* Yale University Press, New Haven.

Hale, J. 1967. "A World Elsewhere," In *The Age of the Renaissance,* ed. D. Hay, Thames and Hudson, London.

Hale, J. 1971. "Sixteenth-Century Explanations of War and Violence," *Past and Present,* 51, 3-26.

Haller, W. 1957. *The Rise of Puritanism: Or, The Way to the New Jerusalem as Set Forth in Pulpit and Press from Thomas Cartwright to John Lilburne and John Milton, 1570-1643*, Harper Torchbooks, New York.

Haller, W. 1963. *The Elect Nation: The Meaning and Relevance of Foxe's Book of Martyrs*, Harper and Row, New York.

Handlin, O. 1967. *The History of the United States*, 2 vols. Holt, Rinehart and Winston, New York.

Hanke, L. 1959. *Aristotle and the American Indians: A Study of Race Prejudice in the Modern World*, Henry Regnery, Chicago.

Hatch, C. E., Jr. and Gregory, T. G. 1962. "The First American Blast Furnace, 1619-1622: The Birth of a Mighty Industry on Falling Creek in Virginia," *Virginia Magazine of History and Biography*, 70, 259-296.

Hay, D. 1968. *Europe: The Emergence of an Idea*, Edinburgh University Press, Edinburgh.

Heather, P. J. 1948-1949. "Color Symbolism, I, II, III, IV," *Folklore*, 59, 165-183, and 60, 208-216, 266-276, 316-331.

Heimert, A. 1953. "Puritanism, the Wilderness, and the Frontier," *New England Quarterly*, 26, 193-218.

Hill, C. 1958. "God's Englishmen and his Empire," *The Spectator*, June 20, 809.

Hill, C. 1961. *The Century of Revolution, 1603-1714*, Thomas Nelson and Sons, Edinburgh.

Hill, C. 1964. *Society and Puritanism in Pre-Revolutionary England*, Secker and Warburg, London.

Hill, C. 1965. *Intellectual Origins of the English Revolution*, Clarendon Press Oxford.

Hill, C. 1975. *Change and Continuity in Seventeenth-Century England*, Harvard University Press, Cambridge, Mass.

Hodgen, M. T. 1964. *Early Anthropology in the Sixteenth and Seventeenth Centuries*, University of Pennsylvania Press, Philadelphia.

Huddleston, L. E. 1967. *Origins of the American Indians: European Concepts, 1492-1729*, University of Texas Press, Austin.

Hudson, C. M. 1976. *The Southeastern Indians*, University of Tennessee Press, Knoxville.

Hulton, P. 1972. "Introduction" to Thomas Harriot, *A Briefe and True Report of the New Found Land of Virginia, 1590*, Dover Publications, New York.

Hulton, P. and Quinn, D. B. 1964. *The American Drawings of John White, 1577-1590*, Trustees of the British Museum, London.

Illick, J. E. 1974. "Child-Rearing in Seventeenth-Century England and America," In *The History of Childhood*, Psychohistory Press, New York.

Illman, J. 1974. "GPs studying the Witch-Doctors," *The Sunday Times of London*, 14 July.

Jacobs, W. R. 1972. *Dispossessing the American Indian: Indians and Whites on the Colonial Frontier,* Scribner's, New York.

Jacobs, W. R. 1974. "The Tip of an Iceberg: Pre-Columbian Indian Demography and Some Implications for Revisionism," *William and Mary Quarterly,* 3rd Ser. 31, 123-132.

Jacobs, W. R. 1975. "Native American History: How it Illuminates our Past," *American Historical Review,* 80, 595-609.

Jennings, F. 1971a. "Goals and Functions of Puritan Missions to the Indians," *Ethnohistory,* 18, 197-212.

Jennings, F. 1971b. "Virgin Land and Savage People," *American Quarterly,* 23, 519-541.

Jennings, F. 1975. *The Invasion of America: Indians, Colonialism, and the Cant of Conquest,* University of North Carolina Press for the Institute of Early American History and Culture, Chapel Hill.

Johnson, R. R. 1977. "The Search for a Usable Indian: An Aspect of the Defense of Colonial New England," *The Journal of American History,* 64, 3, 623-651.

Johnson, R. C. 1970. "The Transportation of Vagrant Children from London to Virginia, 1618-1622," *Early Stuart Studies,* ed. H. S. Reinmuth, University of Minnesota Press, Minneapolis.

Jordan, W. D. 1969. *White Over Black: American Attitudes Toward the Negro, 1550-1812,* Penguin Books, Baltimore.

Kelly-Gadol, J. 1976. "The Social Relation of the Sexes: Methodological Implications of Women's History," *Signs,* 1, 4, 809-823.

Kelso, R. 1956. *Doctrine for the Lady of the Renaissance,* University of Illinois Press, Urbana.

Kelso, R. 1964. *The Doctrine of the English Gentleman in the Sixteenth Century: With a Bibliographical List of Treatises on the Gentleman and Related Subjects Published in Europe to 1625,* Peter Smith, Gloucester, Mass.

Kenyon, J. P. 1967. *The Stuarts: A Study in English Kingship,* John Wiley and Sons, New York.

Kermode, F., ed. 1964. *The Tempest,* The Arden Edition of the Works of William Shakespeare, Methuen & Co., London.

Kerridge, E. 1973. *The Farmers of Old England,* Allen and Unwin, London.

Knowlson, J. 1975. *Universal Language Schemes in England and France: 1600-1800,* University of Toronto Press, Toronto.

Kolodny, A. 1973, "The land-as-woman: Literary Convention and Latent Psychological Content," *Women's Studies,* 1, 167-182.

Kupperman, K. O. 1977a. "English Perceptions of Treachery, 1583-1640: The Case of the American 'Savages,' " *The Historical Journal,* 20, 2, 263-287.

Kupperman, K. O. 1977b. "Thomas Morton, Historian," *The New England Quarterly,* 50, 4, 660-664.

Kupperman, K. O. 1978. "British Attitudes Toward the American Indian, 1580-1640," Unpub. Ph.D. Dissertation, Cambridge University.

Kupperman, K. O. 1979a. "Apathy and Death in Early Jamestown," *The Journal of American History*, 66, 1, 24-40.

Kupperman, K. O. 1979b. "Nature's 'rude Garden:' English and Indians as Producers and Consumers of Food in Early New England," *Comparative Civilizations Review*, 1, 64-78.

Langdon, G. D., Jr. 1966. *Pilgrim Colony: A History of New Plymouth, 1620-1691*, Yale University Press, New Haven.

Lamont, W. M. 1969. *Godly Rule: Politics and Religion, 1603-60*, Macmillan, London.

Lankford, John, ed. 1967. *Captain John Smith's America: Selections from his Writings*, Harper Torchbooks, New York.

Lappé, F. M. 1973. *Diet for a Small Planet*, Ballantine, New York.

Laslett, P. 1965. *The World We Have Lost*, Charles Scribner's Sons, New York.

Leach, D. E. 1966. *The Northern Colonial Frontier, 1607-1763*, Holt, Rinehart and Winston, New York.

Levin, H. 1969. *The Myth of the Golden Age in the Renaissance*, Indiana University Press, Bloomington.

Levy, B. M. 1960. "Early Puritanism in the Southern and Island Colonies," *Proceedings of the American Antiquarian Society*, 70, 69-348.

Loewenberg, P. 1970. "The Psychology of Racism," In *The Great Fear: Race in the Mind of America*, ed. G. B. Nash and R. Weiss, Holt, Rinehart and Winston, New York.

Lurie, N. O. 1959. "Indian Cultural Adjustment to European Civilization," In *Seventeenth-Century America*, ed. J. M. Smith, 33-60.

Macfarlane, A. 1970a. *The Family Life of Ralph Josselin, A Seventeenth-Century Clergyman: An Essay in Historical Anthropology*, Cambridge University Press, Cambridge.

Macfarlane, A. 1970b. *Witchcraft in Tudor and Stuart England: A Regional and Comparative Study*, Harper Torchbooks, New York.

Maclean, U. 1974. *Magical Medicine: A Nigerian Case-Study*, Penguin Books, Harmondsworth.

Maclear, J. F. 1975. "New England and the Fifth Monarchy: The Quest for the Millenium in Early American Puritanism," *William and Mary Quarterly*, 3rd Ser., 32, 223-260.

Martin, C. 1974. "The European Impact on the Culture of a Northeastern Algonquian Tribe: An Ecological Interpretation," *William and Mary Quarterly*, 3rd Ser., 31, 3-26.

Martin, C. 1975. "The Four Lives of a Micmac Copper Pot," *Ethnohistory*, 22, 111-133.

Martin, C. 1978. *Keepers of the Game: Indian-Animal Relationships and the Fur Trade*, University of California Press, Berkeley.

Maycock, A. L. 1963. *Nicholas Ferrar of Little Gidding*, Society for Promoting Christian Knowledge, London.

McCary, B. C. 1957. *Indians in Seventeenth Century Virginia*, Virginia 350th Anniversary Celebration Corporation, Williamsburg.

Miller, P. 1964. "Religion and Society in the Early Literature of Virginia," *William and Mary Quarterly*, 3rd Ser., 5, and 6 (1949), rpt. in *Errand into the Wilderness*, Harper Torchbooks, New York.

Miller, P. and Johnson, T. H. 1938 rpt. 1963. *The Puritans*, rev. ed., Harper Torchbooks, New York.

Morgan, E. S. 1958. *The Puritan Dilemma: The Story of John Winthrop*, Little, Brown, Boston.

Morgan, E. S. 1971. "The Labor Problem at Jamestown, 1607-18," *American Historical Review*, 76, 595-611.

Morgan, E. S. 1975. *American Slavery—American Freedom: The Ordeal of Colonial Virginia*, Norton, New York.

Morison, S. E. 1935. *The Founding of Harvard College*, Harvard University Press, Cambridge, Mass.

Morison, S. E. 1953. "Introduction," to William Bradford, *Of Plymouth Plantation*, Knopf, New York.

Morrison, K. M. 1974. " 'That Art of Coyning Christians:' John Eliot and the Praying Indians of Massachusetts," *Ethnohistory*, 21, 77-92.

Nash, G. B. 1972. "The Image of the Indian in the Southern Colonial Mind," In Dudley and Novak, eds., *Wild Man Within*, 55-86.

———. 1974. *Red, White, and Black: The Peoples of Early America*, Englewood Cliffs, New Jersey.

Nicholas, J. 1828. *The Progresses, Processions, and Magnificent Festivities of King James the First, His Royal Consort, Family and Court, collected from Original Manuscripts, Scarce Pamphlets, Corporation Records, Parochial Registers, etc. etc. Comprising Forty Masques and Entertainments: Ten Civic Pageants; Numerous Original Letters; and Annotated Lists of the Peers, Baronets, and Knights, who received those Honours During the Reign of King James Illustrated with Notes, Historical, Topographical, Biographical, and Bibliographical*, 4 vols., Printed by and for J. B. Nichols, Printer to the Society of Antiquaries, London.

O'Gorman, E. 1961. *The Invention of America: An Inquiry into the Historical Nature of the New World and the Meaning of its History*, Indian University Press, Bloomington.

Parry, J. H. 1963. *The Age of Reconnaissance: Discovery, Exploration and Settlement, 1450-1650*, Weidenfeld and Nicolson, London.

———. 1969. *Europe and a Wider World, 1415-1715*, 3rd ed., Hutchinson University Library, London.

———. 1973. *The Spanish Seaborne Empire*, Penguin Books, Harmondsworth.

Pearce, R. H. 1952. "The 'Ruines of Mankind:' The Indian and the Puritan Mind," *Journal of the History of Ideas*, 13, 200-217.

———. 1957. "The Metaphysics of Indian-Hating," *Ethnohistory*, 4, 27-40.

———. 1965. *The Savages of America: A Study of the Indian and the Idea of Civilization*, rev. ed. Johns Hopkins Press, Baltimore.

Pearl, V. 1961. *London and the Outbreak of the Puritan Revolution: City Government and National Politics, 1625-43*, Oxford University Press, London.

Peckham, H. H. 1964. *The Colonial Wars, 1689-1762*, University of Chicago Press, Chicago.

Phillips, P. L. 1897. "List of Books Relating to America in the Register of the London Company of Stationers, from 1562 to 1638," *Annual Report of the American Historical Association, 1896*, American Historical Association, Washington.

Porter, H. C. 1979. *The Inconstant Savage: England and the North American Indian 1500-1660*, Duckworth, London.

Powell, W. S. 1958. "Aftermath of the Massacre: The First Indian War, 1622-1632," *Virginia Magazine of History and Biography*, 66, 44-75.

Preston, R. A. 1953. *Gorges of Plymouth Fort: A Life of Sir Ferdinando Gorges, Captain of Plymouth Fort, Governor of New England, and Lord of the Province of Maine*, University of Toronto Press and Royal Military College of Canada, Toronto.

Quinn, D. B. 1973. *Ralegh and the British Empire*, Penguin Books, Harmondsworth.

———. 1974a. *England and the Discovery of America, 1481-1620: From the Bristol Voyages of the Fifteenth Century to the Pilgrim Settlement at Plymouth: The Exploration, Exploitation, and Trial-and-Error Colonization of North America by the English*, Allen and Unwin, London.

———. ed. 1974b. *The Hakluyt Handbook*, 2 vols. Hakluyt Society, London.

———. 1976. "Renaissance Influences in English Colonization," *Transactions of the Royal Historical Society*, 5th Ser., 26, 73-92.

Quirk, R. E. 1954. "Some Notes on a Controversial Controversy: Juan Gines de Sepulveda and Natural Servitude," *Hispanic American Historical Review*, 34, 357-364.

Rabb, T. K. 1967. *Enterprise and Empire: Merchant and Gentry Investment in the Expansion of England, 1575-1630*, Harvard University Press, Cambridge, Mass.

Rabb, T. K. 1974. "The Expansion of Europe and the Spirit of Capitalism," *Historical Journal*, 17, 675-689.

Ronda, J. P. 1974. "Red and White at the Bench: Indians and the Law in Plymouth Colony," *Essex Institute Historical Collections*, 110, 200-215.

Ronda, J. P. 1977. " 'We Are Well As We Are': An Indian Critique of Seventeenth-Century Christian Missions," *William and Mary Quarterly*, 3rd Ser., 34, 66-82.

Rose, J. 1955. "The Merchandize of Light; being A Study of the Impact and Influence of the New Knowledge of the Non-European World on some Aspects of English Thought, in the Seventeenth Century," Diss. King's College, Cambridge University, Cambridge.

Rowe, J. H. 1964. "Ethnography and Ethnology in the Sixteenth Century," *Kroeber Anthropological Society Papers*, 30, 1-19.

Rowse, A. L. 1959. *The Elizabethans and America*, Macmillan, London.

Russell, C. P. 1962. *Guns on the Early Frontiers: A History of Firearms From Colonial Times Through the Years of the Western Fur Trade*, University of California Press, Berkeley.

Rutman, D. B. 1964. "The Virginia Company and Its Military Regime," In *The Old Dominion: Essays for Thomas Perkins Abernathy*, University of Virginia Press, Charlottesville.

———. 1967. *Husbandmen of Plymouth: Farms and Villages in the Old Colony, 1620-1692*, Beacon Press for Plimoth Plantation, Boston.

———. and Rutman, A. H. 1976. "Of Agues and Fevers: Malaria in the Early Chesapeake," *William and Mary Quarterly*, 3rd Ser., 33, 31-60,

Salisbury, N. 1974. "Red Puritans: The 'Praying Indians' of Massachusetts Bay and John Eliot," *William and Mary Quarterly*, 3rd Ser., 31, 27-54.

Salmon, V. 1972. *The Works of Francis Lodwick: A Study of his Writings in the Intellectual Context of the Seventeenth Century*. Longman, London.

Sanford, C.L. 1961. *The Quest for Paradise: Europe and the American Moral Imagination*, University of Illinois Press, Urbana.

Scammell, G.V. 1969. "The New Worlds and Europe in the Sixteenth Century," *Historical Journal*, 12, 389-412.

Shakespeare, W. 1972. *The Tempest*, Methuen, London.

Sheehan, B.W. 1969. "Indian-White Relations in Early America: A Review Essay," *William and Mary Quarterly*, 3rd Ser., 26, 267-286.

Shirley, J.W., ed. 1974. *Thomas Harriot: Renaissance Scientist*, Clarendon Press, Oxford.

Shuffelton, F. 1976. "Indian Devils and Pilgrim Fathers: Squanto, Hobomock, and the English Conception of Indian Religion," *The New England Quarterly*, 49, 1, 108-116.

Simpson, A. 1955. *Puritanism in Old and New England*, University of Chicago Press, Chicago.

Slater, M. 1976. "The Weightiest Business: Marriage in an Upper-Gentry Family in Seventeenth-Century England," *Past and Present*, 72, 25-54.

Slotkin, R.L. 1973. *Regeneration through Violence: The Mythology of the American Frontier, 1600-1860,* Wesleyan University Press, Middletown, Conn.

Smith, H.N. 1950. *Virgin Land: The American West as Symbol and Myth,* Harvard University Press, Cambridge, Mass.

Smith, J.M., ed. 1959. *Seventeenth-Century America: Essays in Colonial History,* University of North Carolina Press for the Institute of Early American History and Culture, Chapel Hill.

Stearns, R.P. 1970. *Science in the British Colonies of America,* University of Illinois Press, Urbana.

Stone, L. 1966. "Social Mobility in England, 1500-1700," *Past and Present,* 33, 16-55.

Stone, L. 1974. "The Massacre of the Innocents," *New York Review of Books,* 14 November, 25-31.

Stout, H.S. 1976. "The Morphology of Remigration: New England University Men and Their Return to England, 1640-1660," *The Journal of American Studies,* 10, 2, 151-172.

Street, B.V. 1975. *The Savage in Literature: Representations of "Primitive" Society in English Fiction, 1858-1920,* Routledge and Kegan Paul, London.

Swanton, J.R. 1946. *The Indians of the Southeastern United States,* U.S. Government Printing Office, Washington, D.C.

Swanton, J.R. 1952. *The Indian Tribes of North America,* U.S. Government Printing Office, Washington, D.C.

Taylor, E.G.R. 1934. *Late Tudor and Early Stuart Geography, 1583-1650,* Methuen, London.

Taylor, E.G.R. 1968. *Tudor Geography, 1485-1583,* Octagon Books, New York.

Thirsk, J., ed. 1970. *Land, Church, and People,* British Agricultural History Society, Reading, England.

Thomas, G.E. 1975. "Puritans, Indians, and the Concept of Race," *The New England Quarterly,* 48, 1, 3-27.

Thomas, K. 1973. *Religion and the Decline of Magic: Studies in Popular Beliefs in Sixteenth- and Seventeenth-Century England,* Penguin Books, Harmondsworth.

Vaughan, A.T. 1965. *New England Frontier: Puritans and Indians, 1620-1675,* Little, Brown, Boston.

Vaughan, A.T. 1973. "The Evolution of Virginia History: Early Historians of the First Colony," In *Perspectives on Early American History: Essays in Honor of Richard B. Morris,* ed. A.T. Vaughan and G.A. Billias, Harper and Row, New York.

Vaughan, A.T. 1975. *American Genesis: Captain John Smith and the Founding of Virginia,* Little, Brown, Boston.

Vaughan, A.T. 1978. " 'Expulsion of the Salvages': English Policy and the Virginia Massacre of 1622," *The William and Mary Quarterly*, 3rd Ser., 35, 1, 57-84.

Wallace, A.F.C., with the assistance of Sheila C. Steen. 1969. *The Death and Rebirth of the Seneca*, Random House, New York.

Walzer, M. 1964. "Puritanism as a Revolutionary Ideology," *History and Theory*, 3, 59-90.

Washburn, W.E. 1959. "The Moral and Legal Justifications for Dispossessing the Indians," in J.M. Smith, ed., *Seventeenth-Century America*, 15-32.

Washburn, W.E. 1971. *Red Man's Land, White Man's Law: A Study of the Past and Present Status of the American Indian*, Scribner's, New York.

Washburn, W.E. 1975. *The Indian in America*, Harper and Row, New York.

Wasserman, M.M. 1954. "The American Indian as Seen By the Seventeenth Century Chroniclers," Diss. University of Pennsylvania.

Webster, C. 1975. *The Great Instauration: Science, Medicine and Reform, 1626-1660*, Duckworth, London.

Williams, J.G. 1972. "History in Hawthorne's 'The Maypole of Merry Mount,' " *Essex Institute Historical Collections*, 108, 173-189.

Willison, G.F. 1966. *Saints and Strangers: The Story of the Mayflower and the Plymouth Colony*, Heinemann, London.

Willson, D. H. 1956. *King James VI and I*, Jonathan Cape, London.

Wilson, C. 1965. *England's Apprenticeship, 1603-1763*, St. Martin's Press, New York.

Wright, L.B. 1943. *Religion and Empire: The Alliance between Piety and Commerce in English Expansion, 1558-1625*, University of North Carolina Press, Chapel Hill.

Ziff, L. 1973. *Puritanism in America: New Culture in a New World*, Viking Press, New York.

Zolla, E. 1973. *The Writer and the Shaman: A Morphology of the American Indian*, trans. Raymond Rosenthal, Harcourt Brace Jovanovich, New York.

Zuckerman, M. 1977a. "The Fabrication of Identity in Early America," *William and Mary Quarterly*, 3rd Ser., 34, 183-214.

Zuckerman, M. 1977b. "Pilgrims in the Wilderness: Community, Modernity, and the Maypole at Merry Mount," *The New England Quarterly*, 50, 255-277.

Index

Alexander, Sir William, Earl of Stirling, 71, 106 fn, 109, 119, 129, 161
Allerton, Isaac, 134
Alston, William P., 72 fn.
Amadas, Philip, 14
Andrews, Kenneth R., 10 fn.
Aquiday, 184
Archer, Gabriel, 52, 55, 57, 59, 69 fn, 73, 76, 82-83, 84, 87, 92-93, 96-97, 128, 131, 143, 173
Argall, Samuel, 13, 45, 77, 146, 173
Axtell, James, 156

Bacon, Sir Francis, 151-152
Baltimore, see Calvert
Barbour, Philip L., 1 fn, 24 fn, 45, 67, 98, 126
Barlowe, Arthur, 14, 69, 70, 82, 92, 94, 103, 143, 147, 149
Battis, Emery, 22
Benson, George, 160
Bering Strait, migration across, 5, 109-110
Bermuda, 18
Bernheimer, Richard, 40, 46 fn, 67
Best, George, 36, 40
Best, Thomas, 137, 140
Boorstin, Daniel, 1 fn, 4 fn, 114
Boxer, C. R., 12 fn, 161
Bardford, William, 7, 27, 37, 39, 52, 68, 83, 84, 86, 88, 91, 93-94, 99-100, 125, 130, 132, 134, 137, 144-145, 158 fn, 172 fn, 174, 183-186
Brereton, John, 16, 37, 89, 92, 96-97, 100, 162 fn.
Brerewood, Edward, 109
Bridenthal, Renate, 61
British Library, 48
Brooke, Lord, 21
Broude, Ronald, 126
Brown, Alexander, 12 fn.
Buck, Rev. Richard, 119

C., T., 162
Cabot, John, 12
Cabot, Sebastian, 13, 113
Calvert, George, Lord Baltimore, 22, 132-133
Calvert, Leonard, 53, 157
Calvin, John, 28, 70

Cambridge University, 9, 24, 27, 149
Capps, William, 178
Caribbean, 10
Carleill, Christopher, 164
Carroll, Peter N., 27 fn.
Cawley, Robert Ralston, 165
Ceci, Lynn, 84
Charles I, 11, 51
Chesapeake Bay, 13, 15, 174; early exploration in, 16
Cicero, 70-71
civil man, English definition of, 46, 81-82, 105-106, 186-187
Clarkson, L. A., 2 fn.
Clayborne, Capt. William, 132-133
Coldham, Peter Wilson, 136
colonists, selection of; inclusion of children, 135-136; craftsmen, 11, 17, 20; gentlemen, 17; women, 10, 155-156; poor quality of, 122-123, 135, 153; unwilling, 3, 12, 135
colonization, effect on English culture, 22, 26, 148-158
Columbus, Christopher, knowledge of English exploration, 12
Connecticut, 184; *Records*, 123, 131, 134, 154, 174, 185
Connecticut River, 7, 22, 132
Connors, Donald F., 26
Cook, Sherburne F., 6
Copland, Patrick, 66, 116, 122 fn, 153
Cotton, John, 22
Cradock, Matthew, 21, 172
Crakanthorpe, Richard, 106 fn, 162
Crashaw, William, 36, 69, 106 fn, 113, 122 fn, 123 fn, 143, 149, 151, 161, 162 fn, 164, 166-167
Craven, Wesley Frank, 10 fn, 19, 36, 60, 102, 138, 165
Crosby, Alfred W., 5 fn.
Croshawe, Raleigh, 183
Curtis, Mark, 12
Cushman, Robert, 6, 26, 38, 48, 113, 123, 127, 142-143, 147, 160 fn, 162, 167

Dale, Sir Thomas, 18, 119, 122 fn, 123, 126-127, 159, 174
Dare, Virginia, 15
Davies, K. G., 12 fn.

219

Day, Gordon, M., 91
DeBry, Theodore, 33-34, 82
Dermer, Thomas, 112
disease, effect on colonists, 17, 19, 133; Indian deaths from, 5-6; interpretation of, 31-32, 111, 115-118, 133, 186-187
Dobyns, Henry F., 6
Donne, George, 113, 133 fn, 153 fn, 183
Donne, John, 69, 109, 142-143, 151, 159-160, 172
Dorey, Grigory, 135
Douglas, Mary, 67, 158
Drake, Sir Francis, 14
Drayton, Michael, 107, 139
dress, as indicator of status, 16, 34-35, 37-39, 41-42, 44, 48, 154-155, 187
Driver, Harold E., 102
Dudley, Thomas, 116, 183
Dunn, Richard S., 27 fn, 159 fn.

Eburne, Richard, 106 fn, 113 fn, 120, 123 fn, 143, 160, 162-164, 172 fn.
Eliot, John, 110
Elizabeth I, 51
Emerson, Everett, 134 fn, 136 fn, 174
English Civil War, 11, 12, 26

Fernandes, Simao, 15
Ferrar, Nicholas, 30, 164
Floyd, John, 69, 165
food, sources of; failure of colonists to grow food, 17, 24, 172-174, 179-183; starving time in Jamestown, 18, 127
Foss, Michael, 165
France, 39, 130; Huguenots, 13; North American colonization, 13, 132, 156; reports of, 104-105
fur trade, 20, 26, 132

Gates, Sir Thomas, 18, 83
Gilbert, Sir Humphrey, 10, 14, 16, 22-23, 150
Gilbert, Raleigh, 16
Gordon of Lochinvar, Robert, 93, 101, 160, 163
Gorges, Sir Ferdinando, 26, 123, 185
Gosnold, Bartholomew, 16, 131
Gray, Robert, 106 fn, 113 fn, 124, 142, 161, 167
Gregory, Thurlow G., 165
Grenville, Sir Richard, 14-15
Gresham, Sir Thomas, 150
Griffin, Owen, 74
Guy, John, 103

Hakewill, George, 90, 105, 113

Hakluyt, Richard (lawyer), 9, 23, 162 fn, 170-171
Hakluyt, Richard (younger), 9, 23-24, 33, 41, 42, 65, 96, 102, 109, 113, 125-127, 129, 135, 143, 149-150, 171, 174
Hall, Clayton C., 131
Hall, Thomas, 39-40
Haller, William, 28-29, 166
Hamor, Ralph, 59, 91, 103, 111, 113, 120 fn, 123-124, 126-127, 146, 159, 182-183
Hanke, Lewis, 163
Hariot, Thomas, 6, 14, 25, 31-33, 47-48, 54, 70-77, 81-83, 86-88, 91-94, 96, 98-101, 103, 111-112, 115-116, 120 fn, 126, 146-147, 150, 164, 172, 174
Hartford, 21
Hatch, Charles, E., 165
Hawkins, Arthur, 166
Hayes, Edward, 14, 23, 122 fn, 160-162
Heather, P. J., 36
Higginson, Francis, 69, 70, 87, 98-99, 115, 120
Hill, Christopher, 2 fn, 26, 28, 120, 142, 152
Hodgen, Margaret T., 4 fn, 40, 106 fn, 113 fn.
Holland, 130, 161, 171; colony in North America, 13, 20, 132; Pilgrims in, 11, 20; wealth from fishing, 9, 152
Hore, M., 127
Hoskins, Nicholas, 91
Huddleston, Lee E., 110
Hudson, Charles, 53
Hulton, Paul, 33 fn, 113
Hutchinson, Anne, 22, 28-29, 155-156

Iapaseus, 77
Illick, Joseph, 146
Indians; Algonquians, 7, 25, 43, 47-48, 53; Iroquois, 7, 43; Sioux, 7
agriculture, 82-85
Blacke Boy ceremonies, 64-68
burials, 74-76
cannibalism, issue of, 43, 127
canoes, 102-104
characterizations of (by English), 110-114, 120-122, 143-148, 170-171
color, 35-37, 112
conversion, 42, 64, 111, 160-166
diet, 82, 87-88, 92-94, 147
dignity, 4, 37, 50-52
dress, 34-42, 50
fishing and hunting, 88-89
games, 56
government, 48-56
hair, 39-40

houses, 86-87
inheritance, 53
language, 47-48, 108-109
marriage, 58-60
medicine, 72, 97-98, 116-118
metalwork, 96-97
monstrous, reports of, 42-44, 48
nakedness, issue of, 39-42
nature, relationship to, 89-91
origins, debate on, 108-109
physique, 37
pottery, 94
priests, role of, 72, 98, 116-118
record-keeping, 95
religious beliefs, 68-79
sexroles, 60-62, 82-84, 88
society, regulation of, 52-55, 58-62, 143-146
technology, compared to European, 88, 102-106, 111, 172-174, 186-187; useful to English, 88, 96-100
towns, 81-82
trade networks, 56-58
treachery, issue of, 127, 175-176
wampum, 57-8, 174
warfare, 55-56
weapons, 44, 100-102
weaving, 94, 99-100
Indian tribes: Abnaki (Tarrentines), 43-44, 156; Chesapeakes, 7, 16; Chickahominies, 50, 111, 174; Croatoan, 15; Mahicans, 7; Mohawk, 43-44; Narragansetts, 56, 58, 74; Pamunkeys, 181; Pawtuxet, 20; Pequots, 7, 43, 126, 132, 175, 184-185; Powhatans, 43-44, 67, 72; Rappahannocks, 146; Susquehannocks, 37, 43; Wampanoags, 7
Ingram, David, 42, 44, 59, 69, 92, 96, 109
Inns of Court, 24, 142
Ireland, 5, 25, 171
Israel, Menassah ben, 110
Iyanough, 52, 144

Jacob, Henry, founded Jacobopolis, 30
Jacobs, Wilbur, 4 fn, 82, 89, 91, 164
James I, 8, 11, 28-29, 49-51, 100, 111, 135, 145, 152
James River, 7, 17-19, 45, 120, 165
Jamestown, 3, 7, 8, 20, 24-25, 30, 45, 64, 66, 87, 92, 97, 102, 104, 118, 122-123, 126-127, 144, 146, 148-149, 171, 173; changes in government of, 18-19, 24, 138
Jefferson, Thomas, 7
Jennings, Francis, 4 fn, 6 fn, 22 fn, 27, 30 fn, 43, 55 fn, 106 fn, 111-112, 126, 164

Jesuits, 13, 69, 135; Jesuit letters, 38, 49, 59, 113, 135
Johnson, Robert, 46, 48, 65, 106 fn, 113, 122 fn, 123 fn, 160 fn, 166, 167, 170
Johnson, Robert C., 136 fn.
joint-stock organization, 11, 20
Jordan, Winthrop, 36, 111, 139, 165

Kelly-Gadol, Joan, 61
Kelso, Ruth, 24 fn, 170
Kenyon, J. P., 51
Kermode, Frank, 126
Kerridge, Eric, 119
King, Gregory, 4
Koran, 76
Kupperman, Karen Ordahl, 20 fn, 36 fn, 106 fn, 115, 126, 129-130

Lamont, William, 28-29
Lane, Ralph, 14, 50, 57, 75 fn, 82-83, 88, 96-97, 100, 111, 115, 146-147, 166, 171-173
Langdon, George, Jr., 20 fn, 29-30
Lappé, Frances Moore, 82
Las Casas, 163
Laslett, Peter, 2 fn, 59
Laud, William, Archbishop of Canterbury, 11, 28
L'Estrange, Hamon, 110
Levett, Christopher, 31, 48, 50, 54 fn, 59, 69, 70, 96, 101, 108, 116, 125 fn, 145, 156
Levy, Babette, 29-30
London, colonial leadership in, 16, 124, 133-134, 136
Lurie, Nancy Oestreich, 8, 60, 117, 126 fn, 128, 157

Macfarlane, Alan, 116, 146, 170, 175
Madoc, 109
Magnel, Francis, 69, 116
Maine, 13, 132; Sagadahoc colony, 16, 43-44
Manteo, 111
Martin, Calvin, 89, 114
Martin, John, 49, 157-158
Maryland, 7, 22, 27, 30, 38, 49, 53-55, 57, 132-133, 135, 137; *Relation of Maryland*, 31, 53-55, 57, 58-59, 68, 71, 73, 76, 81, 83, 87, 92-94, 96-98, 104, 133, 143-147, 157, 171-172
Massachusetts, 7, 11, 12, 16, 31, 132, 153-154, 156, 169, 184-186; Massachusetts Bay, 21-22, 25-26, 29, 38, 52, 126, 184-185; Cape Cod, 20-21
Massachusetts Bay Company, 21, 25-27,

76-77, 171-172; *Records,* 21, 113, 118, 123, 125 fn, 130 fn, 131, 134, 137-138, 154, 156, 172, 174
massacre of 1622, 19, 66, 121, 129, 139, 165, 176-178
Massasoit, 7
Maycock, A. L., 30, 164
Mayflower Compact, 20
McCary, Ben, 6, 8
Mercator, 161
Miller, Perry, 29-30
Morgan, Edmund, 8, 17, 19-22, 30, 90-91, 119
Morrell, William, 31, 36, 54, 59-60, 70, 75, 77, 83, 85, 94-95, 98, 116, 144-145, 155, 161-162
Morton, Thomas, 21, 25-26, 31-32, 36, 37, 39, 41-42, 48, 50, 56, 57-58, 71-72, 75-77, 81-82, 85-87, 90-94, 98, 103-105, 109-110, 112, 115-117, 119, 125, 131, 137, 144-147, 150, 154, 156-158, 163, 167, 169-170, 187; Ma-re Mount (Merrymount), 25-26, 122, 137
Mosco, 40, 111

Namontacke, 118
Nash, Gary B., 4 fn, 106 fn, 110, 128, 176
Nemattanow (Jack of the Feather), 177
New England, 3, 7, 14, 16, 24, 27, 48, 49, 57, 74, 80, 82, 88, 90-91, 95, 103, 119, 121, 123, 131, 134, 157, 159, 162-163, 174, 185; Council for, 20-21, 26
New Haven, 21; *Records,* 125 fn, 134, 138, 174
New York, 7
Newfoundland, 10, 12, 14, 22, 65, 163; Ferryland, 22; international fisheries, 13
Newport, Christopher, 17-18, 118, 146
North Carolina, 7, 14
Nova Scotia, 13

Old Testament precedents, 64-65, 77, 101, 108, 110, 118-119, 159-160, 166-168, 175, 188
Opechancanough, 19, 49, 51, 54, 66, 87, 157, 177
overpopulation of England, 3, 12, 135
Oxford University, 9, 24

Parkhurst, Anthony, 14, 65, 110-111, 162
Parkinson, Marmaduke, 57
Parry, J. H., 12 fn, 126
Paspiha, 67
Pearce, Roy Harvey, 4 fn, 27 fn, 31, 70, 106 fn.

Peckham, George, 41, 42-43, 109, 143, 150-152, 160 fn, 161-163, 166, 170-171
Peckham, Howard H., 27 fn, 30 fn.
Pelham, Sir William 162
Penn, William, 110
Pennsylvania, 7
Penreis, John, 174-175
Peppet, Gilbert, 182
Pequot War, 7, 22, 43, 55, 127, 132, 154, 175, 184-186
Percy, George, 73-74, 78, 83, 93, 98, 100-101, 103, 112, 121
Pierce, John, 186
Pierce, Lt., 153
Pilgrims, 6, 7, 11, 20-21, 25, 29-30, 36, 88, 134
Plymouth Colony, 6, 7, 11, 20, 25, 26-27, 29, 30, 32, 41, 52, 71, 83, 88, 123, 125, 132, 134, 150, 153, 154, 167, 183-184; *Records,* 123, 125 fn, 131, 134, 136-138, 154, 174
Pocahontas, 4, 18, 37, 61, 65, 67, 79, 95, 111, 118-120, 146
Poole, Robert, 157
Popham, George, 16
Popham, Lord Chief Justice, 16, 31
Portobacco, 53
Portugal, 166; ship pilots from, 9, 15, 130, 150
Pory, John, 53, 58, 66, 154
Potomac River, 57
Powell, William S., 179
Powhatan, 7, 8, 16, 18-19, 37, 45, 49-51, 53, 54-55, 61, 66, 77, 95, 118-119, 126, 145-146, 173
Preston, R. A., 16
Price, Daniel, 142, 161, 166-167
Pringe, Martin, 36, 90, 101, 103
privateering, 9-10, 15
Purchas, Samuel, 23-24, 40, 43-44, 45, 59, 65, 66-67, 77, 79, 83, 87, 95, 97-98, 106 fn, 109, 111-112, 120, 122 fn, 127, 130, 148, 157, 162, 165, 167, 176-178, 183
Puritans, Puritanism, 6, 11, 20, 25-26, 27-32, 38, 41, 70-71, 120, 143, 159-161, 166-167, 169, 185-186; separatists, 29-30
Pythagoras, 76

Quakers, 28
Quinn, David B., 8, 12, 15, 16, 22, 30, 96-97, 113, 141, 150

Rabb, Theodore K., 10 fn, 123

INDEX

Raleigh, Sir Walter, 10, 14-16, 25, 33-34, 150
Rhode Island, Providence, 22
Rich, R., 149
Roanoke, 3, 7, 10, 14, 15, 25, 33-34, 49, 57, 70, 88, 96, 99, 111; Lost Colony, 15-16, 130, 171-174
Robinson, John, 183-184
Rolfe, John, 18, 65, 108, 113 fn, 132, 137, 153 fn, marriage to Pocahontas, 17, 118-119; work with tobacco, 17-18
Roman Catholics, 11, 13, 14, 22, 27, 28-29, 31, 64, 66, 69, 130, 135, 137, 143, 159-161, 163, 165-166
Romans, conversion of English by, 113
Rosier, James, 16, 40, 61, 74, 80-81, 92-94, 96, 99-100, 103-104, 111-112, 144-145, 147, 161
Rowe, John H., 4 fn.
runaways to Indians, 118-119, 127, 139, 156-158, 173
Russell, Carl P., 102
Rutman, Anita, 19-20
Rutman, Darrett, 19-20

Salisbury, Neal, 113 fn.
Sandys, Sir Edwin, 136, 138
Sandys, George, 25, 107, 153, 179, 181
Sanford, Charles L., 159
Sauer, Carl O., 91
Savage, Thomas, 118, 146, 157
Saybrook, 21, 184
Saye and Sele, Lord, 21
Scandinavia, 5; settlement of New Sweden, 13
sectarianism, 21-22, 28-29, 38
Sequin, 184-185
Shakespeare, William, *The Tempest*, 18, 74
Shirley, John W., 31, 47, 116 fn.
Simpson, Alan, 28
Skelton, R. A., 33 fn.
Slater, Miriam, 170
slavery, Africans in Virginia, 19, 187; for English servants, 137-140
Slotkin, Richard, 26, 27 fn, 31 fn, 169 fn.
Smith, John, 4, 8, 17-19, 23-24, 30-31, 36, 37, 40, 43-44, 45, 50-52, 53-55, 58-61, 66-76, 80-85, 87-90, 92-95, 111-113, 115, 122-125, 127, 129-131, 142-150, 152, 155-157, 161-163, 165-166, 171, 173-174, 176-178, 181
Smith, Sir Thomas, 138-139
social change in England, 8-9, 141-149; economic change, 11
social control in colonies, 122-127, 148-158

South Sea, search for passage to, 17, 47, 57, 96
Spain, 10, 132, 150, 163; Armada, 15; colonization efforts, 13; peace with, 16; perfidy, 130; reports of Indians, 109, 113; wealth from colonization, 9, 80, 152, 166
Spelman, Henry, 45, 51, 55, 56, 58, 59, 66, 69 fn, 70, 73, 75, 82, 87, 89, 91, 110, 116, 118, 145-146, 156-157
Squanto, 6, 20, 84, 88
St. Augustine, 28, 126
status distinctions, 134; in English society, 3, 148-155; in Indian society, 2, 34, 58, 122
Stockam, Master, 78
Stone, Lawrence, 2 fn, 145
Stout, Harry S., 12
Strachey, William, 23, 25, 35 fn, 49, 56, 59, 61, 65, 66, 68-70, 73-77, 82-83, 85, 87-89, 92-97, 100-103, 109, 113, 116, 123-124, 130, 145, 148, 152, 153 fn, 164
Street, Brian V., 114 fn.
Swanton, J. R., 8, 57-58, 67, 84
Symonds, William, 65, 100-101, 106 fn, 113 fn, 118-119, 142-143, 152, 159-160, 162, 164, 167
syphilis, 5, 59, 97, 115

Tanner, R. H. C., 100
Tanx-Powhatan, 45, 120
Thomas, Keith, 115-118, 141-142, 175
Thorowgood, Thomas, 110
Thorpe, George, 177
Throckmorton, Elizabeth, 126
tobacco, 178; effect on organization of Virginia, 19; Indian pipes, 100, trade, 133
Tomocomo, 79, 95
Town life, importance of, 46-47, 81-82
Tynley, Robert, 106 fn, 166

Underhill, John, 37-38, 55, 94, 126, 154-155, 175

Vane, Henry, 22
Vaughan, Alden T., 17 fn, 22 fn, 24 fn, 27 fn, 29, 48, 71-72, 156, 158 fn, 159 fn, 165
Vaughan, William, 113, 147, 161, 163, 170
Varrazano, Giovanni da, 13
Vincent, Philip, 43, 86, 108, 113, 126-127, 172, 175
Virginia, 3, 7, 8, 10, 11, 13, 14, 16-19, 24-25, 27, 29-30, 38-39, 49-50, 51, 54,

55, 57, 58, 66, 75, 82, 90, 95, 99, 107, 120, 124, 131, 132-133, 135-137, 142, 148, 151, 153-154, 156-157, 159, 161-162, 164, 167, 173-174, 176-184; particular plantations in, 19, 20, 22, 30
Virginia colony, records, 39, 116, 118, 124-125, 127, 130 fn, 131, 133 fn, 134, 136-140, 154-156, 158, 172-174, 179-183
Virginia Company, 10, 11, 16, 19, 54, 120, 123, 135, 136, 148, 151, 155, 176; dissolution, 19, 21, 138, 178; expectations and instructions, 17-18, 49, 104, 125, 178-179; motivations of, 30, 64, 135, 161, 164-165; *Records* and publications, 10, 17, 19, 38-39, 49, 51, 54, 69 fn, 71, 76, 82-83, 87, 96, 100-101, 110-111, 120, 124-126, 129-140, 145, 148-149, 152-158; 160, 163, 167, 172-175, 178-183

Walsingham, Sir Francis, 9
Washburn, Wilcomb, 56, 89, 120, 128, 164-165, 181
Waterhouse, Edward, 57, 83, 87, 91, 129, 164, 174, 176-178, 180-181
Waymouth, George, 16
Webster, Charles, 159
Wessagusset, 21, 157, 174, 183
West, Thomas, Lord de la Warr, 18
West Indies, Old Providence, 184
Weston, Thomas, 137, 174
Wethersfield, 184-185
Whitaker, Alexander, 26-27, 29, 66, 69, 70, 86, 101, 108, 110, 113 fn, 116, 123, 127, 142-144, 149, 161-162
Whitbourne, Richard, 40, 86, 93-94, 113 fn, 121, 163-164, 171
White, Fr. Andrew, 53, 59, 69, 83, 87, 92, 101, 110, 131-133, 157

White, John (painter, governor), 10, 14-16, 25, 39, 70, 111, 130; paintings, 33-34, 70, 73, 74, 81-82, 88, 94, 101-103, 113
White, John (minister), 25, 70, 76, 78, 110, 113 fn, 160-161, 163-164
White, William, 66-68
Wild Man of Middle Ages, 40, 45-46
Williams, Roger, 22, 28, 110
Willison, George F., 20 fn, 21, 30
Willson, David H., 51
Wilson, Charles, 2 fn.
Wingfield, Edward Maria, 59, 73, 131, 143
Winslow, Edward, 6, 26, 27, 31, 37, 39, 48, 52, 56, 59, 67-77, 83-84, 86, 88, 91, 93-96, 99-100, 110, 115-116, 123, 125, 144-146, 156, 161, 166, 171, 172 fn, 174
Winthrop, John, 21, 38, 50, 52, 58, 82, 103, 116, 125 fn, 127, 130 fn, 132, 134-136, 138, 153-154, 156, 172, 183-186
Winthrop, John Jr., 21
witchcraft, 2, 72, 116-118, 175
Withers, George, 89
Wood, William, 25-26, 31, 36, 37, 39, 41-42, 43-44, 48, 54-56, 57-62, 69-76, 83-90, 92-95, 98-100, 103-104, 108-109, 115, 117, 121, 144-145, 147, 155, 157-158, 172 fn, 187
Wyatt, Sir Francis, 178-179, 182
Wyatt, George, 156, 178-179
Wyatt, Lady Margaret, 133, 180

Yeardley, Sir George, 136, 153
Yong, Capt. Thomas, 133, 157

Ziff, Larzer, 31, 165
Zolla, Elemire, 31
Zuckerman, Michael, 26, 169 fn.